# A Guide to
# Greek Theatre
# and Drama

KENNETH McLEISH's translations, of plays by most of the Greek and Roman dramatists, Ibsen, Feydeau, Molière, Strindberg and others, have been performed throughout the world on stage, film, TV and radio. His original plays include *I Will If You Will, Just Do It, The Arabian Nights, Omma* and *Orpheus*. His books include *The Theatre of Aristophanes, A Pocket Guide to Shakespeare's Plays* (with Stephen Unwin) and *The Bloomsbury Good Reading Guide*. He was editor of the Drama Classics series for Nick Hern Books and a Fellow of the Royal Society of Literature. He died in 1997.

TREVOR R. GRIFFITHS is Professor of Theatre Studies at London Metropolitan University. His publications include *A Midsummer Night's Dream* in CUP's Shakespeare in Production series, *Stagecraft*, seven volumes in the Nick Hern Books Drama Classics series of which he is associate general editor, *British and Irish Women Dramatists since 1958* (joint editor with M. Llewellyn-Jones) and the *Bloomsbury Theatre Guide* (with Carole Woddis). He is one of the editors of *Theatre Notebook* and was chair of the board of Foco Novo Theatre Company.

*Methuen Classical Greek Dramatists series*

AESCHYLUS PLAYS: ONE
Persians, Seven Against Thebes, Suppliants,
Prometheus Bound

AESCHYLUS PLAYS: TWO
Oresteia: Agamemnon, Libation-Bearers, Eumenides

ARISTOPHANES PLAYS: ONE
Acharnians, Knights, Peace, Lysistrata

ARISTOPHANES PLAYS: TWO
Wasps, Clouds, Birds, Festival Time (*Thesmophoriazousai*),
Frogs

ARISTOPHANES AND MENANDER: NEW COMEDY
Women in Power, Wealth, The Malcontent,
The Woman from Samos

EURIPIDES PLAYS: ONE
Medea, The Phoenician Women, Bacchae

EURIPIDES PLAYS: TWO
Hecuba, The Women of Troy, Iphigenia at Aulis, Cyclops

EURIPIDES PLAYS: THREE
Alkestis, Helen, Ion

EURIPIDES PLAYS: FOUR
Elektra, Orestes, Iphigeneia in Tauris

EURIPIDES PLAYS: FIVE
Andromache, Herakles' Children, Herakles

EURIPIDES PLAYS: SIX
Hippolytos, Suppliants, Rhesos

SOPHOCLES PLAYS: ONE (*The Theban Plays*)
Oedipus the King, Oedipus at Colonus, Antigone

SOPHOCLES PLAYS: TWO
Ajax, Women of Trachis, Electra, Philoctetes

# A Guide to Greek Theatre and Drama

KENNETH McLEISH

completed by TREVOR R. GRIFFITHS

Methuen

1 3 5 7 9 10 8 6 4 2

This edition first published
in the United Kingdom in 2003 by
Methuen Publishing Limited
215 Vauxhall Bridge Road
London SW1V 1EJ

Copyright © 2003 by Trevor R. Griffiths and the Estate of Kenneth McLeish

The rights of the authors to be identified as the authors of
this work have been asserted by them in accordance with the
Copyright, Designs and Patents Act, 1988

Methuen Publishing Limited Reg. No. 3543167

A CIP catalogue record for this book
is available from the British Library

ISBN 0 413 72030 6

Typeset by Deltatype Limited, Birkenhead, Merseyside

Printed and bound in Great Britain by
Creative Print and Design (Wales)
Ebbw Vale

# CONTENTS

*Introduction*                                          vii

ATHENIAN THEATRE                                          1

AESCHYLUS                                                31
  Oresteia                                     39
  Agamemnon                                    42
  Libation-Bearers (*Choephoroi*)              45
  Eumenides                                    48
  Persians                                     51
  Prometheus Bound                             55
  Seven Against Thebes                         59
  Suppliants                                   63

SOPHOCLES                                                67
  Ajax                                         76
  Antigone                                     80
  Elektra                                      84
  Oedipus at Kolonos                           88
  Oedipus Tyrannos                             92
  Philoktetes                                  96
  Women of Trachis                            100

EURIPIDES                                               105
  Alkestis                                    114
  Andromache                                  119
  Bacchae                                     124
  Cyclops                                      128
  Elektra                                     132
  Hekabe (Hecuba)                             136
  Helen                                       140
  Herakles (Hercules)                         144
  Herakles' Children                          148

Hippolytos                                      153
Ion                                             157
Iphigeneia at Aulis                             161
Iphigeneia in Tauris                            165
Medea                                           169
Orestes                                         173
Phoenician Women                                178
Rhesos                                          183
Suppliants                                      187
Women of Troy                                   191

ARISTOPHANES                                    195
Acharnians                                      203
Birds                                           208
Clouds                                          213
Festival Time (*Thesmophoriazousai*)            217
Frogs                                           222
Knights                                         227
Lysistrata                                      231
Peace                                           236
Wasps                                           240
Wealth                                          244
Women in Power (*Ekklesiazousai*)               248

MENANDER                                        253
The Malcontent                                  260
The Woman from Samos (*Samia*)                  265

ARISTOTLE'S *POETICS* AND GREEK TRAGEDY         269

*Key Myths*                                     275
*Glossary*                                      293
*Chronology*                                    297
*Bibliography*                                  300
*Index*                                         304

# INTRODUCTION

The purpose of this book is to provide a general survey of the place and purpose of theatre in ancient Greece, of the conditions and styles of performance, of all the extant plays and their authors. The focus is on what remains of the dramatic output of the Greek theatre from the fifth to third centuries BC. Inevitably some judgements about theatrical practices are speculative and subject to revision in the light of new archaeological evidence – a theatrical excavation, a re-examination of a vase, or even the unwrapping of a mummy may yield new evidence that will overturn cherished ideas about the achievements of the ancient Greek theatre. While we have only a small part of the output of just five dramatists we know the names of many of their plays that are now lost, just as we know the names of many other dramatists and the titles of their plays and plays by other still unidentified writers. In some cases, like Menander, we have substantial fragments of other plays, in some cases works are known only because later scholars quoted them, we even have some Roman plays that were based on two or more Greek originals. All of this contextual evidence has a bearing on this book but much of the argument about what the evidence means is highly technical and speculative. It is tempting to speculate about the exact nature of the satyr play or the details of the transition from Old to Middle to New Comedy, or the relationship between theatrical practice outside Athens and that of the Athenian festivals, or to try to reconstruct Greek originals from the Roman plays of Plautus and Terence, but these are complex issues and the scholarly arguments about them depend on conflicting interpretations of fragmentary evidence. Readers who wish to pursue such issues will find that many of the books in the bibliography offer useful starting points.

The first section covers the *raison d'être* and style of the ancient performances – why and where they were done, how the plays were selected, how dramatists went to work, who the performers were and how they were chosen, how plays were performed, what drama meant to (and did for) ancient Greeks. The key topics addressed include when the festivals took place, what were they for and how were they organised, the physical nature of the festival, the theatre, the performances. Who were the playwrights, the actors, the chorus-members, and the audience? Sections on literary and dramatic technique deal with such matters as why are the plays in verse, how the verse is organised, and the function of rhetoric. Other elements of dramaturgy considered are how the experience is articulated (e.g. by chorus scenes and dialogue scenes, by monologues and dialogue, by single and half lines) and the functions of music, dance and slapstick routines.

The next section covers the writers (Aeschylus, Sophocles, Euripides, Aristophanes, Menander) whose work survives, in chronological order of birth. There is little accurate information available about the dramatists' lives and many of the anecdotes about them appear to have been derived from the plays themselves, as Mary R. Lefkowitz* has shown. The surviving biographical material reflects an ancient view of what the authors ought to have been like, tempered by a few facts. The biographical account that begins each author's section in this volume takes these limitations into account in offering some details of his life before discussing the general characteristics of his approach. Each of his plays then has a section of its own (the plays are treated in alphabetical order of title) which includes a character-list, and plot summary; details about first performances are given where known (date; accompanying plays; prize) and a discussion of the play then follows, relating it to its author's other work and to its period, analysing points of interest and importance in attitude, style or performance needs and discussing how the piece works in literary and dramatic terms.

The first appendix considers Aristotle's extant remarks on drama (known as the *Poetics*), both what Aristotle actually said

*Mary R. Lefkowitz, *The Lives of the Greek Poets*, Duckworth, 1981.

and his influence on later writers. Aristotelian theory is described as it relates to the plays and to subsequent theatre. The second appendix gives an account of key myths; the third is a glossary of technical terms.

## A note on Greek names

Many characters from ancient Greek life, myth and drama such as Aeschylus, Ajax or Phaedra are more familiar to us in versions of their names transmitted through Latin or Anglicised in ways that do not closely reflect the original Greek (Aischylos, Aias or Phaidra). In this book each name is treated consistently but there is no attempt at uniformity in adopting a consistent policy of, for example, direct transliteration from Greek. The reasons for this are entirely pragmatic: where there is an established familiar version of a name, such as Crete or Aeschylus, Circe or Oedipus it would create a barrier to understanding to insist on using more literally accurate forms such as Kriti, Aischylos, Kirke or Oidipous. The broad aim is to be as faithful as possible to the original Greek names while not interposing an extra difficulty for the modern reader. Judgements about names where traditional English usage has softened 'k' to a soft 'c' (Eurydice, Circe) are particularly difficult, but the guiding principle has been to use a familiar form where it will aid comprehension. However where an accurate transliteration appears to be less of an obstacle, particularly with names beginning with a hard 'c', where the familiar name is pronounced in the same way as the transliterated name would be, a more accurate rendition is used: Kassandra and Kleon, rather than Cassandra and Cleon, for example. Sometimes this policy produces anomalies.

Names like Dionysos and Theophrastos and Olympos are given in their Greek rather than Roman forms (Dionysus, Theophrastus, Olympus). In some cases characters such as Herakles and Hekabe may be more familiar under their Roman names (Hercules and Hecuba) but where there is a substantive discussion of the character, the Roman name is also mentioned.

Such compromises are the result of a desire to encourage readers to engage actively with the achievements of Greek drama without undue distraction. What this policy may mask is the fact while such names as Antigone, Elektra, Klytemnestra, Oedipus may recur from play to play, each play treats its characters differently so that a character with the same name may be very different from play to play.

## A note on authorship

This book was unfinished on Kenneth McLeish's untimely death in 1997. At the request of Valerie McLeish, it has been completed and seen through the press by Trevor R. Griffiths.

# Athenian Theatre

## Athens and the origins of drama

Forty-six complete plays survive from ancient Greece, between one and five per cent of the total number written. All are by Athenians. The earliest is Aeschylus' *Persians* (472), the latest the plays of Menander from the last decades of the fourth century BC. The surviving tragedies were all produced between 472 (*Persians*) and 401 (Sophocles' *Oedipus at Kolonos*). All surviving comedies except Menander's *The Malcontent* and *The Woman from Samos* were produced between 425 (Aristophanes' *Acharnians*) and 388 (his *Wealth*). The span of time is not long, and the number of masterpieces produced within it and in a single city and dramatic community – the majority of the surviving plays, no less – is remarkable. In later Western theatre, only Shakespeare's London and Spain in the 'Golden Century' offer similar packed excellence.

We are too distant from ancient Greece to know if this constellation of talents was coincidence – the right people in the right place at the right time, striking sparks off each other – or if what we call 'Greek' drama was exclusively an Athenian phenomenon. There may have been earlier dramatic performances, of one kind or another, in Minoan Crete or the Southern Peloponnese. But whichever other states had claims on the art, Athens was where it reached its peak. Athenian dramatists and companies regularly took plays elsewhere (Aeschylus to Sicily, for example, Euripides to Corinth and Macedonia), and most surviving Greek theatres were built, centuries after the Athenian heyday, for revivals and imitations of Athenian plays.

The heart of the Athenian experience was celebration of Dionysos, first in village shrines outside the city and then at his cult centre at the foot of the Acropolis. Dionysos was the god of ecstasy, supervising the moment when human beings surrender to

1

unstoppable, irrational feeling or impulse. His devotees worked themselves into trances, during which they thought that they lost themselves in God, changed their nature (for example, becoming wild beasts) and briefly enjoyed the powers, visions and happiness of gods before returning to human reality. Because wine, supposedly Dionysos' gift to mortals, was thought to be a human simulacrum of nectar (the gods' drink which guaranteed immortality) and to allow us a moment's glimpse of that timeless joy, the god was particularly worshipped at the beginning and end of the wine-making season. As well as processions, prayers and sacrifice, the celebrations included singing and dancing, some of it formal ('dithyrambs'), some of it informal and exuberant.

Aristotle, writing a century and more after the heyday of Athenian drama, but still the commentator nearest in time to it, claimed that theatre arose out of these Dionysian celebrations. The serious singing and dancing, he said, led to tragedy, the unserious to comedy and to the 'satyr play' or pastoral. The statement may contain a grain of truth. Dionysian celebrants, early on, seem to have divided into groups, answering one another in words, music or dance and so varying the myth narrative with elements of response, even confrontation. Each group may have had a leader, a solo performer – and an anonymous, late writer claims that at some early stage in the development of these performances, in the mid 500s, someone 'climbed on a table' and 'answered' the chorus. (The Greek word for actor, *hypokrites*, literally means 'answerer'.) Then, the theory goes, a writer called Thespis standardised the practice of balancing a solo performer against the chorus – and drama was born. (Very little else is known about Thespis, but Thespians still honour his name.)

Alongside such Dionysian developments, and probably just as influential, was the annual public recitation in Athens of Homer's *Iliad* and *Odyssey*, a practice begun at about the same period (mid 500s). These recitations, given by single speakers or relays of speakers, were part of the Panathenaic Festival, a celebration of the city's political, military and mercantile grandeur. Unlike the

Dionysian celebrations described above, Homer's *Iliad* and *Odyssey* are not devoted to the exploits and worship of any particular god. Based on enormous cycles of ancient myth, they tell the stories of part of the Trojan War and of Odysseus' return home afterwards, concentrating on character and incident, putting words directly into the mouths of such individuals as Agamemnon, Athene, Circe or Polyphemos and drawing from the myths a wide range of philosophical and political point-making, wit, pathos, contradiction and irony – in a word, attitude.

The moment you characterise individuals in telling a story, it turns into drama. The *Iliad* opens with a row between Agamemnon and Achilles and ends as Priam, Andromache and the Trojan people lament the death of Hektor. The *Odyssey* pits Odysseus against supernatural and natural adversaries of all kinds, and shows him defeating them as often by quick-witted dialogue as by physical prowess. A major theme in both epics is the way domestic life and ordinary human feelings impinge on and are affected by the grand schemes and strategies of the gods, heroes and supernatural beings of the main myth narrative – and a similar unpacking of the energies and implications of basic myth material is the stuff of Greek drama, from Sophoclean solemnity to Aristophanic rudery, from Aeschylean philosophising to Euripidean scepticism. As Aeschylus said, 'We all feast on crumbs from Homer's banquet.'

## The festivals

The two main Athenian festivals at which drama featured each year were the Lenaia and the City Dionysia. The Lenaia (named after Dionysos Lenaios, 'ecstatic Dionysos') was held in December–January, and the difficulty of winter sea travel to Athens tended to make it a local affair, smaller-scale than the City Dionysia. The City Dionysia, celebrating Dionysos' arrival in Athens in mythical times, was held in March–April and was lavish, spectacular and crowded with visitors.

# Festival Days

## City Dionysia

Day 1:    Processions, speeches, as the statue of Dionysos
         was taken from its temple to Eleutheria on the
         outskirts of the city, then back, and was set up
         in the theatre

Day 2:    Dithyramb competition. Ten choruses, five of
         boys and five of men

Days 3–5: Drama. Mornings: three tragedies, one (shorter)
         satyr play. Late afternoon: one comedy. (Later, a
         separate comedy day was established, with five
         plays in all)

Day 6:    Prizegiving and closing ceremony

## Lenaia

The only details known are the numbers of plays. Five
comedies were performed (perhaps on a single day), and
two tragedies by each of two writers (perhaps also on one
day). If the festival opened with a day of processions and
speeches, and closed with a day of prizegiving and
celebrations, that means four days overall.

## Performers and audiences

Each dithyramb chorus consisted of fifty people, and the
chorus of each play involved some 12–24 people. If no
performer appeared twice in a year's competitions, then
something like 1,000 amateurs were involved altogether in
these choruses. The audience, if it included relatives,
friends and performers from other shows in competition,
would have been both knowledgeable and partisan.

As well as drama, each festival included processions, speeches, religious ceremonies, competitions for music and dance and other less formal jollifications. At the Lenaia, two tragic dramatists entered two plays each in competition, and five comic dramatists entered one play each. At the City Dionysia, three tragic dramatists each entered four plays (three tragedies and a satyr play), and five comic dramatists entered one play each. (These numbers were sometimes reduced, for example in wartime.) Thus, some two dozen new plays, half each of tragedies and comedies or satyr plays, were performed each year. Surviving lists show that most authors were what we might think of as 'Sunday' writers, producing only a handful of plays in an entire lifetime. Outputs as large as those of Sophocles (who had 96 plays accepted in 24 competitions) or Aristophanes (some 40 plays in as many competitions) were rare.

In fifth-century Athens, each play was performed once only, in the competition for which it was entered. After Aeschylus' death a law was passed allowing his plays, and his alone, to be repeated. Otherwise, runs were unknown, and revivals practically non-existent (Aristophanes' *Frogs* was an exception, and his *Clouds* and Euripides' *Hippolytos* were performed in revised versions). Successful plays may have been circulated after the competitions in private performances or in script form, and the actors almost certainly toured. But it was not till the fourth century, long after the heyday of Athenian drama, and when theatregoing had become a pastime rather than part of festival celebration, that old plays were regularly revived as staples of the repertoire.

Each festival was organised by a state official, as part of his one-year term of office. To enter a drama competition, playwrights submitted ideas to this official or his committee, outlining the main themes and points of interest. The authors were chosen and each was allocated a backer. Backing plays was a form of taxation, and some aristocrats specialised in it, favouring it over such other choices as sponsoring warships or paying for public works. Depending on the backer's generosity and the demands of the play, it cost some 1,600 drachmas to mount a comedy in the late fifth century, and twice as much to mount a tragedy. To give a perspective, an adult male slave could be bought at the same time for 150–300 drachmas, and it cost some 3,000 drachmas to build and equip a warship.

The order of plays in competition was decided by lot – and must have been awaited with considerable interest. When Aristophanes' *Clouds* (a satire on advanced 'modern' education, with Socrates as a main character) was first performed, it was allotted third position on a day where the two previous plays also featured Socrates. The effect of such a billing, compared (say) to being placed on the same day as *Medea* or *Women of Troy*, must have been considerable. At the end of the competition, ten judges each wrote an order of merit on a clay tablet, and the senior official chose five at random to determine the result. Prizes, as in all Greek competitions, for example in athletics, were wreaths of honour – plus the ensuing reputation, with its almost certain guarantee of a place in next year's competition.

## The Theatre of Dionysos

The Theatre of Dionysos, home of the drama competitions, lay between the fortified hill of the Acropolis and a large temple complex of Dionysos (still not excavated and partly underneath the modern road). All surviving plays were first performed there. Although the remains we now see are partly Romanised, they give an excellent idea of the original theatre, and particularly of its size and openness (in striking contrast to the closed, formal design of later buildings like the nearby Theatre of Herodes Attikos).

The hub of the theatre was the *orchestra* or 'dancing circle', a floor of hard-packed earth in a circle of stone and some 18.5m in diameter. Round this on three sides, built up on the slope of the Acropolis, were tiers of audience seats. Facing them, on the fourth side across the *orchestra*, was an area of flat ground some 60m long and 6m wide, backed by the wall of the shrine. On this was erected the *skene* ('booth'), a building some 30m long and 3.5m wide. In

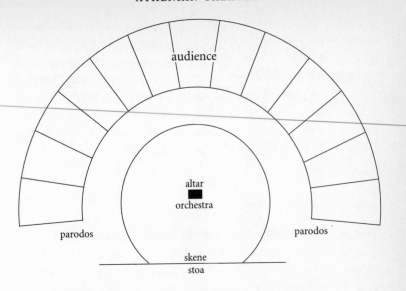

A possible configuration of the Theatre of Dionysos
in the mid-fifth century (not to scale)

later times this building was made of stone, but in the original
theatre it may have been largely a façade of wood or canvas on a
wooden frame, similar to the street façades used on modern film
and TV sets. In the centre of this structure was a doorway, possibly
with a low platform in front of it. Part of the building had a flat
roof strong enough to allow actors to stand on it; the rest was
probably open. Walkways (*parodoi*), like wings in a modern
theatre, led from the acting area and *orchestra* to the temple
precinct and street beyond.

Scholars argue about almost all these features, and the discussion is not helped by the fact that surviving theatres tend to be
either much later or smaller and worse preserved. But although
there is dispute about detail, the balance of probability is that what
we see as we sit in the Theatre of Dionysos today is substantially
similar to the experience of ancient visitors. When full, the theatre
held some 14,000 spectators. This has suggested to some that
seeing and hearing the actors may have been difficult. But anyone

who has ever visited an ancient Greek theatre will have experienced the astonishing clarity of the acoustics, and we know from modern experience, for example at sports meetings or rock concerts, that visibility, even in crowds much larger than 14,000, is perfectly possible. When we watch Greek plays in the original theatres today, difficulties of hearing and seeing are the last matters on our minds – and there is no reason to suppose that things were radically different in ancient times.

### Scenery, costumes, props, masks

Little is known about scenery. Most surviving plays are set in the open, usually in front of a building, and the setting is often described in detail, much as in Shakespeare's plays. There is no need for elaborate scenery. Several plays require actors to play scenes on an upper level, perhaps the flat roof of the stage building. This was the *theologeion* ('god-speaking-place'), and was probably used for those scenes where gods start plays (as Poseidon and Athene begin *Women of Troy*) or end them (as Herakles rounds off *Philoktetes*), and for a few spectacular sequences like the moment in Euripides' *Suppliants* when Evadne hurls herself into a funeral pyre below. Two pieces of stage machinery also feature. The crane (*mechane*, 'machine') was used to fly actors, perhaps in tragedy (for example, Ocean in *Prometheus Bound*) and certainly in comedy (for example, *Peace*, *Festival Time* and *Birds*), where its ricketiness and unpredictability were mocked. The 'roll-out' (*ekkuklema*) was used in tragedy, perhaps to reveal the results of murder 'inside' (for example, the corpse of Klytemnestra in the *Oresteia*), and in comedy for jokes, as when Euripides in *Acharnians* is too lazy or too busy to come to his own front door, and has himself 'rolled out' instead. It used to be thought that the 'roll-out' was some kind of wheeled platform or sofa, but it is more likely to have been a screen or screens, wheeled aside at the appropriate moment.

Costumes and props are another little known area. Some plays – Aeschylus' *Suppliants* or Aristophanes' *Birds*, for example – offer

8

scope for particularly elaborate costumes, giving the backer a chance to show munificence. Most plays, however, require nothing especially out of the way. Many characters in tragedy are rich aristocrats, and the costumes may have been designed accordingly: vase paintings show embroidered, fringed fabrics and the soft leather boots called buskins. Exotic locations, such as the Persian setting of *Persians* or the Egyptian setting of *Helen*, and foreign characters, such as the Scythian policeman in *Festival Time*, may have inspired the designer; we have no evidence. Props in tragedy are sometimes crucial, such as the carpet and the net in the *Oresteia*, the urn in *Elektra*, the bow in *Philoktetes*; they might include a prop baby for Andromache in *Women of Troy*, perhaps a prop head for Agave to carry in *Bacchae* and for Elektra to insult in Euripides' *Elektra*. (It is possible that these heads were replaced by the actors' masks.) In comedy props proliferate. The range is from portable altars to chamber pots, from offal carts to vine poles, from sheep, puppies and birds to Athene's golden helmet from the Parthenon.

One thing known for sure is that all performers wore masks made from stiffened linen or thin clay. Although the masks were made to resemble characters (old people, for example) and had wide funnel mouths, they were not there to make performers easier to see and hear. The main purpose was religious. Dionysos' worshippers surrendered their identity to the god, submerging themselves in him, and the actor's taking on of a character symbolised this process. Some actors, we are told, prayed to the god before putting on their masks, and treated them with respect and dignity as if they contained the character they represented. Modern actors who use masks find two things which can surprise those not familiar with theatre practice. Wearing a mask does not inhibit or restrict the portrayal of character but enhances it, allowing more, not less, fluidity and suppleness of movement; and the character created by or embodied in the mask and the actor who wears it can feel as if it has an independent identity which is liberated at the moment of performance – an unsettlingly Dionysian experience.

## Actors and chorus

By modern standards, the number of actors was small: two in Aeschylus' time, three in later tragedy, three or four in comedy. The parts were divided among them, and doubling probably drew on actors' individual abilities – in music or dance, for example, or the difficult technique of travesty acting. All actors were male. There were also extras (eloquently called 'silent masks') playing attendants, soldiers and the like. Scholars think that in tragedies, at least, the playwrights themselves also acted. When one adds this to their other responsibilities – rehearsing the company, training the chorus, composing and directing music and (perhaps) choreography, liaising with the backer and the authorities, all this for a total of four plays on a single day, their involvement must have been exhausting. In comedy matters are less certain. Aristophanes is thought to have performed in some of his early plays, but the names of his later leading actors are known, and perhaps he gave up acting or took smaller parts in the later plays. Certainly, about halfway through his career, there is a marked change in the style of comic acting he requires from his leading actor.

The chorus originally consisted of a dozen people, all men or boys, but Sophocles increased it to fifteen, and all surviving fifth-century plays apart from those of Aeschylus used that number. The size of Menander's chorus is unknown. The chorus members were amateurs, and each was picked to represent his local area in the festival: an honour. They sang and danced, and their leader (perhaps an experienced professional) also took part, representing their voice, in the spoken scenes. In the *Oresteia*, for example, the chorus leaders have long stretches of dialogue with Klytemnestra in *Agamemnon*, with Elektra and Orestes in *Libation-Bearers* and with Apollo and Athene in *Eumenides*. In satyr plays, where the singing and dancing of the satyr chorus were main attractions, the dialogue scenes may have been trimmed accordingly: this is certainly the case in the only such play to survive, Euripides' *Cyclops*. In Euripides' and Aristophanes' later plays, the writers fragmented the chorus in various ways, letting them speak as groups or individual voices with conflicting attitudes. In the fourth century, for example in Aristophanes' *Wealth* and in Menander, the chorus became increasingly marginalised, their part consisting of sung and danced interludes, often indicated in the scripts by the single word *chorou* ('something by the chorus').

As we read the surviving texts of the plays, used as we are to theatre which is predominantly non-choral, the chorus can seem awkward to place in the dramatic ebb and flow. In practice, however, their presence articulates the entire performance and contributes tone, pace, style and mood. Without the choruses, *Antigone* (say) or *Agamemnon* would lack the general philosophical point of view to which the acted scenes give specific dramatic focus; without the chorus, plays like *Persians*, *Peace* or Euripides' *Suppliants* would lose most of their lyrical context and energy; the choruses are essential components of such otherwise unlikely dramatic bedfellows as *Seven Against Thebes*, *Bacchae* and *Birds*. Many choral odes are fine examples of Greek poetry, and there is evidence that they were widely appreciated and admired. The writer Plutarch, for example, recounts how Athenian soldiers captured by the Sicilians were exempted from slavery and sent home simply for reciting to their culture-hungry conquerors such Euripidean lyrics as they could remember.

## Later Greek theatre

In the time of Menander, a century after the heyday of Athenian theatre, superficially similar conditions masked substantial changes in detail and emphasis. Competitive festivals were still held in Athens, but the new tragedies were by all accounts inept and have not survived. In comedy, there was a shift in emphasis from political and personal satire towards rustic knockabout on the one hand, and on the other the genial, domestic drama of which Menander was the acknowledged master, and which became the dominant form of the somewhat marginalised theatre of the succeeding centuries.

From the fourth century onwards, theatres were built all over the Greek world and were focal areas for their communities. Some were large – those which survive at Ephesus and Taormina are cases in point – but many were small, seating as few as two or three hundred spectators, and doubled as venues for civic assemblies and other gatherings, for example slave auctions and produce markets. (St Paul held evangelistic meetings in theatres; one of these, at Ephesus, is described in the Acts of the Apostles.) Although such events and other kinds of entertainment (ballet, mime and, in Roman-dominated areas, gladiatorial displays) shared the theatre bills, it was possible for dramatic actors to make a full-time living, touring old plays and creating new ones to suit local audiences.

In modern times, these developments have sometimes been deplored as a decline from the intellectually more rigorous theatre of fifth-century Athens. But although much of the theatre entertainment in Menander's time and later was ephemeral, it was also vibrant, popular and highly successful. It could even be argued that it, and not the comparatively highbrow drama which survives, was the dominant ancient Greek theatrical form.

## Language and music

All plays, tragedy and comedy alike, were written throughout in verse. This was partly convention. Since Homer's time, verse had been used for what we would think of as 'imaginative literature', and prose had been reserved for what we might call 'non-fiction': speeches, public records, philosophical and historical writing. If anyone had asked, Greek writers might also have said that once Homer had shown how to articulate action, character and emotion in verse, any other medium seemed second-rate. And in the theatre at least, the reason was also to do with physical movement. Ancient Greek verse was organised in patterns based on the different 'lengths' of syllables – a 'long' syllable (say, the 'hope' in 'hopeless') was considered three times as long as a 'short' syllable (say, the 'hot' in 'hothouse') – and each of the available patterns gave the verse its own unique speed and character. (Thus, the name Oidipous – Oedipus – has three syllables, long-short-long or

3-1-3.) Since, in the danced sections of plays, verse rhythms were also those of the choreography, the patterns crucially affected the look as well as the sound of the action in performance. The exact movements are now lost to us, but a moment's reflection will show the different effects which will be produced in an actor's body when the physical appearance of each instant of a performance is as precisely notated, and observed, as is its sound. Use of the word 'feet' for verse patterns is not an accident. When this choreography is observed by large groups of people, for example the chorus, the effect is astounding, more systematic than anything practised in current Western theatre – and, alas, hard to recreate by performers and audiences using translated texts.

The simplest pattern, used in most spoken dialogue, was based on the *iambos*, a short syllable followed by a long syllable, with the verse stress on the short syllable. (Satisfyingly, in all Greek poetry, verse stress is not always the same as the natural stress of the words, so that there is a constant effect of syncopation, the ear being tickled when the stresses do not coincide and seduced when they do.) Six *iamboi* made one line of verse, and in performance they produced an effect of fast, rhythmic everyday speech, in a way similar to the blank verse lines which predominate in Shakespeare. The pace and emotional intensity of spoken dialogue could be changed by incorporating passages based on the *trochee* (the mirror image of the *iambos*, a long syllable followed by a short one). Here the lines were often arranged with four *trochees* each, and the stress pattern, still on the first syllable of each *trochee*, coincided less often with the words' natural stresses, producing an unsettled and edgy effect.

At moments of highest tension, and in choruses, lyric rhythms were used, and the playwright had access to a couple of dozen groupings, each with its own impact on emotion and performance rhythm. *Anapaests*, for example (patterns of two short syllables followed by one long one, with the stress on the first syllable), were used for striding passages in tragedy – for example when the chorus first entered the theatre – and in comedy for arguments. *Tribrachs* (short-short-short), *choriamboi* (long-short-short-long), *epitrites* (long-short-long-long), *dochmiacs* (short-long-long-short-long or long-short-short-long-short-long) and others were used as needed to give colour and impetus to lyric passages of all kinds; the choruses in particular were virtuoso pieces of rhythmic and musical construction. The nearest Greek equivalent to this today is the exuberant, multi-rhythmed complexity of folk dance, especially in Crete and Macedonia. Rhythmic nuance of a similar kind is still characteristic of Arabian and Indian music.

To speakers of a non-quantitative language like English, these details can seem both complex and arcane. The idea of syncopation is easy enough. It happens in English verse, as when the rhythmic stress of Hamlet's 'To be or not to be, that is the question,' a 'bump' every second syllable with the last syllable hanging from the end of the line as if rhythmically redundant, is not identical to the natural stress of the spoken words, where we might emphasise 'that' and skip over 'is the'. But English verse which uses heavily stressed and complex patterns, such as the mixed *tribrachs* and *trochees* of a limerick, tends to sound comic rather than subtle. Ancient Greek listeners, by contrast, must have been seduced by endless tiny nuances; the analogy for us is less with poetry than with the inflexions and subtleties of music.

Lyric sections of the plays – that is, most of the chorus's material, and passages of heightened emotion in the dialogue scenes – were accompanied by a wind-player and a percussionist, and were sung or declaimed in a manner hard to reconstruct today. Once again, the basic idea was varied in every conceivable way. The final sections of many surviving tragedies are predominantly in lyric metres, so that the plays end in a more heightened emotional state than they began – and tension is increased by having the characters use different lyric metres from one another, and from the chorus, so producing rhythmic and lyrical counterpoint of considerable complexity. Another idea, particularly common in Euripides, is to create a dislocated emotional dialectic by giving one character in a scene lyric metres and the other *iamboi*. Hekabe's character in *Women of Troy* is articulated in this way, the dislocation between her rhythms and those of other characters creating a distance between herself, as queen, and the other women, and bridging or emphasising it according to the emotional situation.

In Aristophanic comedy, lyric metres are largely confined to the chorus, except where characters parody the lyrical style, as Philokleon does from his 'prison' in *Wasps*, or break into unrestrained joy or ecstasy, as Dikaiopolis does in *Acharnians* when contemplating peace. Many of Aristophanes' surviving comedies end with a metrical riot, a finale involving music, solemnity, comic songs and eccentric dance. The wedding processions which end *Birds* and *Peace* are typical. Menander's verse is almost entirely in *iamboi*, ordinary speech made poetry, and moves with a spring-heeled elegance which was much admired. Lyrical complexity in productions of his plays would be provided during the interludes, but they do not survive and their nature can only be imagined.

## The style of tragedy

Although the surviving tragedies differ (sometimes considerably) in detail, all follow the same basic conventions. With one exception (*Persians*) each draws its story from ancient myth, sometimes relevant to Athens and/or Dionysos, more often not. The characters have a dimension larger than life – they are gods, heroes and heroes' wives, surrounded with all the penumbra of legend – and they are set in the context of a chorus which does not share this dimension, which indeed is determinedly, sometimes aggressively, unheroic. (Two plays are exceptions: sea goddesses are the chorus of *Prometheus Bound*, and Furies are one of the two choruses of *Eumenides* – the other is Athenian citizens.) Use of myth also lets the playwright assume that his audience will know the bones of the story, allowing him to focus attention on the particular meanings he wants to draw out from it.

In performance, the chorus articulated the entire progress of a tragedy. Their first entrance was sometimes delayed for several minutes, during which gods, supernatural spirits or individual humans set out, in a prologue, the place, time and background to the action which was to follow. The entry of the chorus was usually a spectacular set piece, poetically rich and establishing the emotional landscape of the play much as the prologue had set out its narrative parameters. Sometimes there was an ironical clash between the two events, as in *Seven Against Thebes* when the chorus's articulation of panic and distress contrasts with the triumphant bravery of Eteokles' speech which precedes it. In one play, *Orestes*, Euripides subverts the whole tradition, making Elektra try to stop the chorus singing in case they wake the sick Orestes.

Once in the *orchestra*, the chorus normally remained in the theatre for the duration of the play, a kind of living and reactive reminder of the human dimension of what was being enacted in the dialogue scenes. Three or four times during the action, they performed long passages of lyric movement and dance, of high poetic and emotional intensity. On the page, especially to readers concentrating on the 'meaning' of the dialogue scenes, these choruses can sometimes seem to interrupt the action or be thematically irrelevant. In the theatre, they reassert or redirect the emotional narrative. The energy of each dialogue scene spins out of the preceding chorus, the actors' words taking up or contrasting with what has gone before. The choruses are not interludes and do not end scenes; they begin them.

The dramatic narrative, articulated by actors in dialogue with one another or with the chorus – never more than three speaking characters onstage at once, and often only two or one – sets out the intellectual and emotional dilemma which the playwright has drawn from the central myth. The audience already knows that Oedipus is to discover the truth and blind himself, that Orestes will avenge his father or that Prometheus is being punished for giving divine fire to mortals; the dialogue scenes set out the moral, philosophical, intellectual, political and personal background and implications of these events, examining both them and the (often mistaken) attitudes of the characters and using every dialogue strategy, from argument to storytelling, from monologue to repartee, to do so.

Three kinds of scene were particularly favoured, and appear in most surviving plays. In one, two characters set out opposing points of view in long rhetorical speeches without interruption, and then draw out the emotional implications in a passage of *stichomythia* ('rapid dialogue') in which characters each say one line, or half a line, in alternation. In the second, a soldier, servant or other 'ordinary' person appears, to announce, in a long monologue, the suffering and death of the central character – usually to an interested party, a relative or friend, who then has a scene of lyrical regret and mourning with the chorus. In the third, in the final section of the play, actors and chorus share a scene of lyric grief or acceptance, a kind of musical rounding-off and winding-down of the emotion which the action has generated and expressed. In some plays – Sophocles' *Ajax* and *Philoktetes*, and half a dozen of Euripides' later plays – this scene is replaced or followed by one of increasing emotional tension between two characters, interrupted at its climax by the appearance of the *deus ex machina*, 'god from the machine', who stops the action, bluntly announces how the story will end and orders the characters to accept their destiny.

## The style of comedy

The form of Aristophanic comedy is as controlled as that of tragedy. The play begins with a prologue setting out some problem or injustice and announcing the hero's extravagant plan to put things right. The chorus then enters, usually hostile, and the hero has to win their support. The argument between them is partly in dialogue, partly lyric, and often involves a formal, rhetorical debate. It is followed, about halfway through the play, by the *parabasis* ('stepping aside'), in which the chorus, in character, directly address the audience, commenting on the situation, the state of city affairs and the profession of comedy, the advantages of ensuring that Aristophanes wins the competition, and any other matters on the playwright's magpie mind. The second half of the play consists of a series of slapstick scenes, as cheats and frauds try to take advantage of the hero's new-found success and are repulsed. In between these scenes, the chorus perform short, satirical pieces of song and dance, sometimes related to the story and always attacking well-known 'real' individuals by name. Most plays end with orgies of lyric celebration, sometimes wedding processions: music (serious and silly), dance (lyrical and eccentric), prayers, jokes and slapstick, the Aristophanic mixture in microcosm.

In the bulk of Aristophanes' surviving plays, energy is shared between chorus and actors in a way different from tragedy (where choral energy predominates). In the early plays, the chorus begin by attacking the hero, but as soon as they are won over they become subordinate, urging him on and expanding on the benefits his grand new scheme will bring. Performance energy comes initially from the hero's need to convince the chorus, then passes to him as he baffles and outwits the frauds, and is finally shared in the all-engulfing, riotous finale. In later surviving plays, for example *Lysistrata*, *Festival Time* and *Frogs*, Aristophanes varied this structure, dividing the chorus, reallocating energy between the actors (using double acts, for example, in *Frogs* and *Festival Time*), and not clustering the fraud scenes but incorporating them in the ongoing story – in *Frogs*, for example, they occur almost from the start of the action, with the arrival of the corpse who refuses to carry Dionysos' luggage down to the Underworld. Each of the last surviving plays, *Women in Power* and *Wealth*, has its own unique form and prefigures the sequential, five-section narrative structure favoured in New Comedy.

Scholars often divide Aristophanes' 'Old Comedy' from Menander's 'New Comedy' and describe the (lost) products of the years between as 'Middle Comedy'. However, even in the later works of Aristophanes we can see the beginnings of the development away from the characteristic elements of 'Old Comedy' into those of 'New Comedy'. The chorus has a reduced role, represented increasingly by a stage direction indicating that there was a choral interlude rather than any text, the *parabasis* disappears, topical satire is reduced and the free-wheeling episodic anarchy gives way to a more domestic drama and a concern with plot and character that represent the beginnings of the traditions of situation comedy, romantic comedy and comedy of manners.

## Representation and narration in tragedy

It is often said, and it is generally true, that 'nothing happens in Greek tragedy'. Modern, realistic drama, whether on stage, film or television, is a ceaseless presentation of people doing things: eating, fighting, kissing, reading and so on. Physical action predominates; what we see is a simulacrum of the bustle of everyday real life. For example, Macbeth is the host of a dinner party before our eyes; Othello strangles Desdemona in plain view; Claudius watches a play while we absorb both it and his reaction. In Greek tragedy, by contrast, the main dramatic 'actions' are people talking or people listening. Most significant action is reported, and our interest is in the attitudes to that action of the narrator or the listener. When significant action *does* occur onstage – in recognition scenes, for example, or in such moments as the pinioning of Prometheus in *Prometheus Bound*, the letter scene in *Iphigeneia in Tauris* or the suicides of Ajax in *Ajax* and Evadne in Euripides' *Suppliants*, it is usually prepared and surrounded with so many layers of irony that it itself acquires a kind of iconic status, becomes the presentation of an attitude as well as a performed action.

Throughout the plays, articulation of attitude is the playwright's main concern. Each character has a standpoint, and that is revealed, reinforced or changed during the course of the play. No character in Greek tragedy is colourless: even a two-line messenger or attendant has, and expresses, a view about what is being revealed. Some attitudes are articulated in rhetorical, formal speeches, others in rapid dialogue, others in lyrical assertion, others again – something often forgotten by people who read the plays on the page rather than seeing them in performance – in the reactions of those actors who are onstage, by silence. (In each moment of an argument, for example, the attitude of the listener is as crucial as that of the speaker.) Greek tragic dramatists constantly prepare their characters, and us their audience, for an oncoming narrative: 'Here comes X. How sad she looks'; 'It's a messenger. What terrible news is coming now?'; 'Hear what I say: God speaks'. Such announcements, apparently bald and 'primitive', are in fact a principal dramatic strategy, setting up expectation and creating a mood and rhythm which give energy to the scene which follows. The person arriving, and those who are already onstage to respond to his or her arrival, are, so to speak, framed and presented to us. Before a scene even starts, its boundaries are established in our minds and resonate in the theatre.

This kind of drama relies heavily on irony. There are always spectators and auditors; no statement is made without an audience. This is different from realistic theatre. In a realistic *Oedipus*, Jokasta might hang herself and Oedipus might blind himself before our eyes, and our interest would be partly voyeuristic – 'How do they do that?' When the same actions are narrated, and the mood of the scene of narration is previously established, our interest is focused not only on the detail of the events but also on their effects: on the narrator, on the listeners, on our own appreciation of the 'deeper' meaning of the play. When a narrator layers his or her account with detail, as Euripides' 'messengers' often do, or with emotional colouring, as is common in Sophocles, the playwright is extending not the event but its meaning – a characteristic Greek dramatic strategy. The process is deepened by specific ironies of all conceivable kinds. What we think of each statement, each narration, is coloured by what we know of the speakers, their hearers, the over-riding 'meaning' of the play, our previous knowledge and expectation of the myth and the characters within the myth. The interface between such expectation and what actually happens, moment by moment, is where the play takes place. Dionysos, patron of drama, was among other things the god of change, of perception acquired through metamorphosis.

## The rationale of tragedy

Because tragedies were performed at a festival which was at least in part religious, and because in his treatise on tragedy, *Poetics*, Aristotle chose, as prime exemplars of the form, plays concerned with destiny and acceptance of the will of heaven (notably *Oedipus Tyrannos*), it is sometimes assumed that Greek theatre was a predominantly religious art form. The surviving plays hardly bear this out, particularly if one thinks of 'religious drama' as solemn, didactic and ritualistic. It is really only in *Oedipus Tyrannos* and *Antigone* that 'destiny' is seen in such stark and unflinching terms. In most plays the gods are capricious, cruel, deceitful and subject to human emotion, and their interaction with mortals, like that of mortals with each other, is subject to all kinds of slyness, wit and irony – not qualities the later Christian West liked to associate with religion, but quintessentially theatrical. Compassion and redemption are not attributes of the gods in Greek tragedy, and very few plays end with the protagonists understanding the purposes of heaven. Acceptance is mandatory and imposed, and the message presented to the audience, often explicitly by the chorus, is not that the gods are all goodness and all mercy but that they are beyond our comprehension and that when we try to understand them we discover more not about them but about ourselves.

If dogma did have any part in Greek tragedy, in the surviving plays it is more often political than religious. Clear strands in the work of all surviving dramatists are patriotism for Athens and its institutions and a series of 'lessons' (in Aristophanes' sense) about the ethics and morality of different systems of government, in peace and war. Sometimes the didacticism is overt, as in the pro-Athenian fanfares which end the *Oresteia* or run through *Oedipus at Kolonos* and Euripides' *Suppliants*. In other plays the messages are no less clear but more discreet. *Prometheus Bound*, *Antigone* and *Herakles* are, in part and in their different ways, meditations on the nature of power, and the tyrant rulers and commanders of *Agamemnon*, *Ajax*, *Philoktetes*, *Hekabe* and *Medea* are drawn with a two-dimensional harshness only just this side of melodrama. A main theme of *Persians*, *Ajax*, *Women of Troy* and Euripides' *Suppliants* is the effect of war. Euripides' plays regularly set personal and interpersonal politics in the wider context of affairs: examples are the way such characters as Ion and Kreusa in *Ion*, Theseus in *Suppliants* and Menelaos in *Helen* change and grow in response to developments in the plot – and, equally strikingly, the way others (for example, Hippolytos in *Hippolytos*, Jason in *Medea* and Menelaos in *Orestes*) do not.

## Drama and politics

To the original Athenian audiences, all such matters would have had more than the abstract philosophical interest the same plays may kindle in us today. They arose directly out of the political situation of the city and its people, and descanted upon it in ways which were, no doubt, often unexpected but none the less relevant. This unspoken relevance is one of the most 'political' aspects of Greek drama. Its pungency in a city first basking in the glory of its triumphs in the Persian War and then gradually collapsing and losing hope in the generation-long Peloponnesian War against the Spartans is hard to recapture or imagine nowadays. Greek playwrights, again in Aristophanes' metaphor of the teacher, did present their audiences with a series of ideas to reflect on – and, in a way characteristic of Greek thought in general, those points were regularly not the ones that might have been expected.

The defeat of a huge invasion force from Persia in the 490s–480s, culminating in two significant victories each only a few kilometres from Athens itself (the land battle of Marathon in 490, the sea battle of Salamis in 480), led to an explosion of self-confidence and civic energy in Athens. As one of the co-leaders (with Sparta) of the Greek defence, Athens was famous wherever Greek was spoken, and quickly became the hub of a large admiring empire. Trade and tribute boosted the city's wealth, and – in particular under the leadership of Pericles (c.495–429) – its civic institutions, buildings, artists, soldiers and thinkers were widely admired and imitated. The decades after the Persian War, nicknamed in Athens 'the Fifty Years', saw the building of the Parthenon, the consolidation of 'democratic' rule and a respected legal system, an upsurge of 'philosophy' (scientific, moral and political thought), and a flowering in the arts of every kind, from sculpture and the writing of history to drama.

The bubble burst in 431. Throughout 'the Fifty Years', Athens' former co-leader against the Persians, Sparta, had been amassing an empire and dependencies of its own, and Athenians and Spartans had challenged each other in a dozen small-scale squabbles. In 431 open war was declared, and was fought as viciously as any civil war, Greek against Greek, neighbour against neighbour, friend against friend. At first the Athenians, flushed with their own greatness, imagined that they would crush the Spartans in a matter of months. In fact the fighting lasted on and off for twenty-seven years. In 404 the Athenians capitulated, and the Spartans imposed a form of rule which wiped out many of the political institutions which had underpinned the flowering of 'the Fifty Years'. This, coupled with the fact that there can hardly have been a family in the city and surrounding area which had not lost men and property during the fighting, left the population exhausted and sceptical about many of the ideas and beliefs in which they had formerly gloried.

The 'Fifty Years' and the Peloponnesian War are the background to the entire great period of Athenian drama, and – since theatre was, after architecture, the main public artistic medium of the Athenian democratic state – each surviving play is, in part, a mirror of its audience and the circumstances in which it was performed. No tragedies are untouched by politics, whether obliquely (as in Sophocles' surviving plays) or more overtly (as in those of Aeschylus and Euripides). Political pungency is a feature of all Aristophanes' surviving comedies except *Wealth*, as he makes his characters hark back to the glories of the 'good old days' of the Persian War, underlaying the hilarity with a melancholy and lyrical nostalgia whose effect on audiences in general must have been profoundly moral. The plays he wrote after the fall of Athens include the cynical *Women in Power*, about an 'ideal' society which comes hard up against human passion and venality, and *Wealth*, an almost apolitical social farce about the effects of healing the blind god of Wealth and letting him see his potential beneficiaries. Fifty years after *Wealth*, by the time of Menander, this kind of non-political comedy had become the norm, satirising the follies not of groups but of individual people.

## Characterisation

Ancient Greek playwrights and audiences were as interested in character as we are, but in a completely different way. Modern audiences are, in the main, fascinated predominantly by the individuality of literary and dramatic characters, the way their uniqueness is revealed and impinged on by the events in which they take part, and its effect on those events. If Macbeth had Othello's character, not his own, the action and meaning of the play *Macbeth* would be considerably affected. In Greece, by contrast, people were fascinated with characters as types, and individuals were interesting inasmuch as they conformed to or deviated from those types. In the time of Menander, Aristotle's disciple Theophrastos wrote thirty thumbnail sketches of such people: the busybody, the flatterer, the superstitious person and so on. The work was called *Characters* (literally 'impressions', images like those a sealstone makes on clay) – and grew out of Aristotle's work on *Ethics*, which deals with the virtues which enhance 'ideal' human behaviour and the vices which detract from it.

It is easy to see this kind of fascination as the root of character creation in New Comedy – where people are resourceful slaves, innocent virgins, toadies, harassed parents, boastful soldiers and so on – and also to project it back into the work of Aristophanes and the tragic dramatists. There is a 'type' of ruler, for example, and Greek interest in the characters of, say, Klytemnestra in *Agamemnon*, Kreon in *Antigone* or Theseus in Euripides' *Suppliants* would be partly in the ways they conformed to or deviated from that type. Similar tragic types – suffering hero, noble stripling, grieving mother – are found, not only in the plays, but also as subjects in

24

the fine art of the period. Comic types – farmer, hag, slave, soldier – were equally well established.

This is not to say that character drawing in the plays was formulaic, rather that it took formula as its starting point, making dramatic and literary use of each individual's relationship with his or her character stereotype. The tragic dramatists used myth stories in a similar way, creating and exploring points of difference, of focus, between the received myth story, known to the audience, and their own individual treatment. No one reading the unadorned myth accounts of (say) Prometheus, Oedipus or Medea could have predicted in advance what Aeschylus, Sophocles or Euripides was to make of them; our reading nowadays of the myths is skewed if we come to them first in tragedy. In the same way, character drawing exploits prior knowledge and expectation in a creative way, often by combining two or more character types in the same individual – as when Aeschylus depicts Prometheus as a combination of counsellor and suffering hero, or Sophocles makes Ajax a combination of ruler, father, fool and victim. Euripides' character drawing, even more complex and more suggestive, plays variations on a dozen stereotypes (as in the cases of, say, Phaedra in *Hippolytos* or Hekabe in *Women of Troy*) without ever losing sight of the basic nature of Greek dramatic characterisation, its ironising of expectation. (We are never interested in Phaedra or Hekabe as individuals in their own right, as we are with, say, Lear or Shylock. What matters is their character in the action and in the meaning of the action. Everything they do, say or are is relevant only to the situation and story in which they appear.) Aristophanes used a similar ironical strategy, giving mythical characters (such as Dionysos or Iris) everyday, bathetic and ludicrous tics of behaviour and attitude, and drawing people from real life – Socrates, Lamachos, even his audience itself, characterised in *Knights* as the gross and venal Demos – into his comedies and deconstructing them to make myth beings or stereotypes.

As with so much else in Greek drama, the precedent for these approaches to character drawing was the work of Homer. He removed inertness from his chosen myth stories (the inertness we find, for example, in Hesiod) by constantly altering the focus between grandeur and intimacy, showing large in small and small in large. His Trojan War is both an epic struggle on the mightiest human scale and a series of individuals fussing about their armour, relaxing with friends, boasting to enemies, meeting sordid deaths or bewailing the loss of those they loved. The societies he shows – in Zeus' palace on Olympos, on Circe's island, on the walls and plains of Troy, in the Greek camp, in a swineherd's hut or a rich man's hall on Ithaka – are presented with a realism, or at least verisimilitude, quite unlike the blunt assertiveness of myth, and his characters, similarly, are drawn with an attention to tiny, often irrelevant-seeming detail which gives them the sap of life. Over-riding themes are addressed in the same way, not with assertion but by accumulation of detail. Examples are the way the *Iliad* handles the nature of command by focusing on a score of different characters and instances, showing the futility of war not in epic panoramas but in the pain and tears of a dozen individuals, and the *Odyssey* builds up the picture of what makes a human being gradually, piece by piece, so that we observe and learn it as Odysseus lives and discovers it in himself.

Homer's specific characterisation of some of the major people in the myth stories was followed by most later writers, including dramatists, as if it was canonical. Andromache is normally noble and suffering, Menelaos vacuously boastful, Odysseus devious and irresistible. More importantly, Homer's method of revealing rather than declaring the point of a story, and doing so by the way he organises the balance between event and character, incident by incident, was a major influence on drama. Each of the dramatists has his own style of character drawing, and the art of character drawing itself changes as the century proceeds, from the blunt, declarative typologies favoured in Aeschylus' surviving plays through Sophocles' more complex psychological exploration of the stereotypes to the impassioned, often self-baffling mixtures of inner turmoil and outward self-possession shown by many Euripidean characters. Examples of all of these can be multiplied in Homer. But he also gave the dramatists another character, undeclared but vital to their art. In Homer's epics, the principal character of all is the narrator, framing, selecting, presenting, controlling the focus and guiding audience enjoyment and understanding. In drama, both tragedy and comedy, this function is taken over by the playwright, whose 'attitude' predominates in the play in a way unmatched in later drama (for example in Shakespeare, who wrote in a dozen different styles and modes, or Racine, who avoided authorial attitude altogether) but commonplace in prose fiction (for example that of Jane Austen or James Joyce). None of the tragic dramatists' plays, as they survive, could have been written by either of the others, and their respective treatments of incident and character in the two surviving myths which all three *do* use (the stories of Elektra and the Seven Against Thebes) show just how much each is, throughout, his own most important character.


## Translation

It is a truism that no translation can ever fully represent the original. In earlier times, when Greek plays were rarely performed and the minority who read them were educated in the original language, translation was regarded as at best irrelevant and at worst impertinent. But nowadays, when performances are common and the plays are widely enjoyed, the matter of translation is crucially important. The whole issue has been bedevilled in the West by the facts that in the Middle Ages the chief use for 'translations' was in church, and that, for reasons of dogma and interpretation, the sacred writings had to be rendered as literally as possible. The tradition grew – and still persists in some quarters – that this word-by-word literality is what 'fidelity' in translation means, and this is borne out by the need for literal translation in such nuance-free areas of modern international traffic as contracts, instruction manuals, appointment diaries, menus and airport signs.

Imaginative literature is completely different. Its lifeblood is not particularity but nuance, and the nuances are manifold: between two cultures, those of the original audience and the new audience; between two systems of thought, each embodied not merely in the words people speak but the implications and undertones those words have accumulated; in the case of Greek drama, between two historically remote periods, and in the case of all drama by the fact that the original author wrote not to be read from a book but to make a bridge in a theatre between performers and spectators. Bluntly, if translators of plays fail to move spectators or make them laugh, they fail their authors.

All this makes literary translation in general, and drama translation in particular, a subjective and ephemeral art. Good translations may outlive their original commissioning, may even set agendas and send awareness of the art in new directions. But by and large translations are dead (or should be dead) within a couple of generations. One of the problems with Greek drama in the past has been that some old translations have lingered well past their sell-by dates and have seriously skewed both understanding and enjoyment. The difficulty is not principally one of ideas or cultural awareness, since these can be studied in the abstract. It arises from the natures of the two languages, ancient Greek and (in our case) modern English. The Greek playwrights wrote in a language which was full of precise rhythmic nuances which made a subtle but clear distinction between lyricism and bluntness. English, by contrast, is organised by stress and its sounds are brisker. Greek is a language of accumulation, in which words can grow like coral reefs (for imposing effect in Aeschylus; for comic effect in Aristophanes), and in which sentences can be prolonged almost indefinitely by subordinate clauses and other syntactical subtleties. English, by contrast, uses unaccreted words and a minimum of syntax. The result is that when Greek is plain and blunt, it is an effect as carefully deployed as when English is ornate and ponderous. To replicate the 'wrong' structure at the 'wrong' moment in a translation is like automatically withholding the verbs to the ends of phrases or sentences in a version from German – an effect to be sure, but hardly one which represents the original.

The language of Greek plays is not uniform. Each surviving playwright has his unique style, and moments when the writers imitate, parody or borrow from each other are obvious and make a deliberate effect. Within the same author's work, within the same plays, the same speeches, even the same sentences and phrases, the language can change in a moment from one mode to another. Dialogue scenes, for example, are often written in 'simpler' Greek than anything else – except when a character colours an idea with poetry or rhetoric, or when emotion irradiates the thought being articulated. The plays include long rhetorical scenes, whose language is as ornate as the intellectual rationale it articulates – or is not, for irony is a favourite strategy even at such moments. Lyrical passages are syntactically looser and freer than such dialogue, both in the image-packed choruses and the many moments of ecstasy, grief or yearning which fill the plays. At regular points, syntax and rhetoric collapse altogether and are replaced by pure sound, emotion articulated in wordless cries which are none the less precisely notated. (In *Persians* there are over a hundred such utterances.)

The translator must bear all this in mind, but not necessarily replicate it in her or his own language. In any case, the problems are perhaps less urgent for readers or performers of the plays than for those who translate them. What does remain to be said is that, with very few exceptions, the surviving ancient Greek plays are masterpieces of art, and that if their qualities fail to leap from stage or page, the fault is that of specific interpreters, including translators, and not the playwrights.

# Aeschylus

## Life

Aeschylus is the earliest world dramatist any of whose works survive. He was born in about 525 BC. His father Euphorion was an aristocrat from Eleusis, a town near Athens which had been independent and prosperous since Minoan times, partly because of its fertile land and partly as home of the Eleusinian Mysteries. In such an area, a man of Euphorion's rank would probably have owned farming estates, or had some connection with the Mystery shrine, or both, but no information survives.

Dates are conjectural, but Aeschylus may have competed at the City Dionysia as early as 500. His first surviving play, *Persians*, dates from some thirty years later. In the intervening years, as well as working in drama, he spent some time fighting the Persians, in the infantry at the battles of Marathon (490) and possibly Plataia (479) and in the navy in 480, perhaps at Artemision (where his brother was killed) and certainly at Salamis, so graphically described by the messenger in *Persians*. His self-composed epitaph, which mentions none of his dramatic achievements, talks with pride of this military service.

Defeating the Persians was the high point of a growth in Athenian civic and political self-confidence during Aeschylus' lifetime. In 510, when he was about fifteen, the unpopular autocrat Hippias was driven into exile, and the citizens, led by Kleisthenes, developed a political system in which new laws were discussed and passed by a representative Assembly and supervised by elected officials responsible to that Assembly. Although to modern eyes this 'democracy' (as the Athenians proudly called it) was remarkably partial, ignoring the rights of women, slaves, resident foreigners and other non-citizens, some two-thirds of the population, it worked well both in the crucible of the Persian War and in the period of triumph and prosperity which followed, 'the Fifty Years'. Aeschylus is the only surviving Athenian playwright to live in an age gilded by triumph and untouched by self-doubt – and his work seemed to later generations both to express and to validate the human qualities and energies which made possible such an explosion of honour, justice, creativity and material and political success.

Aeschylus wrote some eighty to ninety plays altogether (that is, entered for some twenty to thirty competitions). The surviving plays date from his fifties and sixties. He visited Sicily at least twice, at the invitation of the theatre-loving ruler Hieron. In 472 he revived *Persians* there, and wrote *Etneans* (now lost) to inaugurate a theatre in the newly built city of Etnea. Some time after the Athenian production of the *Oresteia* in 458, he went back to Sicily, and died there in 456 aged about sixty-nine.

## Works

Alone of the surviving dramatists, Aeschylus specialised in sequences of linked plays, on different stories from the same myth-cycles. Although other groupings were possible (for example, pairs of plays), the commonest arrangement was three tragedies and one satyr play, performed on the same festival day in sequence. Except for *Persians*, each of his surviving works, the Oresteian trilogy and the four individual plays, is a torso whose effect was not as a separate unit but as part of a longer and more complex experience. (Even the celebrations which close the surviving *Oresteia* must be imagined in relation to the satyr play which followed them.) His surviving plays were originally no more self-standing works of art than are the Parthenon remains or the now armless and unpainted Venus de Milo. Extant titles suggest that his lost plays include sequences on the myths of the Trojan War, the Argonauts, Odysseus and, not least, Dionysos himself. He was a master of the satyr play, and this perhaps led to his reputation for being, in Aristophanes' phrase, 'a Bacchic king', writing lines which admirers said were 'full of Dionysos' and detractors said must be composed when he was drunk. Seven plays survive: *Persians* (472), *Seven Against Thebes* (467), *Suppliants* (463), the *Oresteia* trilogy (*Agamemnon, Libation-Bearers, Eumenides,* 458) and *Prometheus Bound* (no recorded date; some dispute whether the play is actually by Aeschylus).

## Style and approach

Taken as a whole, Aeschylus' surviving plays are remarkably diverse in structure, style and approach. He used the same elements each time, but varied their placing, length and density, sometimes for clear dramatic or conceptual reasons, sometimes for purposes which, in the absence of context, are less apparent. One example, taken at random, makes the point: messengers' speeches. None of the surviving plays contains a messenger's speech of the type which seems later to have become standard. In *Persians* the messenger reports 'real' events (the battle of Salamis and its aftermath) in such a way that they seem remote from the time of the play's action, are given an almost mythical, Homeric aura. In *Agamemnon* the messenger puts a kind of common-man's gloss on the epic grandeur of the Trojan War, whose causes, sorrows and outcome the chorus and Klytemnestra have already presented to us. The messenger's speeches in *Libation-Bearers* and *Seven Against Thebes* are no more than bald announcements of long-expected events (the deaths of Aigisthos and of Eteokles and Polynikes), and attention is focused not on the deaths themselves but on the effect of the announcement on the messenger's hearers (respectively, Klytemnestra and the chorus of Theban women). In *Seven Against Thebes*, at least as it stands, the power of an extended messenger's speech might well have been undercut by the long scene in which the soldier describes the seven champions and Eteokles responds. In *Libation-Bearers*, during the servant's announcement of Aigisthos' murder, the focus is so tightly on Klytemnestra that it is almost as if we have entered her private thoughts, an intimacy essential for the following scene between her and Orestes, which an orotund messenger's speech would dissipate. There are no messenger speeches at all in *Eumenides, Suppliants* and *Prometheus Bound.* In *Eumenides,* Athene announces the result of Orestes' trial in two lines, and the scene focuses on his reaction and that of the Furies. In *Suppliants* there is nothing substantial for a messenger to report: the main issue, whether the Argives will welcome the Danaids or leave them to the Egyptians, is resolved onstage. In *Prometheus Bound* the messenger's role (and, to some extent, style) is taken over by two of the characters. Io tells the causes of her madness and wandering, and Prometheus outlines the cosmic events which led to his punishment and foretells Io's future and the resolution of the story.

In a similar way, Aeschylus' characters and chorus constantly reflect on the entire continuum of the myth of which each individual play is part, looking back at past events and forward to what may happen, placing moments of specific action (Agamemnon's murder, for example, or the homecoming of Xerxes) in contexts which are far more the focus of the play than are those individuals. His drama is not one of consecutive narrative (of the kind which predominates in Sophocles' and Euripides' surviving plays, where action is continuous) but of a systematic alteration of focus, pulling away from intimacy to reveal the wider perspective, and then closing back on another specific instance and another confrontation. In pre-Aeschylean drama, the hero's main action might have been the subject of an entire play; in Aeschylus it is shown to be part of a much larger 'action', of wider significance than the fate of a single individual.

The analogy for this method is not drama but Homer's *Iliad.* In that, the narrative constantly changes perspective, moving rapidly from scene to scene, dislocating the time sequence, focusing on individual reactions or the meaning of specific events and then returning to the sweep of the story and its over-riding meaning. In public readings of the *Iliad* (such as those given annually in Athens), the experience was corseted by the narrator's single voice, impersonating not only the characters in the action but also Homer himself. Even sequences in the *Iliad* which might now seem quintessentially 'dramatic' (for example, Achilles' and

34

Agamemnon's quarrel at the beginning, the moment in Olympos when Zeus refuses to reveal his purposes to Hera, or Priam's visit to Achilles to beg Hektor's body for burial) are modulated through the narrator. We are always aware of the context both of the story and of the 'performance' we are witnessing, live in ancient Athens, in our minds as we read from the page today.

Aeschylus found a way to replicate this double perspective onstage, replacing the narrator in moments of dramatic intimacy by actors playing individual characters, and constantly using other characters and the chorus to give epic and philosophical perspective. His dramatic predecessors, using a single actor and the chorus, were able to present the climactic moment of suffering at the centre of each myth story, and to give a context of grief or joy. But without Aeschylus' addition of the second actor, and the variety of dramatic strategies this allowed, their work must have been predominantly lyrical, static and presentational (of situation, not character or attitude) rather than critical, ironical and devious in the Aeschylean manner.

In particular, the panorama of cause and effect, the continuum of cosmic and human meaning of which the individual's suffering was part, could in pre-Aeschylean drama only be narrated, not shown. An example is Agamemnon's entry into Mycenae. Homer would have described it, perhaps giving voice to Klytemnestra and Agamemnon as Aeschylus does, embodying the choral foreboding in narrative and dwelling on the detail of the crimson carpet in ways which he would pick up later, when describing the net in which Agamemnon was trapped and butchered in the bath-house. A pre-Aeschylean dramatist such as Thespis might have made Agamemnon *describe* his intention to enter on the crimson carpet, and let us hear the choral anxieties and reflections, but the moment of entrance itself, even if *described* by the chorus (in lines like 'The king goes in, treading the carpet of blood to his death'), would have remained inert, all resonance left to the spectator's imagination. In Aeschylus' *Agamemnon*, by presenting a four-cornered dialectic scene, in which Agamemnon, Klytemnestra, the chorus leader (trying to warn Agamemnon of danger without actually declaring it) and the chorus themselves (full of anxiety and then of a kind of resigned distress) each has a different level of understanding of what is happening, the playwright is able to show event, context, character and meaning in a single theatrical experience – and Aeschylus trumps even this with Klytemnestra's speech beginning 'The sea is there, and who shall drain it dry?'. The apparent whimsicality of this first line ushers in a moment of deepest irony and equivocation, so that the speech not only hands Agamemnon into the palace, and to his death, with language of fanfare-like richness but also sets the entrance in the framework of duplicity and discord which are part of the story's whole architecture and meaning.

As such sequences suggest, Aeschylus was a master of apposite surprise. His art was quintessentially theatrical, making metaphors for thought and experience which could seem more compulsive than reality itself. Several of the surviving plays include 'turns' which are at once stagy and thrillingly effective. Kassandra's scene in *Agamemnon* focuses the panic and separation from cosmic and intellectual order which underlie the whole situation in Mycenae. The stirring of the Furies in *Eumenides* makes explicit the nature of the cosmic malignity directed at Orestes and so prefigures both the trial scene and the 'softening' of the Furies at the end of the play. The ghost scene in *Persians* articulates the grandeur and helplessness of the 'old' Persia before the arrival of Xerxes who destroyed that glory. Io's appearance in *Prometheus Bound* simultaneously parallels and contrasts with Prometheus' helplessness at the hands of the gods. Prometheus is tethered, Io free, Prometheus able to soar in imagination, Io shackled to her own small suffering and destiny. In many sequences, time seems to collapse and expand before our eyes, as the immediate situation dissolves to show enormous vistas of events and consequences. In less than 250 lines, the opening chorus of *Agamemnon* relates the situation in Mycenae to the entire back history and meaning of the Trojan War. In some 300 lines of *Seven Against Thebes*, Eteokles and the soldier set out the glory and futility of war – and the scene ends by narrowing the focus to Eteokles' own heroic and patriotic determination and the certainty of his death. The choruses of *Libation-Bearers, Suppliants* and *Prometheus Bound* offer a seething emotional background (respectively, compassionate hope, panic and uncomprehending pity) against which immediate events are set.

## Metaphor and language

Such examples can be endlessly multiplied – the surviving plays are alert with dramatic cunning. But Aeschylus' metaphorical art works in small matters as well as large. At the time he was writing, people were not accustomed to discussing abstract matters in a logical, analytical fashion, and lacked the words to do so. The history of fifth-century philosophy is, in part, the invention of ways to tackle 'big' intellectual ideas, and it was not till the following century, with Plato and Aristotle, that a specialist vocabulary (terms like 'morals', 'ethics', 'politics', 'character' and 'virtue') became established. At the start of the process, with ideas far outsoaring the language needed to express them, thinkers like Homer and Hesiod devised a way of metaphorising abstractions by giving them personal identity and character ('lovely Hope', 'grim Death', 'brave Honesty' and so on) – and Aeschylus used a similar technique, extending it to the point where the cynic might say he became reluctant ever to call a spade a spade at all. ('Fish', to one of his characters, are 'silent children of the Unbounded'.)

The result is that language itself acquires a kind of mythic density, always seeming to suggest more than is actually expressed. 'Hope fluttered for a moment, and then was gone'; 'Happiness is a chalk drawing, cancelled by a damp sponge'; 'The trumpet flamed and fired their ranks'; 'Waves of the myriad-laughing sea' – such constant tripping of the audience's imagination ironises language itself. Nothing is quite what it seems or sounds like, a cloud of association surrounds every idea presented, and the effect is to involve the spectator, instant by instant, in creating both the nature and meaning of the spectacle. This elevation of ordinary matters to magnificence allows Aeschylus also to express the magnificent in terms of the ordinary – and places him, as a creator, in the rarefied company of a handful of the greatest geniuses in the history of the arts.

# Oresteia

The *Oresteia* was first performed at the City Dionysia of 458. Its four parts were the surviving tragic trilogy (*Agamemnon, Libation-Bearers, Eumenides*) and the lost satyr play *Proteus*. Proteus, in myth, knew the secrets of the universe. He evaded capture by taking on any shape at will, but if you could hold him despite his transformations, he answered your questions. In one version of the myth of the Trojan War (the one on which Euripides based *Helen*), the Queen of Sparta never went to Troy; instead the gods sent a phantom Helen in her place and left her under Proteus' protection. After the war Menelaos visited Proteus and discovered the truth. How Aeschylus used this myth is unknown – and its effect on the audience for the *Oresteia*, after the Panathenaic celebrations which end the trilogy we have, can only be imagined.

As the name *Oresteia* suggests, the sequence centres on the story of Orestes. Its anchor point is the moment when he murders Klytemnestra. Aeschylus makes this the heart of an exploration of the events and meaning of the entire myth cycle, tracing its causes back through the story (to Agamemnon's sacrifice of Iphigeneia at Aulis) and forward to Orestes' acquittal by Athene in Athens. In this sequence, the killing of Klytemnestra is one moment of frozen time, focusing the entire meaning of the myth on a single racked individual. Later, single plays on the subject (such as Sophocles' *Elektra*) make the tyrant-queen's death a deed of vindication and triumph, purging the evil in the royal house. Aeschylus makes it clear that there are still paths to tread and sufferings to bear before true understanding and resolution are achieved.

At a straightforward, storytelling level, the *Oresteia* is impressive for its range of dramatic strategies and techniques. Aeschylus' handling of time is particularly striking. At moments of close focus he slows down the action to draw out individual emotions. Examples are Agamemnon's entrance into Mycenae, Klytemnestra's murder, the stirring of the Furies and the end of Orestes' trial.

At other times, he uses poetry and choral movement to evoke enormous stretches of events – the first chorus of *Agamemnon* is typical. The characters (save, perhaps, for Apollo and Athene) are never one-dimensional, but varied and thrillingly theatrical: Agamemnon, Orestes, Elektra, and above all Klytemnestra, the watchman, the soldier and Kilissa. Each play has its eye-catching theatrical 'turn': the Kassandra scene in *Agamemnon*, Elektra's and Orestes' invocation of Agamemnon's ghost in *Libation-Bearers*, the stirring of the Furies and the trial in *Eumenides*. Poetic and rhythmic density in the writing is subtly varied, so that despite the trilogy's enormous span (3,900 lines, some five hours' continuous performance time) we are constantly refreshed, surprised and challenged. On the page, the *Oresteia* can seem leisurely and expansive; in the theatre, one is surprised at how fast it moves.

If storytelling were all, the *Oresteia* would be masterpiece enough. But Aeschylus also has points to make about grander matters. The immediate action is a metaphor, allowing exploration of an edifice of imposing philosophical enquiry. In all ancient Greek arts at the time, a favourite theme was *theomachy*, 'god-war', the struggle between the Olympians (led by Zeus) and the giants, Titans and supernatural monsters who challenged their authority. In most treatments of this conflict – for example, those depicted on the Parthenon marbles – the battles are straightforward affairs of spears, bows, rearing horses, contorted victims and triumphant victors. Aeschylus, by contrast, sees the struggle as a series of experiments in justice, an evolution from primitive chaos (symbolised by the Furies), through the partial order enforced by such gods as Zeus and Apollo (whose will is autocratic but whose nature admits benevolence) to the point where gods and humans seek to understand one another, producing justice by a process of partnership and co-operation (symbolised by Orestes' trial and Athene's part in it). In the myths, *theomachy* was a dynastic affair, each generation directly challenging its parents; by using as his metaphor a similarly dynastic myth, and teasing out not only the nature of absolute right and wrong but also the relationships between members of the same family and between males and females, Aeschylus is able to make his points not directly and didactically but by open-ended allusion and suggestion. Finally, in *Eumenides*, he stirs Athenian politics into the mixture, focusing the whole debate, specific and general, on the 'democratic' court of the Areopagus (whose nature and duties were a matter of controversy at the time of the original production), and ending the tragic portion of the sequence with a re-enactment of the main procession of the Panathenaia, a festival instituted to celebrate, precisely, the pre-eminence of Athens, its goddess and its people.

# Agamemnon

## Characters

WATCHMAN
KLYTEMNESTRA, *Queen of Mycenae*
SOLDIER (MESSENGER)
AGAMEMNON, *King of Mycenae*
KASSANDRA, *Trojan prophet, Agamemnon's concubine*
AIGISTHOS, *Klytemnestra's lover*
GUARDS, SERVANTS (*silent parts*)
CHORUS OF OLD MEN

## Synopsis

A watchman on the palace roof at Mycenae sees the beacon announcing that Troy has fallen. He is full of foreboding about Agamemnon's return. The chorus tell of events before the war started: the Greeks becalmed at Aulis; the prophet urging Agamemnon to ensure fair winds by sacrificing his daughter Iphigeneia; the moment of sacrifice. Klytemnestra describes the beacons and the victory they proclaim. The chorus sing how the gods punish human arrogance, and weep for the deaths of so many innocent men in the war 'for a worthless wife'. A soldier, coming to announce Agamemnon's arrival, tells of the physical hardship of the war, and of the storm which savaged the returning fleet. Klytemnestra proclaims her loyalty to Agamemnon, and the chorus sing of dynastic evil engulfing generation after generation.

Agamemnon enters with Kassandra and the rest of his booty. Klytemnestra begs him to walk into the citadel on a crimson carpet – an invitation he first rejects (on the grounds that it is fit only for a god) and then accepts. Again proclaiming her loyalty, Klytemnestra follows him, then returns and orders Kassandra inside to join the sacrifice. In a huge outburst of prophecy and misery, Kassandra talks of Apollo's cruelty, the fall of Troy, Agamemnon's and her own coming deaths, and the cloud of ghosts and Furies hovering over the royal house. The chorus try to calm her, and at last she goes into the palace. The chorus hear death cries offstage, but before they can decide what to do Klytemnestra is revealed with the bodies of Agamemnon and Kassandra, wrapped in a bloodstained, crimson net.

Klytemnestra tells the chorus that Agamemnon's death was the inevitable punishment for murdering Iphigeneia. Aigisthos claims his share of the triumph, saying that Agamemnon has paid the price for a crime of his father Atreus (serving his brother Thyestes a stew of Thyestes' own children's flesh). The chorus draw swords, but Klytemnestra tells Aigisthos to ignore them. Her words end the play as abruptly as if it had been sliced with a knife.

About the play

Taken on its own, *Agamemnon* is one of the most magisterial of all Greek tragedies, challenging mind and emotions in true Aristotelian fashion. Seen as part of a trilogy, it is also remarkable for what it foreshadows but leaves for later working-out. The theme of dynastic guilt, for example, is stated – when the chorus talk of Iphigeneia's sacrifice, or Aigisthos uses the grisly stew served by Atreus to Thyestes as justification for Agamemnon's murder – but the implications for the future, the way present actions will impinge on what is to come, are left for the next play in the sequence. Orestes is barely mentioned. The gods are presented as aloof and autocratic, beyond human understanding. The world of the play is arbitrary, bleak and violent.

In a similar way, *Agamemnon* sets up but never develops one of the trilogy's main themes, the relationship between male and female. In this play, at least, Klytemnestra is a better man than her husband. He has power but she has moral authority – a striking irony in view of the see-saw of guilt and innocence in the nature and deeds of each of them, and the first statement of an ambiguity which will define and motivate later parts of the trilogy, from Elektra's 'nerving' of Orestes to kill Klytemnestra in *Libation-*

*Bearers* to the moral argument underlying the trial scene in *Eumenides.* Even more unobtrusively, the hesitant, impotent character of the chorus in *Agamemnon* lays a foundation for developments in *Libation-Bearers* (when the chorus press hard for vengeance) and in *Eumenides* (when the chorus must be persuaded, must consent, before true justice can be achieved).

An important strand in Aeschylus' dramatic method is to show how Fate's imperatives impinge on individuals. He pinpoints moments when a character's 'journey' coincides with the workings of a cosmic purpose of which he or she may be only partially aware – and the Kassandra scene in this play is a prime example. Kassandra's fate, like Agamemnon's, like Klytemnestra's, is preordained and inevitable. In the scene before the gates, the progress of Fate coincides exactly with the point each character has reached: Kassandra's helpless despair, Agamemnon's folly and Klytemnestra's imperiousness.

# Libation-Bearers (Choephoroi)

## Characters

ORESTES, *Prince of Argos*
PYLADES, *Prince of Phokis, his friend*
ELEKTRA, *Orestes' sister*
DOORKEEPER
KLYTEMNESTRA
NURSE (KILISSA)
AIGISTHOS
SERVANT
GUARDS, SERVANTS (*silent parts*)
CHORUS OF WOMEN

## Synopsis

Orestes and Pylades make grief offerings at Agamemnon's tomb, then stand unseen while Elektra and the chorus pray to Agamemnon to send Orestes as his avenger. Elektra sees Orestes' offering on the tomb: her prayers are answered. Orestes comes forward, and after a tender scene of recognition explains that Apollo's oracle has sent him to end the evil in Argos.

After a ceremony of grief and prayers to Agamemnon to help restore justice, the chorus tell Orestes that Klytemnestra has dreamed of giving birth to a snake, a serpent son that bit her breast even as it drank her milk. Accepting this omen, he says that he will trick his way into the palace by pretending to be a stranger with news of Orestes' death. Once inside, he will take revenge.

After a choral song about women in myth who betrayed and murdered close relatives, Orestes knocks on the door and gives Klytemnestra the false news that Orestes is dead. Pretending grief, she says that she will decide with Aigisthos what to do. An old nurse, bewailing the death of the beloved Orestes she nursed as a baby, goes to fetch Aigisthos, and the chorus pray the gods to give Orestes courage.

Aigisthos hurries into the palace, and we hear his death cries. Orestes and Pylades, with bloody swords, follow Klytemnestra outside, and Pylades reminds Orestes that killing his mother is ordained by Apollo. Klytemnestra warns Orestes of the Furies' vengeance if he kills her. He and Pylades lead her inside. After the chorus sing how this vengeance was Apollo's will, the doors are opened, revealing Orestes with the bodies of Klytemnestra and Aigisthos. Almost at once the Furies begin swarming in his mind, and the chorus tell him to go to Delphi and beg for purification.

## About the play

After the grand, public sweep of *Agamemnon*, the focus of the action narrows first on intimacy (the ceremony before Agamemnon's tomb and the murderous business between Orestes and Klytemnestra) and then (as it were) on Orestes' mind as madness bites. The raucousness of the end of *Agamemnon* gives way to some of the most limpid poetry in all Greek tragedy, balanced by scenes of a fleet-footed lightness anticipating the style of Euripidean adventure: Elektra's recognition of Orestes, Orestes' and Pylades' welcome at the palace gate, the nurse's speech and the build-up to Orestes' murder of Klytemnestra.

The play is related to the rest of the trilogy chiefly by allusion and metaphor. The moment when Orestes displays the bodies of Klytemnestra and Aigisthos parallels the scene with Agamemnon's and Kassandra's bodies in *Agamemnon*. Images of cancer and corruption, picked up from the earlier play, are given a new association (that Orestes is a surgeon who will cut out diseased material and allow healthy blood to flow), and made to anticipate the Furies' change of heart in *Eumenides*, from blighting the land to protecting it. The gods, who in *Agamemnon* figured only as puppeteers of destiny, are now invited to validate specific human actions and a particular view of justice – a prayer whose fulfilment will be enacted in *Eumenides*.

In particular, *Libation-Bearers* takes up and develops the male/ female theme only briefly touched on in *Agamemnon*. The play is seen almost entirely from the female perspective. The chorus are palace women. Elektra controls both grief for Agamemnon and the impulse for revenge. The nurse reminds us of the (female controlled) continuum in human life which Aeschylus' (predominantly male) theatre audience may have been surprised to hear mentioned in public at all, let alone in such a 'heroic' context. Apart from Aigisthos (who has two speeches) and Pylades (who has three lines), the only man in the play is Orestes himself – and Aeschylus uses his character to explore the whole masculine/ feminine dichotomy. As the play begins, Orestes is unsure and unformed. The purpose of the ceremony between him, Elektra and the chorus (which takes up a third of the play) is as much for the women to 'man' him to kill Klytemnestra as to invoke justice; the invocation *is* the manning. Klytemnestra herself completes the process. By begging Orestes to spare her life, she persuades him, ironically, to murder her. He reaches the moment for which his life has been preparation, nerves himself to become greater than his mother, to become the man his father never was – and then, as madness clouds his mind, we see that the triumph is equivocal, that the issues are unresolved.

# Eumenides

## Characters

PRIESTESS OF APOLLO
APOLLO
ORESTES
KLYTEMNESTRA'S GHOST
ATHENE
HERMES, PILGRIMS, JURORS, ATTENDANTS (*silent parts*)
CHORUS OF FURIES
CHORUS OF CITIZENS

## Synopsis

Outside Apollo's shrine at Delphi, the priestess tells pilgrims of a terrifying sight. Orestes, surrounded by the terrible shapes of the sleeping Furies, has taken refuge at the omphalos (navel stone) at the heart of the shrine. The doors open to reveal them. Apollo tells Orestes that he must go to Athens, where his case will be tried. He (Apollo) will stand by him. As soon as Orestes leaves, Klytemnestra's ghost rouses the Furies and tells them their prey has escaped. After an argument, Apollo drives the Furies from the shrine.

In Athens, the Furies find Orestes in Athene's temple, and dance their binding spell, their death dance, round him. Athene intervenes. She hears the two sides of the argument (that Orestes' murder of Klytemnestra categorically deserves punishment; that it was just) and summons a jury of Athenians to judge the case. Apollo speaks for Orestes, saying that Klytemnestra deserved to die and was killed on his orders. The Furies' leader says that all must die who murder relatives: blood for blood. They argue whether the father or mother is the 'true parent', and Apollo uses Athene's birth (from Zeus' forehead, with no mother) to show that the father is supreme. The jury votes, Athene gives the casting vote, and Orestes is acquitted.

Orestes and Apollo leave the stage, and the Furies round on Athene, threatening to blight the city and land of Athens. Athene invites them, instead, to accept Zeus' justice and to become protectors of the city – no longer Furies but Eumenides, 'well-disposed ones'. The Furies accept, proclaim their love and support for the city, and a chorus of citizens take them in procession to new homes in caves under the Acropolis.

## About the play

It was a favourite technique in Greek drama to put gods onstage, giving them human characteristics and emotions as well as human form. (The idea parallels their depiction in the visual arts, and perhaps originated with Homer.) In *Eumenides* the issue of justice, which the human action of the trilogy has so far failed to resolve, is debated face to face by Apollo and the leader of the Furies, and Athene both organises the trial and delivers the casting vote.

This is done not merely for theatrical effectiveness. It objectifies the dilemmas of the story, isolates them and allows them to be 'solved' in a way beyond emotion. In this trial the issue is not really Orestes' personal guilt or innocence, but the abstract nature of those conditions. Once acquitted, he is dismissed from the action as summarily as a piece of forensic evidence might be returned to its cupboard. The remainder of the Orestes myth, in which this trial and its outcome were not the end of the matter, is ignored. The argument surrounding the degree to which blood guilt demands blood punishment is reduced to a few bald statements, such as the Furies' assertion that their avenging role is as old as time, or Apollo's analysis of whether the mother or the father is a child's true parent. Once the verdict is given, the issue is no more mentioned.

The reason for this briskness is suggested by the title of the play. *Eumenides* may be a culmination and resolution of the Orestes trilogy, but it also deals, specifically, with the Furies' manifestation as 'well-disposed ones'. The action shows their evolution from bloodhounds of the Underworld to still terrifying but comparatively benign protectors of Athens and its people, symbolically residing in the heart of the Acropolis rock. The first two-fifths of the play show them as primitive, mindless and hideous, fouling all they touch, conversing with ghosts, bickering with gods, yapping after prey. We see the binding spell, the 'loathsome saraband' with which they ensnare their victims. They agree to the trial only because Athene overbears them; incapable of logic, they threaten the jurors; the verdict enrages them. Then, in the closing scene, speaking for Zeus, Athene soothes them and persuades them to accept that universal order has changed and that they should honour and protect the mortal city where justice, the gods' most prized prerogative, has been manifest. Gods and humans process from the theatre, symbolically joining to celebrate the new order. In modern times, and outside Athens, the speed and assertion with which the ethical and moral dilemmas of the trilogy are resolved can be less persuasive than the anguished interrogations which have gone before. But in Aeschylus' own production, *Eumenides* triumphant, patriotic conclusion may well have carried all before it.

# Persians

## Characters

ATOSSA, *Dowager Queen of Persia*
SOLDIER (MESSENGER)
DARIUS' GHOST
XERXES, *King of Persia*
ATTENDANTS (*silent parts*)
CHORUS OF OLD MEN

## Synopsis

Outside the royal palace at Sousa in Persia, before the tomb of King Darius, the chorus describe the glittering expedition which left to conquer Greece. They are full of foreboding. Queen Atossa tells of a dream forecasting disaster, and it is proved true when the soldier brings news of the destruction of the fleet at Salamis. The chorus mourn for the dead and for Persia's lost glory, and they and Atossa beg Darius' ghost to rise from the grave and advise them. The ghost lays the blame on Xerxes, whose youth and blindness to destiny have caused catastrophe. It announces that he is on his way home, and asks the chorus to comfort him and advise him how to restore Persia's greatness by ruling wisely in future.

The ghost disappears, and the chorus recall Darius' greatness when he was alive, the cities he conquered and the empire he ruled. Xerxes stumbles in, dressed in the rags of his former magnificence, and he and the chorus end the play with a ceremony of grief for the soldiers lost in battle and the greatness of Persia which is now no more.

## About the play

*Persians* was first performed at the City Dionysia of 472, financed by the twenty-three-year-old Pericles (who went on to govern

Athens during its period of greatest glory). It was not part of a sequence, but was performed with three unrelated Aeschylus plays, now lost: *Phineus*, *Glaukos of Potniai* and the satyr play *Prometheus Firekindler*. *Persians* is the oldest surviving Greek play, and the first extant play in Western drama. But it is not therefore 'primitive'; written two-thirds of the way through Aeschylus' career, it is as imaginative and surefooted as any of his surviving plays.

Although Greek dramatists consistently revised and reinvented myth-stories, they rarely wrote plays with wholly original plots or on material not drawn from myth. *Persians* is the main surviving exception. Its subject is a real event, the failure of the expedition led against Greece by King Xerxes of Persia, and it includes an account of the destruction of the Persian fleet off Salamis in 480, only eight years before the play's production. Salamis is a small island in the Saronic Gulf near Athens, and the Persian ships were lured into the narrow straits between it and the mainland, where there was no room to manoeuvre and the (smaller) Greek ships could easily destroy them. Many of Aeschylus' audience took part in the battle, so that the soldier's account of it in this play must have had eyewitness force – something of which Aeschylus took full ironical advantage by telling the story not from the Greek point of view but from that of the defeated Persians.

Similar irony pervades the play. The only other Greek tragedies based on real events, *The Siege of Miletos* and *The Phoenician Women* by Aeschylus' predecessor Phrynichos (the latter play also about Xerxes' invasion), had little scope for irony. Both are lost, but reconstructions suggest that at the start of each of them a disaster was announced (the destruction of Miletos in 494 and the Persian defeat at Salamis), and the 'plays' consisted largely of songs of mourning divided between the chorus and a single actor. Placing the only dramatic event at the start must have made for a linear structure, leaving little opportunity for confrontation or surprise. In *Persians*, by delaying announcement of the defeat until halfway through the action, and the arrival of the main 'tragic' character (Xerxes) until some nine-tenths of the way through, Aeschylus makes possible all kinds of refractions and alternative views of the central events, and is able constantly to second-guess the audience's prior knowledge of the story.

Throughout the play, Aeschylus 'cuts' the narrative more like a modern film writer than a maker of 'well-made' drama. In effect, *Persians* is in four thematic blocks: the chorus's description of the expedition and their own foreboding, the soldier's account of Salamis, the raising of Darius' ghost and the mourning scene between Xerxes and the chorus. These are placed to have dramatic but not temporal logic, not so much telling the story as drawing out its underlying themes (the moral blindness of Xerxes and his people, and the bitter lesson defeat teaches them). In this scheme, space and time need have no literal verisimilitude. Darius' tomb is not a thousand kilometres from the royal palace (as in reality) but just outside the gates; Xerxes appears minutes after we hear of the defeat at Salamis, rather than after the weary months of his real-life journey home. (He is also wearing the same clothes, rags of his former pomp – a costume which perplexed generations of un-dramatically-minded commentators.) Freeing the action from realism allows Aeschylus to enter the minds of his characters, to explore the emotional landscapes of Darius and Atossa (emblems of Persia's ancient glory), Xerxes (embodiment of the rashness which destroyed it) and the dignified, bewildered chorus.

Perhaps the biggest surprise for the original audience, one hard to recapture today, was the play's 'take' on historical events. When we look at a Greek temple, we see predominantly stone: columns, pediments and lintels. But the stone shapes bound and are bound by the spaces between them, and those spaces are as much part of the building's 'meaning' as the stones. In a similar way, Aeschylus presents the defeat of the Persian invasion entirely from the Persian side (the stones, as it were), and allows the Greek triumph (the space, as it were) to make its effect not with patriotic fanfares but by insinuation and juxtaposition. The method allows him simultaneously to show two aspects of the same situation, each depending on and enhancing the other – the quintessence of drama.

In particular, this tactic strips *Persians* of jingoistic smugness.

The play's underlying theme is the working of *ate*, that disastrous blindness to wider moral issues which the gods send on mortals dazzled by their own magnificence. Unlike *hubris*, the conceit which leads mortals to challenge the gods and which can be purged only by death, *ate* falls like a cancer on its victims and requires no intention; since it results from a misreading of destiny, it allows the possibility of survival. Once the blindness is corrected (usually by much suffering – for example, in *Persians*, the loss of a million lives and a nation's self-esteem), a new course can be set which is more in line with the requirements of destiny. At the end of the action Xerxes is redeemed, not dead. As the ghost has predicted, he and the chorus may together find some way to restore Persian greatness, this time unflawed by *ate*. To modern spectators and readers, the point may seem strikingly religious – far more so than the pessimistic grimness of *hubris*-oriented tragedy – and, as with so much else in *Persians*, it is all the more impressive for being not stated but left hanging in the air.

# Prometheus Bound

## Characters

PROMETHEUS
HEPHAISTOS
MIGHT
IO
OCEAN
HERMES
FORCE (*silent part*)
CHORUS OF SEA NYMPHS

## Synopsis

The scene is a remote mountainside. Might and Force bring in
Prometheus, and Hephaistos spikes him to the rock: his punishment for disobeying Zeus. Left alone, Prometheus sings of
injustice and the eternity of his suffering. The chorus enter. They
sympathise with Prometheus, and he tells how he helped Zeus
defeat the Titans, how he stole fire from heaven to help human
beings and how Zeus punished him. Ocean tries in vain to
persuade him to submit. Prometheus likens himself to Atlas,
Typhon and others punished for defying Zeus.

After a chorus of pity, Prometheus describes the blessings he
gave mortals: intelligence, learning, civilisation, respect for the
gods. He mentions a secret he alone knows, which will threaten
the gods unless he is set free to tell it. The chorus pray that they
may never challenge God and suffer Prometheus' punishment. Io
comes in, raving. Because Zeus had sex with her, Hera has changed
her to a cow, sent a stinging fly to drive her mad and left her to
roam the world in search of absolution. Prometheus offers to tell
her either the secret he knows or every detail of her future
wandering. She makes the second choice, and when he has
outlined her future suffering, she leaves the stage. Prometheus

defies Zeus' tyranny and insults Zeus' messenger Hermes, who has
come to order him to give way. As the play ends he and the chorus
are engulfed by thunderbolt and earthquake: injustice, as Prometheus claims in the play's last line, made manifest.

## About the play

*Prometheus Bound* may be related to *Prometheus Freed*, a play
(now lost) which in Greek times was one of Aeschylus' most
celebrated works. In that, Mother Earth persuaded Prometheus to
yield to Zeus and accept his place in the new Olympian world
order. Some authorities think that *Prometheus Bound* and *Prometheus Freed* formed a two-play sequence, moving from chaos to
order and from discord to reconciliation in a way similar to the
philosophical progression in the *Oresteia*. A third play, *Prometheus
Firebringer*, may have preceded them both, creating a trilogy, but
there is no evidence. Others believe that *Prometheus Bound* stood
alone, or that it was written at the end of the fifth century by
someone else, perhaps for production in Sicily, and was attributed
to Aeschylus only because of the fame of *Prometheus Freed*.

The play's apparently extravagant stage demands may support
this last theory. The theatre crane (on which the chorus and Ocean
may have entered the theatre) came into use after Aeschylus' time,
and thunder effects were used in Sicilian theatres but not (so far as
is known) in the Theatre of Dionysos. There is however no reason
why the effects should actually have happened. As the Prologue to
Shakespeare's *Henry V* makes clear, description alone can 'piece
out' the actors' 'imperfections' in an audience's thoughts. Similarly, the staging problems of the opening, where Prometheus is
pegged to the rock, need have been only described, not shown. (In
the late 460s, when the play may have been written, there was a
huge boulder in the *orchestra* of the Theatre of Dionysos, later
removed – a gift to anyone trying to stage the play.)

*Prometheus Bound* is one of the most influential of all Greek
tragedies. In nineteenth-century Europe in particular, the grandeur
of its poetry and the suffering colossus at its centre were so much

in tune with the intellectual mood that it was ranked with *Hamlet* and the Book of Job, and its creator with Dante, Michelangelo and other such artist-supermen. Shelley and Victor Hugo admired its display of an individual spirit fighting unjust oppression. Goethe praised its themes and imitated passages from it, notably Prometheus' description of his benefactions to humanity and his despairing final cry:

> Themis, mother!
> Sky-wheel which turns the stars!
> See how unjust my suffering.

Beethoven planned an opera on the subject, and used parts of the music in his overture *The Creatures of Prometheus*. Fine artists, especially in France (David, Doré, Guéricault, Rodin) made images showing the Titan on his rock with the eagle poised to attack him.

For all its appeal to revolutionary romanticism, the play as it stands poses problems in terms of the religious and ethical philosophy of its own time – particularly so if it was a single, self-standing artistic statement. These problems are to do with the nature of Zeus. He is presented throughout from Prometheus' point of view only, and is characterised as a tyrant, scheming, ill-fitted for rule and ignorant about the workings of Fate and the future. Having unjustly punished Prometheus, who helped him to his power, he will be forced in the end, for survival's sake, to submit and beg forgiveness. This Zeus is a mirror image of the supreme deity as presented in all other Greek myth-based works. In them, Zeus is all-powerful, all-wise, beyond question and understanding. The rest of creation must accept him as he is or take the consequences. If *Prometheus Bound* were part of a sequence with *Prometheus Freed*, and the later action showed Prometheus and the chorus coming to terms with such a Zeus, the audience would have experienced an examination of the 'issues' of the drama (the natures of power, justice and destiny) far more searching than in the play which survives.

However one-sided the play's viewpoint, its merits as dramatic literature are otherwise unquestioned. Its brief span (fewer than 1,100 lines) is belied by the extraordinary breadth and power of its intellectual landscape. Its bizarre-seeming characters (a Titan, a speaking cow, a river, bird women) are elevated by the myth context and the grandeur of both thought and language; they become mysterious and archetypal in a way which other Aeschylean characters (Xerxes, Agamemnon, Eteokles) do not. The poetry, whether by Aeschylus or not, rises regularly to the granitic simplicity of his finest work: examples are Prometheus' opening monologue ('Day-brightness, winds on beating wings'), or his description of his gifts to mortals, after the chorus has called him

> ... rudderless,
> A sickly doctor
> Who dare not dose himself.

The stage picture is an apt metaphor for the central dichotomy of the action, the all-knowing but guilty, tethered and impotent Prometheus contrasted with the restless, innocent, ignorant Io. The play's simple form – essentially a balance between Prometheus' wide-ranging, single-voice rhetoric and the close-focus, emotional music of the chorus – serves the philosophical and intellectual dialectic in a convincing way.

Arguments about the play's authorship depend largely on value judgements. Those who say it is Aeschylean take the views outlined above, those who say it is by someone else say that the quality of the verse is inconsistent (Aeschylean passages perhaps being sewn into a lesser writer's drama), the characters lack dramatic dignity, the physical action is unconvincingly static and the Io scene irrelevant. The issue is, perhaps, less important outside the lecture room than in it. The play's nature, status and influence are hardly affected by its author's name.

# Seven Against Thebes

## Characters

ETEOKLES, *King of Thebes*

SOLDIER

MESSENGER

ANTIGONE

ISMENE

HERALD

POLYNIKES, SOLDIERS, ATTENDANTS, TOWNSPEOPLE (*silent parts*)

CHORUS OF WOMEN

## Synopsis

At his palace gates, Eteokles reassures a group of townspeople that he will defend Thebes against Argive attack. A soldier urges haste, and he leaves to take command. The chorus enter, singing of the pain and grief of war and praying to the gods to help them. Eteokles returns, shouting that their fear will sap the spirit of the defenders, but they ignore him and sing once more of their hopelessness and panic.

The soldier describes the seven invading champions, one at each city gate. Eteokles replies with a description of each defending champion, and the chorus pray for Theban success. The last attacker is Polynikes and the last defender his brother Eteokles. The chorus beg him not to fight, but he says that death is his destiny, that it will save the city and end the curse on the royal dynasty. He leaves, and the chorus describe the curse and its effects, generation after generation.

A Messenger reports that the attackers have been defeated and that Eteokles and Polynikes are dead. Their bodies are brought in, attended by their sisters Antigone and Ismene, and the chorus mourn them. A herald announces the counsellors' decision that Eteokles is to be buried with honour but Polynikes left to rot, and

Antigone says that she will give her brothers equal burial. After a final prayer that the Furies will be satisfied with the princes' deaths, actors and chorus leave the stage in a procession of mourning.

## About the play

*Seven Against Thebes*, first performed at the City Dionysia of 467, was the third play in a sequence which included *Laios*, *Oedipus* and the satyr play *Sphinx* (all now lost). One of the main themes in the sequence may have been the working-out of a dynastic curse, similar to the one which afflicts the royal family in the *Oresteia*. The curse began when Laios, brought up in exile at the court of King Pelops of Pisa, angered the gods by raping Pelops' son Chrysippos – homosexuality until then was a prerogative of immortals only – and then caused Chrysippos' death when he tried to kidnap the boy to Thebes. (In some accounts Chrysippos fell out of Laios' chariot and broke his neck; in others his mother crept into his and Laios' bedroom at night to stab Laios, and murdered Chrysippos by mistake.) Pelops cursed Laios, asking the gods to prevent him ever having a son, or if he did, to make that son his murderer.

These events may have been the subject of *Laios*, the first play in Aeschylus' sequence. The second play, *Oedipus*, may have covered similar ground to Sophocles' *Oedipus Tyrannos*. Oedipus, born after Laios' return to Thebes, was the son mentioned in Pelops' curse, fated to murder his father and marry his own mother Jokasta. His parents tried to prevent the curse by exiling him, but he returned and unwittingly fulfilled it. He also passed it to the next generation, prophesying that his sons Eteokles and Polynikes would fight for the succession and go to the Underworld on the same day, dead at each other's hand. If the theory is correct that the play-sequence concerned a dynastic curse, *Seven Against Thebes* shows the working out of this destiny in Eteokles.

In the *Oresteia*, Aeschylus altered the end of the Argos myth-cycle to make points about the nature of justice, universal order and the relationship between mortals and immortals. Without *Eumenides*, the story would end bleakly and without resolution – precisely what happens in *Seven Against Thebes*. Eteokles, a noble and heroic figure, behaves for most of the action as if blind to destiny and the dynastic curse. Then, reminded of it just as he is about to fight his brother, he accepts his fate for the glory of his city. The contrast with Oedipus' 'blindness' to Fate, and his behaviour when he discovers the truth about himself, is striking.

Scholars say that Aeschylus wrote only the first four-fifths of *Seven Against Thebes* as we have it. His contribution ends not with resolution and catharsis, but with a brief report of the princes' deaths (8llff), a reminder that 'God's knife is whetted still', and a chorus of desolation balancing the chorus of distress at the beginning. Later hands added the Antigone/Ismene material we now possess – and they unfocused the meaning of the action, introducing a completely new strand (Antigone's defiance of the council) without integrating it, and – because the quality of the verse is poor – reducing the impact of Aeschylus' chorus, which returns with full power only at line 1054 ('High-necked Furies, demons of death/That haunt this house . . .'). How Aeschylus resolved the issues raised by the play and its predecessors in the sequence is now unguessable.

Interpolation apart, *Seven Against Thebes* is of a poetic splendour matched in the surviving plays only by the choruses of *Agamemnon*. Physical action is minimal; the play's energy comes from the verse itself. The structure is an arch, two outer sections in similar style supporting a central, contrasting scene. The outer sections, dominated by the chorus, are grief-racked and lyrical; there is a constant pull in them between emotional engagement and the objectivity and formality of both style and structure. In modern productions they are also dominated by female voices – one wonders if Aeschylus intended this contrast with the male-voice dominated central section, and if so, how his (male) chorus made the distinction in performance. The central scene, the description of the champions, is a sevenfold repetition of the same formal pattern (Soldier's speech, Eteokles' response, choral reflection), reaching climax at the end as Eteokles realises and accepts his destiny. The language is rhetorical, martial and majestic: in ancient Greek literature, only Homer's battle-descriptions in the *Iliad* rival its swagger and imagistic resonance.

The play's strong formal armature allows Aeschylus to enrich his writing with every skill at his disposal. The outer sections are resonant with sweeping, extended similes which seem to draw the emotion away from specific pain, specific apprehension into enormous panoramas of human experience. (A good example is the section beginning, 'He speaks; but my mind is on guard for fear . . .' (287ff), where the precision of the images is offset, at least in Greek, by delirious rhythmic swirl.) The central scene, by contrast, offsets rhetorical pomp by cramming the lines with tiny, ear-catching ideas which irradiate the imagination. Kapaneus is a 'blabberer' (447), his opponent Polyphontes the 'breastplate of Thebes' (449). The horses' cheek-pieces are 'muzzle-pipes' that play 'shrill, proud music, the breath of war' (463). The boy Parthenopaios is 'halfway to a man./Down furs his cheeks; close curls, spring blooms' (533ff), and he talks to his spear like a lover, impiously calling it 'more precious,/More reliable than God' (530). Amphiaraos' mind is a 'fertile field,/Its crop good counsel, common sense' (592ff). Writing of this quality suggests that the loss of the rest of Aeschylus' Theban sequence may be one of the greatest blows time has dealt Greek drama.

# Suppliants

## Characters

DANAOS
KING OF ARGOS
EGYPTIAN CAPTAIN
SOLDIERS (*silent parts*)
CHORUS OF DANAOS' DAUGHTERS
CHORUS OF WOMEN

## Synopsis

The setting is a grove of trees near Argos. The chorus of Danaos' daughters (the Danaids) appear. They have fled to Greece from Egypt, where they were threatened with forced marriage to their cousins. Argos was the home of their ancestor Io, and they hope that its people will give them sanctuary. Danaos tells them to stay in the sacred grove while he goes into the city to present their case to the assembly. The King of Argos arrives with soldiers. Though sympathetic to the chorus's claims of kinship, he is reluctant to risk war with Egypt. But when the Danaids threaten to hang themselves from the gods' statues, he agrees that they can stay in sanctuary until the people decide the issue. He and Danaos leave for the city.

After another anxious chorus, Danaos reports that the Argive people have accepted his daughters' claim. The chorus's rejoicing turns quickly to panic when he says that an Egyptian fleet is even now putting in to land. They are still praying to the gods for help when the Egyptian captain arrives with soldiers to drag them to the ships. His efforts to move them from sanctuary are interrupted by the King of Argos and his soldiers. Temporarily outfaced, the Egyptians retreat to their ships, and the women of Argos welcome the Danaids into their city. The issue of sanctuary is resolved, but there remains the greater problem: what will happen when the Egyptians come back, in force?

## About the play

*Suppliants* is the only surviving play from a sequence dealing with the fifty sons of Aigyptos and the fifty daughters of Danaos, Aigyptos' twin brother. Assuming that the Danaid sequence was structured in a similar way to Greek drama's only surviving trilogy, the *Oresteia*, scholars have suggested that *Suppliants*, first in the sequence, established mood and set up the story, that *Egyptians* described the siege of Argos and ended when the Danaids agreed to marry their cousins, and that *Danaids* dealt with the sisters' trial for murdering their bridegrooms, highlighting the actions of Hypermnestra, the only one to let her husband live. (Part of a speech survives, about the force of love – possibly a speech made by Aphrodite in Hypermnestra's defence.) The satyr play *Amymone* told how Poseidon rescued the Danaid Amymone from a lustful satyr.

Whatever the actual nature of the Danaid sequence, *Suppliants* itself is a piece of persuasive dramatic poetry, balancing emotional rhetoric and lyrical richness in Aeschylus' ripest manner. As in *Seven Against Thebes*, static physical action is the foundation for vivid, varied emotional and poetic movement. The role of the chorus is organised in a particularly ornate way, counterpointing expositions of myth and emotion with multi-voiced sections of panic and distress. In the dialogue scenes, the choral continuum of anguished uncertainty is offset by the qualities of individual characters: Danaos' paternal concern, the Argive king's peremptory generosity and the Egyptian's silkiness and savagery. In the theatre, complete with music and movement, the effect must have been spectacular – especially if, as some authorities claim, all fifty Danaids were represented onstage, each with her accompanying maidservant.

In a way familiar from the *Oresteia*, dialogue scenes in *Suppliants* narrow the focus from this grand choral perspective.

Whereas the chorus take in the whole landscape of myth, looking backwards and forwards in time, seeing causes and effects and speculating on the meaning of events, each individual character concentrates on the dilemmas of his own immediate moment. The Argive king straightforwardly demonstrates forethought, compassion and steadfastness. Danaos at first is longwinded and indecisive, taking no part in persuading the Argive king to grant temporary sanctuary and leaving the argument to the leader of the chorus. Later, however, perhaps anticipating the needs of later plays in the sequence, he shows certainty and purpose. The Egyptian, in a scene which is as much a theatrical 'turn' as Kassandra's appearance in *Agamemnon* or the Io section of *Prometheus Bound*, changes from smiles to roars in the same way as sky moves from sun to clouds.

Declarative characterisation of this kind, also found in *Seven Against Thebes* and to some extent in the *Oresteia*, is different from the type used in most of Sophocles' and Euripides' surviving plays, and serves a different dramatic purpose. With some exceptions, Sophocles' and Euripides' characters – Antigone and the Dionysos of *Bacchae* are typical examples – are established and unvaried from beginning to end, but are revealed gradually and progressively, as one might strip an onion. Developments in the story and its 'meaning' trigger new insights into the character, but do not change it (in the way Lear's character, say, is altered by events, before our eyes). Like one of Socrates' philosophical enquiries, each play moves inexorably towards a conclusion implicit from the start – a progression which is a main point of interest for the spectators, and of which the stripping-down of character is part.

*Suppliants*, by contrast, like all Aeschylus' surviving work except *Persians*, uses a different kind of dramatic dialectic, arising from the fact that each individual play is part of a larger structure. Instead of a feeling of logical progression towards a predetermined goal, we are shown the examination, point by point, of a multifaceted situation – involving, in this case, such things as the nature and demands of kinship and the meaning of social obligation – which can change in a dozen different ways. In a structure where multiple possibility is a consistent feature, there is no place for the progressive revelation of predetermined character. Broad-brush presentation of selected traits is enough both for each individual moment and for ongoing dramatic and thematic movement.

For years, taking their cue from Aristotle, scholars relegated this kind of dramatic structure and the minority of surviving plays which use it. (They claimed, for example, that 'weak' characterisation in *Suppliants* proved that the play was early; they described Euripides' un-Aristotelian late plays as 'perfunctory' or 'not his best work'.) Such views assumed an evolution in Greek drama from 'primitive' to 'sophisticated', and created hierarchies of excellence which had nothing to do with the surviving texts. *Suppliants* represents a kind of Greek tragedy – other examples include *Seven Against Thebes*, Euripides' *Suppliants*, *Herakles' Children*, *Women of Troy* and, to some extent, *Bacchae* – which, stylistically speaking, has little in common with (say) *Oedipus Tyrannos*, Sophocles' *Elektra* or *Hippolytos*, but is hardly the worse for that.

# Sophocles

## Life

Sophocles was born c.496, in the Athenian district of Kolonos (then a village on a small hill some 2km north of the Acropolis). His father Sophilos was a wealthy industrialist, whose business possibly included the manufacture and sale of weapons. As a boy Sophocles was uncommonly handsome and an accomplished musician and dancer; this may have prompted his selection to represent Kolonos in dithyrambic and tragic choruses, and by 480 he was sufficiently skilled to lead part of the musical celebrations of the Greek victory at Salamis. He may have gone on to become more closely involved in theatre, perhaps initially as a singer and dancer. He won first prize at the City Dionysia in 468, defeating no less a personage than Aeschylus; some accounts say that this was his first appearance as author at any dramatic competition. He is known to have performed in several of his own early plays – as the lyre player Thamyras who challenged the Muses to a contest and was defeated and blinded for his presumption; as the ball-playing princess Nausikaa who rescued Odysseus when he was shipwrecked on his journey home from Troy – but his *Life*, published long after his death, says that he gave up performing early in his career either because of voice strain or because of the weakness of his voice (the Greek can mean either).

Weak voice or not, Sophocles may simply have been too busy to devote much time to practice and performance as well as his other duties. He was tirelessly devoted to public service, working for his friend Pericles in the running of the ever-expanding Athenian empire and then in the Peloponnesian War. His expertise seems to have been financial, though on two occasions he was elected *strategos* (army commander) on short-term appointments. He was 'priest in charge' of a healing shrine (possibly the manager of a temple where medical help was available), and later became associated with worship of the healing god Asklepios in Athens, work for which he was given an official state honour. He was a friend of poets, statesmen and philosophers, and went on working until his death in 406 at the age of ninety.

## Works

In a writing career of sixty years, Sophocles wrote some 120 plays, more than any other ancient dramatist. He also composed verse – hymns and prayers for public occasions – and wrote a treatise on *The Chorus*. (None of this work survives.) He won first prizes at 24 competitions (that is, with 96 plays altogether, four plays at each festival), and second prizes at all the others he entered. His main output was tragedies, but he also wrote some 20 satyr plays. He is said to have divided his work into three critical periods: his early plays were 'ornate' in the manner of Aeschylus (the Greek word was used of a heavy, elaborate hairstyle), his second period plays 'experimental and hard to swallow' (the Greek word means 'sour'), his third period plays 'the best, in a style drawing out character'. All seven surviving plays are from this last period. They are *Ajax* (before 440), *Women of Trachis* (date unknown), *Antigone* (*c.*440), *Oedipus Tyrannos* (soon after 430), *Elektra* (between 430 and 413), *Philoktetes* (409) and *Oedipus at Kolonos* (produced posthumously in 401).

## Style and approach

For years Sophocles' reputation depended mainly on *Oedipus Tyrannos*, the chief play chosen by Aristotle (in *Poetics*) to demonstrate how, in his opinion, 'well-made' tragedy should be written for maximum moral and didactic effect. The play's supposed message, that when mortals step aside from or defy the will of heaven, they suffer, chimed in many people's minds with the heroine's speech in *Antigone* about obedience to the 'unwritten laws of heaven', and ensured Sophocles' pre-eminence in Western schoolrooms. The Greek of these two plays also made good teaching material. It is syntactically challenging but not outrageously difficult or bizarre, stylistically admirable and imitable, a satisfaction and a reward to work on in its own right. By the late nineteenth century, Sophocles had become a key member of the pantheon of writers, sculptors, philosophers and statesmen who represented the neoclassical ideal of 'the glory that was Greece', a kind of uncluttered template for the utopian dream of later Western civilisation, simultaneously innocent and intellectually compelling, an embryonic Age of Reason.

Although there is some truth in all these notions, they rely on a remarkably partial view of what ancient Greek culture was actually like, and on a less forgivable relegation of the rest of surviving Athenian drama in general and of Sophocles' other five remaining plays in particular. These plays are nothing like *Oedipus Tyrannos* or *Antigone*, and differ from one another in style, structure, meaning and tone. *Elektra* is the study of a woman driven by suffering to the brink of madness, *Women of Trachis* an examination of the nature of innocence and the nature of love. *Philoktetes* makes a kind of philosophical adventure story from the exploration of personal politics and the different aspects of honour, duty and fidelity. *Oedipus at Kolonos* blends simplicity of plot with wintry mysticism in both character drawing and language. *Ajax* is about the corruption of honour. In each play, Sophocles suits language, structure and style to the needs of his plot and the themes it articulates. These disparities raise questions about the lost sixteen-seventeenths of his output. His seven extant plays show none of the consistency of authorship detectable in what we have left from Aeschylus or Euripides. *Oedipus Tyrannos* and *Antigone* apart, the plays could be by entirely separate people – and even *Oedipus Tyrannos* and *Antigone* are as different from one another as they are alike.

This diversity, so far from being a black mark against Sophocles, is one of the main components of his genius. His long life spanned one of the most turbulent eras in the intellectual history of the

West, a period equalled only by the age of scientific humanism in the last four centuries. The fifth century BC saw the flowering of a new approach to the mysteries of the universe and the imponderabilities of human life and character. Previously, myth had provided the matrix for answers to questions about moral, ethical and social behaviour, the supernatural and the human sense of self. The myth stories had been used, embellished and commented on in a thousand ways, from ritual observance to incorporation in civil laws and constitutions, from artistic creation to 'explanations' of the phenomena of Nature. Now, without sacrificing any of this intellectual and social heritage, the idea grew that it was possible to make objective study both of the natural world and the impulses and tendencies of human behaviour, to create systems of analysis based not on precedent (as was the case with myth) but on rationality. From sixth-century Ionia (the Greek-speaking communities on the west coast of what is now Turkey), the process spread to other areas, notably Sicily and Southern Italy, and reached Athens in the mid fifth century, at the time of Sophocles' artistic maturity.

Each of the surviving tragic dramatists reacted in a different way. A generation older than Sophocles, and at the end of his creative career, Aeschylus seems to have remained untouched by the new thinking, unpacking the grandeur and meaning of his stories in a myth-centred manner inspired by Homer. A generation younger than Sophocles, Euripides seems whole-heartedly to have embraced the new thinking, treating myth characters in a rational, analytical manner often far removed from the strategies of his predecessors. Sophocles, on the cusp of the new thinking, in each of the surviving plays scrupulously respects the dialectical framework of his chosen myth and the characters within it, but uses it to investigate and display a specific philosophical question which remains as it were self-standing, independent of the myth-story. The nature of knowledge, politics, heroism, innocence, honour, law – these are topics of Socratic or Platonic enquiry and main themes in Sophocles' plays. This over-riding intellectuality – often jaggedly and ironically at odds with the racked emotions and agonised plight of the characters in the story, who know nothing of the ideas they embody and articulate – contributes to the sense many people have that Sophocles' main artistic signature is uncommon elegance and distinction of mind. His plays offer a double experience. They are theatrically engrossing, and they challenge our thought processes with a kind of imperturbable unanswerability quite different from Aeschylean grandeur or Euripidean edginess.

Sophocles' verse, similarly, avoids spectacular effect and produces instead a feeling of discreet aptness. It is modulated to suit each new exposition of character, each turn and twist of philosophical exposition – and the changes are so subtly managed that it is only afterwards that we realise that the trick has been done at all. This flexibility can be seen at a peak in *Antigone* – in the way the verse quietly but clearly registers the differences between the utterances of Kreon, Antigone, the guard and Haimon, in the graceful handling of disparate abstract themes in the choruses, and in the way grief is articulated quite differently in the scene where Antigone is led out to die and the scene where Kreon comes in with Haimon's body. In a similar way, although Sophocles' characters are in fact as varied and psychologically as complex as any in Euripides – the range is from Ajax to Antigone, from Deianeira to Elektra, from Neoptolemos and Philoktetes to the very different Oedipuses of *Oedipus Tyrannos* and *Oedipus at Kolonos* – they all somehow seem to breathe the same air, seem (as Aristotle pointed out) to be people of distinction, as much apart from the common herd as the idealised sculpted figures of Sophocles' contemporaries Myron and Polykleitos.

## Technical innovation

In *Poetics*, Aristotle praised Sophocles not only for the moral elevation of his work but also for technical innovation. He was credited with making the chorus bigger, inventing scene painting and adding a third actor to the standard two. (No one knows if

Sophocles simply made these changes in performance, so impressively that they became the norm, or whether he lobbied committees and backers until the new standards were written into the competition rules.)

On the evidence of surviving plays, the importance of the first two changes is hard to see. Painted scenery is neither a better nor a worse way of indicating location than encouraging the audience's imagination by poetic description (as Aeschylus does in his surviving work). Without more knowledge of the way ancient choruses moved and sang, the effect of increasing their number from twelve to fifteen can only be guessed. But the third change is decisive, as crucial for the development of drama as was Aeschylus' doubling of the number of actors from one to two. At a stroke, having three actors onstage instead of two allows infinite possibilities for cross purposes, contrasting perspectives, dialectical twists and turns and irony – possibilities available both when all three characters speak (as in the scene in *Antigone* where Kreon confronts first Antigone alone and then Antigone and Ismene together), and, with equal power, when one of the characters onstage is silent (as with Iole's presence among the captives in *Women of Trachis*). Using three actors affects the balance between spoken dialogue and musical scenes – a factor, again, which Sophocles exploits in many different ways. In *Antigone*, for example, spoken scenes and choral odes have almost equal dramatic weight, like a sequence of panels in a painted fresco, and articulation of the issues oscillates between fast, many-voiced discussion and more measured, solemn musical presentation. In *Elektra*, where all the actors sing as well as speak, the chorus is marginalised and scenes wholly in spoken dialogue (the scene of hate between Elektra and Klytemnestra; the servant's bravura, lying account of Orestes' death; the moving recognition scene) become highpoints of the action.

## Character creation

'The best, in a style drawing out character.' If Sophocles' reported comments on the style of his 'third period' are accurate, then we might ask what he meant by character, and how the surviving plays 'draw it out'. In fact they use several different kinds of characterisation. Two plays, *Oedipus Tyrannos* and *Elektra*, centre on individuals whose characters remain unchanged throughout. The psychic identity of Oedipus and Elektra is the same at the end of each play as at the beginning. Events have moved and shifted all round them, and have altered their physical circumstances, but their inner selves remain unchanged. Other plays use what we nowadays might think of as schematic characterisation. Kreon and Antigone in *Antigone*, for example, are not so much dramatic characters as characters in a drama, and their psychic selves are far less important than the roles they play in the working out of a philosophical dilemma. Deianeira and Herakles in *Women of Trachis*, similarly, are attitudes given physical embodiment, and their individuality is subsumed in what they represent. *Ajax* offers schematic views of half a dozen different attitudes, and the lively personalities of Ajax, Teukros and Menelaos are more like dramatic grace notes than integral to the action. *Philoktetes* forcefully contrasts the learning, maturing Neoptolemos with the emotionally extrovert and racked Philoktetes; *Oedipus at Kolonos* shows us the different attitudes that make an individual personality, but avoids giving Oedipus the emotional empathy which might sentimentalise the action. In all of this, Sophocles' vision of character seems to conform to the literal meaning of the word (the impression made by a sealstone): 'type' rather than 'character' in the modern sense. His plays and the people he creates in them are vividly exciting, and he rivals even Euripides for the emotional flamboyance in which he dresses both principal roles and subsidiary figures. But the overriding impression in his work is one of calculation, of selection and precise control of every inflexion and every moment. Untidiness, spontaneity, rawness – such qualities may belong to some of the characters he creates, but they are absent from the plays.

# Irony

Even so, we must beware. Nothing in Sophocles' surviving work is precisely what it seems. The servant's account of the chariot race in *Elektra* (see below, page 84) shows, in perhaps its most overt form, one of the most important components of Sophoclean dramatic art: his use of irony. The servant's story works because we know in advance that it will be lies from start to finish. That knowledge focuses our concentration on Elektra's (silent) reaction as she hears it, and Sophocles then plays games with us by making the narrative itself so compelling, so circumstantial and so vivid, characterising the race itself, that we are all but convinced by what we hear, almost enter into Elektra's condition as she listens. In *Philoktetes*, similarly, the fact that we know from the start that whatever happens in the play, Philoktetes will be persuaded back to Troy, throws attention on the methods of persuasion rather than on their outcome. Odysseus' strategies, and their effect on Philoktetes and Neoptolemos, become the issue – and once again Sophocles trumps expectation by *not* resolving the action in the expected human terms, in the way the play seems to be tending, but by sending a god to do it. The layering of ironies in *Oedipus Tyrannos* ranges from 'small' (each character knows more, or less, than the others about Oedipus' situation) to 'large' (the questions, left implicit, about how much Oedipus actually knows about his Fate and how much he is dissembling or blotting out that knowledge). Irony is the essence of the play, suffusing our understanding even of the choral odes.

The consistent use of irony, and the many ways it can be layered, are Sophocles' major contributions to the art of writing plays. Aeschylus uses irony, but in a more declared, more Homeric manner, as when he pulls back from the small concerns of characters in individual scenes and shows us the wider perspective of the issues. It was Sophocles' discovery that the presence of the audience in a theatre ironises every event in the performance of a play, even the fact of performance itself, and he uses it consistently to surprise, second-guess, illuminate and confound the expectation of his spectators. In his surviving plays, irony features to an extent unequalled even by Euripides. Only *Oedipus at Kolonos* is free of it. The dazzling and varied use Sophocles makes of it, like the innovations attributed to him by Aristotle and his authorship of the treatise on *The Chorus*, suggests that he was a far more self-conscious and experimental technician than the limpid surface of his plays implies.

# Ajax

## Characters

ATHENE

ODYSSEUS

AJAX

TEKMESSA, *a captive princess, Ajax's concubine*

SOLDIER

TEUKROS, *Ajax's half-brother*

MENELAOS

AGAMEMNON

EURYSAKES, *Ajax's son, a child*, ATTENDANTS, SOLDIERS (*silent parts*)

CHORUS OF AJAX'S SAILORS

## Synopsis

In the darkness before dawn on the plain outside Troy, Odysseus is looking for Ajax, who has committed a senseless crime, torturing and killing a herd of sheep and cattle. Athene tells him that she was responsible. Ajax wanted to kill the Greek leaders for humiliating him, and she drove him mad and turned him instead on the cattle. She summons Ajax and shows him to Odysseus in all his madness. After the chorus have sung of the way Ajax has been slandered in the camp, Tekmessa announces that he has come to his senses and is sitting, stunned, among the carcases of his victims. The tent flaps are opened and Ajax is revealed in a tableau. He sings of his dishonour and despair, refuses the sympathy of the chorus, and to Tekmessa's horror announces that the only way he can retain his honour is to kill himself. The child Eurysakes is brought and Ajax bids him a tender farewell.

After a sad chorus about Salamis, Ajax's island home, and his grieving parents, Ajax says that he will make his peace with God. He goes out, and the chorus sing of their hope and their joy in

God. A soldier reports that Teukros is in camp and reveals that Ajax's madness was a punishment from Athene for defying the gods. He tells Tekmessa the generals' orders: Ajax is to be kept indoors in case he does harm to himself or anyone else. Tekmessa desperately sends the chorus to find him.

The scene changes to a deserted part of the beach. Ajax sets his sword upright in the sand and falls on it, just as Tekmessa and the chorus come searching. They weep over the body, and Teukros joins the lamentation. He intends to bury the body, but Menelaos says that Ajax must be left to rot. After a violent argument Menelaos fetches Agamemnon, who orders Teukros to give way. Odysseus, however, pleads for Ajax's burial, saying that it is an honour all the dead are owed. This argument persuades Agamemnon, and the generals leave Teukros and the chorus to conduct Ajax's funeral and end the play.

## About the play

*Ajax* is the earliest play by Sophocles to survive, though by no means apprentice work: it was first performed some time in the 440s, when he was in his fifties. The story of Ajax is a minor episode in the myth-cycle of the Trojan War, and is told briefly in Homer's *Iliad*. Ajax, prince of the small island of Salamis in the Saronic Gulf near Athens – and in some accounts, a notable pirate and cattle rustler – joined the huge expedition mounted by the Greeks to sack Troy and punish the abduction by the Trojan prince Paris of Helen, wife of King Menelaos of Sparta and sister-in-law of the Greek commander Agamemnon. Ajax was a warrior not a thinker, famous alike for courage and slow-wittedness – and after Achilles' death, when a decision was to be made about who should be given the hero's god-made armour, he lost to Odysseus although he felt that the arms were his by right. Soon afterwards he died. In some accounts he was killed by a poisoned arrow fired by Paris, in others he was trapped by the Trojans and, being invulnerable to mortal weapons, was killed by being buried alive.

Sophocles used, or possibly invented, still another account of Ajax's death. In his version, Ajax's failure to win the arms drives him mad, and he vows to kill not only Odysseus but also Agamemnon and Menelaos, the commanders who voted to deprive him. Athene intervenes and makes him attack a group of sheep and cattle, taking them for the hated Greeks. After he has savaged them, she restores his wits and he is so overcome by remorse that he commits suicide. Later writers embroidered this in the light of Aristotelian ideas about *hubris*, saying that Ajax's madness and death were punishment for defying the gods earlier in his career, when, just before sailing from Salamis, he refused to sacrifice on the grounds that he was strong and brave enough to win without divine assistance.

In outline, this is the slightly ludicrous tale of a muscle-bound fool who meets drastic, if due comeuppance. But Sophocles layers and enriches the story to make points far beyond the bounds of the original story. To do so, he uses a dramatic structure employed later by Euripides in two surviving plays about madness, *Hekabe* and *Herakles*, and in Aristophanes' *Women in Power* to show the effects of an insane decision. The structure is that of a diptych, where the play divides halfway. Each half is apparently self-contained, but the meaning of the whole experience depends on the way the second part involves a complete rethinking of the meaning of the first. (This is a technique of the trilogy employed in the span of a single play, and quite unlike the logical, developmental sequence of the kinds of play discussed in Aristotle's *Poetics*.) In *Hekabe* and *Herakles*, the hinge between the two halves is the tipping of the central character from sanity to madness. In *Ajax* it is Ajax's suicide, performed before our eyes.

In the diptych structure of *Ajax*, the first part is a straightforward account of Ajax's madness, his return to sanity and his determination to save his honour by committing suicide. It is a conventional 'Greek tragedy' in miniature, complete with the appearance of a goddess (Athene) in the prologue, a distraught lover (Tekmessa) and a tender scene between parent and child (Ajax and Eurysakes). Ajax is displayed first as a monster of madness and cruelty and then as a suffering colossus. Then, after the suicide, in which ideas of waste and despair predominate, the focus entirely changes, as Ajax's half-brother Teukros demands from the Greek commanders that Ajax be treated not with the contempt his madness and suicide inspire in them but with respect for the hero who helped them battle Troy. The argument has universal overtones – what is the nature of heroism, and how should we recognise and cope with it? – and they refract our view of what happened in the first half of the play, so that the whole experience becomes not a loosely structured piece about a pathetic loser but a study of human aspiration, folly and disappointment. In a manner unlike that in any of Sophocles' other surviving work, the play also presents the gods in a particularly sharp and critical light. Whatever the *hubris* in Ajax which may or may not have caused Athene's anger, she displays a gloating pleasure in his madness and its punishment which makes us seriously question the impartiality of heaven. Euripides is more usually associated with this kind of ironical questioning of what Christian scholars, at least, assumed were 'traditional Athenian pieties' – but like the squabbling of Athene and Apollo in Aeschylus' *Oresteia*, *Ajax* suggests that it may have been a more common feature of Greek tragedy than is normally assumed.

# Antigone

## Characters

ANTIGONE
ISMENE, *her sister*
KREON, *ruler of Thebes*
SOLDIER
HAIMON, *Kreon's son*
TEIRESIAS, *prophet*
SERVANT (MESSENGER)
EURYDICE, *Kreon's consort*
SOLDIERS, ATTENDANTS (*silent parts*)
CHORUS OF OLD MEN

## Synopsis

Antigone tells Ismene that their brothers Eteokles and Polynikes have killed each other in the siege of Thebes, and of Kreon's decree that Eteokles, loyal to the city, is to be buried with honour while Polynikes, who attacked it, is to be left to rot. She fails to persuade Ismene to help her bury Polynikes and so honour both brothers equally. The chorus sing how the gods destroyed Polynikes, and Kreon repeats his decree, adding that defiance means death. A soldier reports that someone has sprinkled Polynikes' body with dust. Kreon orders him to arrest anyone who performs further burial rituals, and after a choral ode about how humans, who have mastered all other skills, must learn to keep the laws of both mortals and gods, the soldier brings in Antigone. She defies Kreon, saying that God's law outweighs human ordinances, and he orders her execution.

After a choral ode comparing Fate to the sea, Kreon's son Haimon tries in vain to convince his father to spare Antigone. Antigone is led to her death, and the chorus sing of other heroines in myth who were unjustly executed. Teiresias warns Kreon of disaster if the execution proceeds, and Kreon hurries to release Antigone. But he is too late: a servant brings news that Antigone has hanged herself, and that Haimon has found her body and stabbed himself dead before his father's eyes. Kreon carries in his son's body, a servant tells him that his consort Eurydice has also committed suicide, and the play ends with a ritual of mourning between Kreon and the chorus.

## About the play

*Antigone* was first performed some time between 442 and 440; Sophocles was in his fifties. It pre-dates his other 'Theban' plays, *Oedipus Tyrannos* by a decade, *Oedipus at Kolonos* by some thirty years. At the time of its first performance Sophocles was at the height of his political career, and the play was said to be so successful that it earned him election in 440 as co-general with Pericles.

*Antigone* is a textbook example of how to develop one short episode from a myth-story to make a full-scale tragedy articulating universal themes and meanings. The story of how Antigone refused to obey Kreon's order about her brothers' burial, and died for it, is a couple of sentences from the tangled Theban myth-cycle, and Antigone as a person has none of the resonance of such other myth women as Andromache, Klytemnestra or Penelope. The fact that her story has had such an effect on world consciousness – she is one of the best loved characters in all Greek myth – is entirely due to the issues which Sophocles draws from the myth, and to his portrayal of Antigone herself, pulled between heroic certainty and all too human frailty.

Part of the play's secret is extreme simplicity of means. The characterisation is direct and unironic, the issues are clearly articulated, the language is unequivocal and the poetry is limpid and unfussy. Few starker works exist in the surviving canon. The focus is throughout tight on a single issue, the effect on Antigone and Kreon of the collision between their different views of the nature of law. Everything arises from this or impinges on it, and there are no distractions, no allusions even to other details from the myth – nothing for example about Oedipus' curse or what will happen after the events shown in this specific play. Exclusion of other material, coupled with the specificity of the central issue, paradoxically allows Sophocles to draw out universal meanings in a way less like drama than the philosophical exegeses of Plato or Aristotle. *Antigone* is a cerebral argument embodied in emotionally engaging characters, and tension between what the people say and what they feel both epitomises the meaning of the action and gives the play irresistible dramatic impetus.

It is important for Sophocles' purpose that *Antigone* centres on two people (rather than on one, as do *Oedipus Tyrannos* and *Elektra*). Kreon's heroic blindness matches Antigone's at every stage, and leads, albeit by a different path, to similar pain and humiliation. The difference between them is, however, starkly drawn. Antigone remains blind to the end, unaware of or unconcerned about the wider workings of Fate. She knew before she started that death would be the consequence of her actions; she is what she believes and has no need to grow or change; if Haimon's arguments about trees bending before the storm had been made to her she would have ignored them just as vehemently as did Kreon. Her death is a personal tragedy but morally a triumph. Kreon, by contrast, has the scales lifted from his eyes, sees the pattern of Fate, but still has to suffer as the consequences of his actions are worked out in his wife and son. The endings of the two characters' stories, and the contrast between them, make it possible for Sophocles to suggest a moral and ethical closure to the play which – since the main philosophical issues are never actually resolved – is in fact illusion.

Throughout the play, the chorus's contribution is central. Most choral odes in tragedy do not end sequences of action but begin them, the energy of a dramatic scene spinning out of the preceding ode. In *Antigone* the opposite is true. The choral entry, picturing for us Polynikes' eagle-swoop on Thebes and his destruction by the gods, the 'many wonders' chorus which follows the soldier's announcement that Kreon's edict has been defied, the savage reminder of the gods' implacable power after Antigone is condemned and the invocation of Eros which follows Kreon's confrontation with Haimon – each of these is an utterance of uncompromising directness, in sharp ironical contrast to the arguments of its preceding scene and underscoring a view of the inevitability of human suffering which shadows all the action. Apart from these Olympian interventions, the choral parts of the play are passionate and partisan. Examples are the scenes of mourning as Antigone is led out to death and as Kreon appears with Haimon in his arms. These scenes are framed with odes of powerful emotional involvement: a comparison of Antigone with other heroines unjustly immured and a desperate invocation of Dionysos to save Thebes, his city. Together with the bleak final tag, these choruses articulate the moral uncertainty and panic which pervade the play. In other respects, *Antigone* is loosely structured – some have criticised the apparently arbitrary appearances of Ismene and Eurydice and deplored the soldier's garrulity – but in its use of the chorus, both as a major character in the action and as a main determinant of musical and poetic style, it is exemplary.

# Elektra

## Characters

ELEKTRA
ORESTES, *her brother*
CHRYSOTHEMIS, *their sister*
KLYTEMNESTRA, *their mother*
AIGISTHOS, *her lover*
SERVANT
PYLADES (*silent part*)
CHORUS OF WOMEN

## Synopsis

Orestes, Pylades and the servant arrive secretly at the palace gates of Mycenae. Apollo's oracle has ordered Orestes to avenge the murder of his father Agamemnon. His plan is to enter the palace, bringing false news of Orestes' death, and seize his chance to kill Klytemnestra and Aigisthos. The three men hear Elektra calling in grief inside, and go off to Agamemnon's grave. She comes out, joins the chorus in a ceremony of mourning for Agamemnon and talks of her years of ill treatment at Klytemnestra's hands. Chrysothemis, saying that Klytemnestra has had a disturbing dream and sent her to placate the dead, brings offerings for Agamemnon's tomb. Elektra persuades her instead to pray that Agamemnon will help wreak vengeance on his murderers.

After a brief chorus about the Furies who wait to avenge Agamemnon, Klytemnestra comes out to sacrifice, and she and Elektra argue furiously. They are interrupted by Orestes' servant, who tells a long, circumstantial account of Orestes' death in a chariot accident at the Pythian Games. Klytemnestra is overjoyed that danger has passed for her; Elektra is torn by a mixture of anguish for Orestes and fury with her mother. She tries in vain to persuade Chrysothemis to join her in taking Orestes' place and killing Klytemnestra, and the chorus pray to the gods to help Elektra's vengeance. Then Orestes appears, carrying an urn which he says holds Orestes' ashes. Elektra's outburst of grief so affects him that he reveals his true identity, and brother and sister fall into one another's arms. Orestes and Pylades go inside, and Elektra waits tremulously until she hears Klytemnestra's death cries. Orestes and Pylades bring out the body, shrouded in a sheet – and Aigisthos, returning from his country estates, sees it and takes it for Orestes. Orestes follows him inside the palace to kill him.

## About the play

*Elektra* was written between 430 and 413 BC. Some scholars think that it preceded Euripides' play on the same subject, others that it came afterwards. Like two other of Sophocles' plays from the same period, *Philoktetes* and *Oedipus at Kolonos*, it centres on a single, all-engulfing bravura role; it is easy to imagine (though there is no proof) that he may have had the same actor in mind for all three of them.

The myth-cycle of Argos, centring on Agamemnon's murder by his wife Klytemnestra and the avenging of this death by his children Orestes and Elektra, was the subject of something like one-fifth of all known Greek tragedies, and plays survive on the subject by all three leading dramatists. Aeschylus' *Libation-Bearers* deals with Orestes' return from exile and the way Elektra and the chorus 'man' him to avenge his father. This 'manning' of Orestes, his growth to accept his destiny, is the main subject of the play, the central panel of the surviving *Oresteia*. Euripides' *Elektra* shows much the same events, but focuses less on Orestes than on Elektra who drives the action through to the murders which are a catharsis necessary to cleanse the royal house. Sophocles, in his *Elektra*, concentrates on Elektra's state of mind, in particular on the effects of her long years of despair and waiting and her hysterical joy when Orestes, against all hope, returns.

The role of Elektra is one of the most technically demanding in all Greek tragedy. Apart from the first few minutes of the play, the actor is onstage throughout, and is required to display a bravura escalation of grief and pain, bursting out finally in hysterical joy when Elektra at last recognises that her brother has returned and her waiting is over. Apart from two brief odes, the chorus perform entirely in counterpoint with Elektra, as if she were their leader. Elektra takes part in every scene, and all other roles – even the demonic Klytemnestra and the servant with his ironical narrative of Orestes' supposed death – are subordinate both technically and psychologically.

In solving the problem of how to show a prolonged period of anguished inactivity in dramatic form, Sophocles makes virtuosic use of the Greek dramatic convention of showing not action but the narration of action. Elektra's narratives are all about her inner self, her emotional and psychological state – and that is busy, ever changing and dramatically charged to the point where even her silence (for example, during the servant's account of the chariot race) is a dominant part of the scene onstage. The emotional release produced when this succession of narratives is replaced by real physical action – her grief over the urn supposedly containing Orestes' ashes and her joyful collapse into his arms when she realises that he is standing before her – is so powerful that many scholars of the past complained that it was unseemly, driving the tragedy to an inappropriate happy ending and a catharsis more appropriate to melodrama than 'serious' dramatic fiction.

These arguments would have force if *Elektra* was a self-contained story with no external correlatives and no myth resonance. In fact, Sophocles uses irony to subvert the ending even as it happens. *Elektra* is the most ironically inflected of all his surviving plays, and the effect is achieved by the simple process of showing us, in the prologue, that Orestes is alive and has returned to seek vengeance. Everything which follows depends on the fact that the audience knows more than the characters do. When Elektra sings or cries of her grief and her longing for Orestes' return, we know that he is already there. When the servant tells of his death, we watch the reactions of his hearers in the knowledge that the story is made up from start to finish. The man Klytemnestra takes to be a stranger, freeing her from the dread of being killed by her own child, is actually that child. The ashes Elektra weeps over are not those of Orestes. And in this context, the happiness she thinks she has found, and the feeling proclaimed in the last scenes of the play, that the deaths of Klytemnestra and Aigisthos are the catharsis which will end misery and bring all joy to Argos – these take place in such a context of irony that we can be sure they are not what the characters think they are. The chorus has already nudged our minds in an ode about the Furies which hover about the royal dynasty of Argos, ensuring death for generation after generation. When we see Orestes follow Aigisthos into the palace to kill him and Elektra standing alone, watching them leave, we know that the ending is no ending, that the rest of the story must mean pain and suffering of which neither she nor Orestes have so much as dreamed. Although Elektra doesn't realise it, she ends the play as alone, bereft and desolate as ever.

# Oedipus at Kolonos

## Characters

OEDIPUS

ANTIGONE, ISMENE, *his daughters*

POLYNIKES, *his son*

THESEUS, *ruler of Athens*

VILLAGER

KREON, *ruler of Thebes*

SOLDIER

ATTENDANTS, VILLAGERS, SOLDIERS (*silent parts*)

CHORUS OF VILLAGERS

## Synopsis

Oedipus, blind and a beggar, is brought by his daughter Antigone to a sacred grove at Kolonos. An outraged villager runs to fetch Theseus, ruler of nearby Athens. Oedipus prays to the gods to grant him rest at last, as prophesied. The villagers treat him roughly despite Antigone's pleas for mercy. Ismene brings news that back at home in Thebes, Oedipus' sons Eteokles and Polynikes are about to fight for supreme power, and that the gods have predicted that only Oedipus' return will save the city. Oedipus sends Ismene into the sacred grove to sacrifice, and reveals his identity to the horrified chorus. Theseus offers Oedipus state protection against the Thebans. He, too, goes to sacrifice.

After a chorus celebrating the loveliness of Kolonos, Kreon of Thebes brings soldiers to kidnap Oedipus. When the chorus intervene, he sends his men to seize Antigone and Ismene instead. Alerted by the shouting, Theseus arrests Kreon and goes with his soldiers to rescue the women. They bring back news of a suppliant at the gods' altar: Oedipus' elder son Polynikes. At first Oedipus will not meet him, but he gives way to the entreaties of Antigone and Theseus. Polynikes begs his father to join him in attacking

Thebes and defeating Eteokles, but Oedipus curses both his sons and predicts that each will kill the other. As Polynikes leaves, the chorus hear thunder, an omen of Oedipus' coming end. Oedipus tells Theseus that he will reveal mysteries to him in the secret place where he is about to die. These must never be disclosed – except to his heir on his own death – and they will protect Athens for ever. He goes into the sacred grove with Theseus, Antigone and Ismene, and after a while a soldier reports that he has miraculously disappeared. Antigone and Ismene enter, grieving. Theseus, who had followed Oedipus to his final moments, now enters and comforts them.

## About the play

*Oedipus at Kolonos* was first produced in 401, five years after Sophocles' death, and may be a work of his extreme old age. Many authorities find in it qualities of mysticism and otherworldliness and claim it as the culmination of a lifetime's work, the elderly dramatist taking a lingering farewell of his art. Just as Shakespeare, on the verge of retirement, is identified with the Prospero of *The Tempest*, so Sophocles is sometimes claimed as the model for this Oedipus.

These ideas belong to romantic fiction rather than dramatic criticism, and can skew the way we see the play. For example, Oedipus is sometimes regarded as very old indeed, several decades older than the Oedipus of *Oedipus Tyrannos* (whose events pre-date those of this play by less than a dozen years) – an assumption which can lead us to read a Lear-like grandeur into the part which is supported by neither the play's language nor its events. Oedipus is soul-sick and physically feeble, but hardly doddering. He is of a similar age to two robust city lords, Theseus and Kreon, and the three of them discuss and argue as equals, princes of power and vigour, not a convocation of dotards. Memories of Lear can similarly affect our view of Oedipus' relationship with his children. But his tenderness towards Antigone and Ismene and his rage at Polynikes and the absent Eteokles are appropriate to the ancient world and have nothing in common with Lear's relationships (which are psychologically more modern and more intimate). This fact is vital to the *dénouement* of the play. Oedipus' departure from the world and transfiguration are presented with grandeur and mystery verging on exoticism – the soldier's speech reporting his disappearance is the only 'mystical' utterance in the play – and belong entirely to the worlds of Olympian religious belief and Athenian folklore. They invite the audience to feel respect and awe, nothing like the cathartic, didactic sympathy which Lear's death evokes.

Oedipus' departure from life is the key event of *Oedipus at Kolonos*. But Sophocles, in a way characteristic of Greek tragedy, makes his play not from that moment itself but out of the events which lead up to and surround it. *Oedipus at Kolonos* is about waiting, about preparation, and is focused on Oedipus' yearning for his earthly life to end and so fulfil God's oracle. In the meantime there are dangers to face, loose ends to tie and scores to settle. The living must be prepared for what is about to happen and the gods must be propitiated – and the play's action shows how, as Oedipus deals with this business, he gradually sloughs the trappings of mortality until the inevitable moment comes.

Sophocles writes for Oedipus in a way different from any other character. For the others, the predominant mode is urgency, a bustle of argument and action. Even when Oedipus takes part in this – for example, in the scene where he reveals his identity to the chorus, or in his confrontation with Kreon – he seems to think in a more measured, more reflective way than anyone else, constantly broadening the perspective to take in ideas of his past, his destiny, the futures of Athens and Thebes, the demands and blessings of the gods. It is as if he stands simultaneously in two kinds of time, two modes of existence. This is the condition from which he is waiting to be freed, and when the soldier reports his release our feeling of satisfaction is conditioned not by events but almost entirely by character, by what we have seen of Oedipus and his dilemma up to this point.

Similarly, in the play's emotional dialectic, all interest lies with Oedipus. Each of the other characters, however warmly drawn, inhabits a single emotional territory: anxious love (Antigone), compassionate strength (Theseus), blustering arrogance (Kreon), feigned devotion (Polynikes). Sophocles deploys them against each other for dramatic effect, but leaves them substantially unchanged. Oedipus, by contrast, constantly reveals new aspects of what we already know of him: he unpeels himself before our eyes. To the people of Kolonos he shows a mixture of helplessness and pride. He makes himself Theseus' suppliant, equal and benefactor. He is contemptuous with Kreon, furious with Polynikes, tender and affectionate with his daughters. Transitions between one state and another are abrupt and untidy. This may not be character drawing of which Aristotle, with his love of the 'appropriate', would have approved, but it animates the play.

*Oedipus at Kolonos* is different from all other surviving ancient tragedies. It belongs to a genre of drama which deals less with the events of myth and the interaction between mortals and the supernatural than with the revelation of a single character at a moment of emotional and psychological crisis. *Medea* and Sophocles' *Elektra* come nearest in the surviving canon, but relate their emotional displays more closely to the enabling myth; Aeschylus' *Suppliants* and *Seven Against Thebes* show the same kind of process in groups of people rather than individuals, and *Prometheus Bound* offers a similar kind of disclosure in philosophical, not emotional, terms. But no other single dramatic character rivals this Oedipus for diversity. In this respect, if no other, he is the most Shakespearean hero to come down to us from ancient times.

# Oedipus Tyrannos

## Characters

OEDIPUS, *ruler of Thebes*
JOKASTA, *his consort*
KREON, *her brother*
TEIRESIAS, *prophet*
PRIEST
CORINTHIAN
SHEPHERD
SERVANT
ANTIGONE, ISMENE (*children; silent parts*)
CHORUS OF CITIZENS

## Synopsis

Oedipus' people beg him to find a cure for the plague which is devastating Thebes. Kreon brings word from Apollo's oracle at Delphi: only when the Thebans find and banish the murderer of Laios, the previous ruler, will their torment end. Oedipus vows to heed the oracle, but when Teiresias says that he, Oedipus, is the killer, Oedipus accuses him of plotting treason with Kreon. Kreon quarrels with Oedipus, protesting his innocence of treason, and Jokasta scolds them for arguing when Thebes is in torment. She tells Oedipus that Teiresias' accusation must be false. Laios was killed by a stranger at a crossroads. The word 'crossroads' horrifies Oedipus. Years ago, just before he came to Thebes, he fought and killed an old man at a crossroads. However, he still thinks that he has cheated an earlier oracle, that he would kill his father and marry his mother. He believes that his father is Polybos, ruler of Corinth, and he left the city for ever to defy the oracle.

After an agitated chorus, a Corinthian brings news that Polybos has died of natural causes. Oedipus shouts in relief, only to be told that Polybos was not his father, that the Corinthian received him from a shepherd who found him in the hills, a baby exposed to die. Jokasta, realising that Oedipus is the son whose death she and Laios ordered because of the prophecy that he would kill his father and marry his mother, tries in vain to warn Oedipus. He sends for the shepherd to hear the truth first-hand, and the old man confirms that Oedipus was, in fact, the baby. Oedipus hurries inside, and after a horrified chorus a servant reports that Jokasta has hanged herself and that Oedipus has used a pin from her dress to blind himself. Oedipus begs Kreon to honour the decree he made about Laios' murderer. After Oedipus' sad farewell to his children Antigone and Ismene, the chorus ends the play with the thought that no mortals should be counted happy until they die.

## About the play

*Oedipus Tyrannos* was probably first produced some time between 430 and 428, at least a decade after *Antigone* and about thirty years before *Oedipus at Kolonos*. The three plays draw on the same myth-cycle, but are otherwise unconnected.

Writing some eighty years after *Oedipus Tyrannos*, Aristotle in *Poetics* mentions it more often than any other play except Euripides' *Iphigeneia in Tauris* – and always with approval, as the tragedy which best exemplifies his theories about form. These were that the material of a play should be organised as a conceptual whole, without loose ends, irrelevancies or inconsistencies. *Oedipus Tyrannos* conforms to this ideal in every particular, the only surviving tragedy to do so. Its logic is all-embracing and its impetus inexorable and precisely paced. Its focus is remorseless on Oedipus' movement from 'ignorance' to 'knowledge' and on the effect this has on him. In the progression, each event is accompanied by its own ironical double, so that everything which happens seems to someone in the action to mean something it does not. (Even the principal metaphor of the play contains its own opposite. When Oedipus is 'blind' to the truth, he has his sight; when he achieves full understanding, he blinds himself.)

The play begins with a ruler accepting the duty of curing his people's suffering. Immediately Kreon announces the first of Apollo's oracles which drive the play: this is to be done by avenging the murder of Laios. In two simple steps, the mechanism of Fate is triggered – and, ironically, none of the characters in the action understands either the oracle or the real meaning of what has happened. In the following scene, similarly, two irreversible steps are taken: Oedipus announces that the murderer of Laios, when found, must be banished, and Teiresias tells him that he himself is guilty. At once, Oedipus' psychological collapse begins (when he rounds on Teiresias), and the exemplary power of tragedy, as described by Aristotle, begins to show itself, as we feel 'pity' (subjective empathy for Oedipus' situation and his blindness to Fate) and 'terror' (objective awareness of and respect for the wider context of human action, the context of which Oedipus is so far oblivious).

The play continues with the same blend of measured logic and escalating psychological tension. Oedipus' quarrel with Kreon, a superb demonstration of a mind in turmoil, triggers Jokasta's revelations that she and Laios tried to cheat the oracle that their son would kill his father and marry his mother, and that Laios was murdered by a stranger. At once, as if frozen by a glimpse of the wider truth, Oedipus stops ranting and tells Jokasta a long story of how he was brought up in Corinth, how a drunk said that he was not Polybos' true son and how, on his way to find the truth in Delphi, he killed a stranger at a crossroads. It is as if he is reviewing his own past, trying to understand it, and he ends by turning coldly on himself: 'If [the old man I killed was Laios] I have cursed myself, pronounced my own banishment'. Even this moment is surrounded with irony. Blotting from his mind the knowledge which we, the audience, possess, that Laios is his father, he singlemindedly pursues the lesser quarry, the truth about Laios' murder. His obsession with this nullifies the wider picture.

The Corinthian announces that Polybos and Merope are dead, and the next steps are taken towards catastrophe. Oedipus, with relief, and Jokasta, in a kind of hysterical attempt to hide the truth she knows in her heart, declare that oracles are worthless, and the

Corinthian reveals that Oedipus was a foundling. For Jokasta, the trap is sprung: she hurries out. Oedipus, still unable to accept or admit the truth, sends for the shepherd who gave the baby to the Corinthian long ago – so putting the last brick in the wall of his own downfall. Predictably, and to the audience's grim satisfaction – this is one of the play's most 'cathartic' moments – the shepherd reveals the baby's true identity.

The progress of the play so far has been what Aristotle calls *desis*, 'ravelling up'. Now begins the second part of what he considers a 'well-made' tragedy, *lusis*, 'unravelling'. Jokasta commits suicide, Oedipus blinds himself, Kreon honours Oedipus' proclamation about the murderer of Laios and banishes him, Oedipus bids farewell to his children and goes into exile, the chorus point a moral which is no moral ('Count none of us happy until we're dead') and the play ends. There is little ceremony and – save for the touching scene with the children – less sentiment. The last minutes, musically the richest part of the action, ritualise and objectify emotion. Since the Renaissance, Western Christian commentators have tried to impose a kind of didactic, moral significance on this conclusion, but it is hard to see precisely what that moral is. Oedipus is not redeemed, reaches no point of accommodation for the future, is as unconsenting in the processes of destiny as a chess piece sacrificed in a game it can never understand. The play's immaculate construction, its blend of irony, emotion and logic and its superb articulation of dramatic tension make it overwhelming to watch or read. But its 'message' is non-existent or remorselessly bleak. More than almost any other tragedy in the repertoire, it makes gods of its audience, and the gods, in ancient tragedy, are heartless.

# Philoktetes

## Characters

ODYSSEUS, NEOPTOLEMOS, PHILOKTETES, *Greek lords*
TRADER (*disguised servant of Odysseus*)
HERAKLES
SERVANT, SAILOR (*silent parts*)
CHORUS OF SAILORS

## Synopsis

Odysseus brings Neoptolemos to the desert island where Philoktetes is in exile, banished because of the stench of his gangrenous
foot. Philoktetes owns Herakles' unerring bow and arrows,
essential for the fall of Troy, and Odysseus tells Neoptolemos to
trick him back to the Greeks. Neoptolemos reluctantly agrees, and
Odysseus leaves before Philoktetes, his mortal enemy, can see him
and kill him. Neoptolemos and the chorus, discussing Philoktetes'
plight, are interrupted by groans, and Philoktetes comes in and
rails at the way the Greeks have ill-treated him. Neoptolemos
repeats the lie Odysseus taught him, that he has quarrelled with
the Greek commanders and is sailing home. Philoktetes begs to go
with him and Neoptolemos agrees. Odysseus' servant comes in,
disguised as a trader, and urges haste, since (he claims) Odysseus
and Diomedes are coming to kidnap Philoktetes. Philoktetes and
Neoptolemos go into the cave to gather Philoktetes' possessions,
and the chorus contrast Philoktetes' exile and the happiness he will
find at home.

Neoptolemos urges Philoktetes to hurry. But Philoktetes is
racked by sudden agony and collapses. The chorus advise
Neoptolemos to leave him and go, taking the bow. But Neoptolemos pities Philoktetes and tells him the truth. Philoktetes begs him
to abandon the Greeks and show the generous spirit of his father
Achilles. As Neoptolemos wavers, Odysseus comes in, says that

now they have the bow they have no need of Philoktetes, and takes Neoptolemos away. The chorus beg Philoktetes to sail for Troy, but he says he prefers suicide and stumbles out.

Neoptolemos returns with the bow, followed by the incredulous Odysseus: the boy is siding with Philoktetes after all. Odysseus tries threats, but Neoptolemos turns the bow on him. Neoptolemos tries to persuade Philoktetes to come to Troy, not for the Greeks but for his own sake, and when Philoktetes refuses, he agrees to abandon Troy and take him home. He gives him the bow and they prepare to leave. But Herakles appears and orders Philoktetes back to Troy: his destiny and that of the city are inextricably entwined. Philoktetes sings farewell to his island home, and the chorus usher him and Neoptolemos offstage.

## About the play

*Philoktetes* was first performed in 409, when Sophocles was in his late eighties. Although the basic story, part of the Trojan myth-cycle, was used by all three great tragedians, only Sophocles' play survives, and only he seems to have included the character of Neoptolemos. His *Philoktetes*, though self-standing, is thematically related to *Ajax* in that both are concerned with the balance between honour, political expediency and treachery.

Centring the action on Neoptolemos allows Sophocles to ironise the confrontation between Odysseus and Philoktetes and between the qualities they represent. They are irreconcilable. When one is up the other must be down, when one has the magic bow, the other must be deprived of it. It would have been possible to write a straightforward – and dramatically compulsive – argument between them. But Sophocles arranges his plot so that each presents his arguments through a third party, Neoptolemos, and the effects are to put a critical distance between the spectators and those arguments, and to show how they impinge on someone untouched by the obsessions of the principals. In the course of the action, neither Philoktetes nor Odysseus changes. All change is in Neoptolemos, and his moral and emotional journey is the backbone of the play. In his oscillations and vacillations, he also embodies one of the play's main philosophical distinctions, between the roles we are assigned, or assign ourselves, and the 'truth' of life.

The role of Philoktetes makes virtuoso demands on the performer: it is one of the most exhausting in extant drama. Like Herakles in Euripides' play, Philoktetes is a version of the wounded god-king common in Western folklore. He has divine power (symbolised by the magic bow), and yet his mortality (symbolised by his wounded foot) disables him. He is Herakles' mirror image: as Herakles must shed mortality to cope with his divine nature, so Philoktetes must shed divine power to cope with his mortality. When he thinks he can evade this destiny by escaping from the island with Neoptolemos, the gods send him agony. When he agreed to light Herakles' funeral pyre and so burn away the god-hero's mortality, he tore the web of Fate and opposed the will of Hera (who was determined not to allow Herakles into Olympos). This act must be put right if universal harmony, and his own peace of mind and body, are to be restored. The putting right affects a second great purpose of Fate, the use of Herakles' bow in the downfall of Troy – and Philoktetes is in too much physical agony, too clay-souled or too intransigent to realise it. His focus is on pain, not cure. He thinks that his wound is physical, and his concentration on gangrened flesh blinds him to the fact that it is also metaphysical, that to cope with it he must come to terms with the gods who hurt him. He is delirious – he peoples a desert by personalising inanimate objects such as his cave, his cup and his water pool – and his delirium prevents him from true understanding right until the closing moments of the play, when his mentor Herakles explains directly how the pattern of the universe is to be restored. All this vastness must somehow be embodied in the playing of the role.

In Homer's *Iliad*, and in all surviving plays using the Trojan myth-cycle, Odysseus is something of a standard 'turn'. In contrast to the long-suffering, morally evolving hero he becomes in Homer's *Odyssey*, he appears in the plays as the incarnation of *poneria* (self-admiring wiliness), a character akin more to the tricksters of folklore than to Achilles, Hektor and the other princes who fought for Troy. Sophocles had already made ironical use of this characterisation in *Ajax*, showing Odysseus not merely as wily but as wiser and more aware of the issues than any other character. In *Philoktetes* he darkens the interpretation – if there is a morally equivocal person in this story, it is Odysseus – but also plays a series of theatrical games which crucially affect the part, and the whole play, in performance. In the original Athenian production, the first actor may have played Philoktetes, the second actor Neoptolemos and the third actor not only Odysseus but also both the trader (Odysseus' servant, or Odysseus himself, in disguise) and Herakles appearing *ex machina*. This would mean that every time Neoptolemos wavers, the Odysseus character appears, in one role or another, to remind him of his purpose. The *ex machina* appearance caps the play by showing that what the Odysseus character wanted in the first place is in tune with the requirements of Fate. Neoptolemos' final lessons, and the final ironies for the audience, are that black was white all along and that both the moral direction the action was taking and Philoktetes' moral understanding were mistaken. The 'happy' ending (in which balance is restored) is by no means the outcome we are encouraged to expect.

It is impossible to tell how much Sophocles' audiences might have been aware of doubling. Modern spectators acknowledge or ignore it as the circumstances of each production demand. But *Philoktetes* is a tragedy – the only one to survive – in which doubling is clearly related to the meaning of the action, by intention or coincidence, one more layer in the role playing and multiple irony which characterise this most devious of dramas.

# Women of Trachis

## Characters

DEIANEIRA, *Herakles' wife*
HYLLOS, *their son*
NURSE
MESSENGER
LICHAS
HERAKLES
OLD ATTENDANT
IOLE, WOMEN PRISONERS, GUARDS (*silent parts*)
CHORUS OF WOMEN

## Synopsis

Outside Herakles' palace in Trachis, his wife Deianeira tells how he won her in single combat against the river god Acheloös, and how she is waiting anxiously for his return after fifteen months' adventuring. Hyllos tells her the rumour that Herakles has in fact been the slave for a year of a princess of Lydia, and is now making war against the Euboians. Deianeira asks him to go and help his father. After a brief chorus comparing Deianeira's anxiety to clouds and waves, Deianeira tells how Herakles prophesied that when he returned it would be either to his death or to peaceful retirement. Lichas announces Herakles' success in Euboia, and brings a group of prisoners including Princess Iole. One of his entourage tells Deianeira that Iole is Herakles' concubine, and Lichas confirms it. Deianeira goes to fetch gifts for Herakles, and the chorus sing of the power of love and the fight between Herakles and Acheloös.

Deianeira brings a shirt she has made for Herakles, and tells the chorus that it is smeared with the blood of the centaur Nessos. Long ago he tried to rape her, was shot by Herakles, and told her with his dying breath that if she soaked a garment in the blood,

Herakles would never again look at another woman. Leaving
Lichas to deliver the gifts, she goes inside, and the chorus sing of
their eagerness to see Herakles home again. Then Deianeira comes
out, distraught. She has discovered that the blood was not a love
philtre, but poison. Hyllos runs in and denounces her for
poisoning his father: the shirt has burned into Herakles' flesh and
he is being carried home in agony. Deianeira goes into the palace,
we hear cries of grief, and the nurse reports that she has stabbed
herself.

After a brief chorus of mourning, Herakles is carried in,
attended by Hyllos and an old man. He rails against Fate, and
against his treacherous wife. But when Hyllos tells him that
Deianeira mistook the poison for a love philtre and has killed
herself, he realises the true meaning of an oracle that he would be
killed 'by no living creature'. He abandons his anger and grieves
for Deianeira. He begs Hyllos to fulfil the rest of the prophecy by
taking him to the top of Mount Oita and burning him on a funeral
pyre, so freeing him at last to join the gods in Olympos. Hyllos
refuses this, but agrees to Herakles' second request, that he marry
Iole.

## About the play

The date and position of this play in Sophocles' career are
unknown. Its form and verse style – not to mention the bleak
attitude it takes to the gods' riddling prophecies – suggest to some
that it may be one of his earliest surviving plays, but convince
others that it is late work, perhaps influenced by Euripides.

The play uses a variant of the two-part form also found in
*Eumenides, Ajax, Women in Power* and half a dozen plays by
Euripides. The halves are markedly different in style, like a pair of
contrasting movements in classical music; perhaps its original
theatrical rationale was also musical. (It differs from the usual two-
part structure, seen in such plays as *Ajax, Women in Power* or
*Hekabe,* in that one section grows out of the other, in contrast to
the more common break-and-contrast diptych method.) The first

'movement', centring on Deianeira, is in a brisk, tripping verse style more like that of comedy (even the New Comedy of a century later) than what we otherwise know of Sophoclean tragedy. In the second 'movement', centred on Herakles, the action is slowed down and focuses on a single event and a single relationship, and the verse style is more formal and syntactically more elaborate.

Sophocles uses stylistic difference to articulate the main contrast in his play, between the feminine and masculine aspects of life – *yin* and *yang* – which together make wholeness. Deianeira embodies many of the qualities Greeks thought of as 'feminine': freshness, intellectual innocence, simplicity, emotional openness and a kind of tremulous eagerness for and acceptance of experience of the world and its ways. Herakles embodies many of the qualities they thought of as 'masculine': strength of mind, assertiveness, decisiveness and a willingness first to challenge Fate and then to embrace what cannot be changed. The 'tragedy' of the play is that they never meet: Deianeira kills herself before Herakles reaches the stage. In this vision of the tear in the net of universal order, *yin* and *yang* are not united and reparation is not achieved.

The hinge between the two parts of the play, the tragic link, is that it is Deianeira's flawed view of the pattern of the universe, her (feminine) trust in what Nessos the centaur told her years before, which brings about catastrophe. Herakles' flawed understanding, his (male) rage at what he takes to be her treachery, is mended before our eyes, when he hears that she gave him the shirt thinking that it was impregnated with love, not death. Sophocles ends the play with a further, over-riding irony. The audience knows that Herakles' story, and the end of his life, are still in the future. The understanding he reaches in the play does *not* mend the net of universal order, because the tear was made much earlier, by Zeus when he had sex with Alkmene and fathered Herakles and by Hera when she refused to accept the child as an immortal. This skewing of universal balance is what must be set right, and the story of Deianeira and Herakles is merely one portion of that process – a process whose next step Herakles himself lays out in his instructions to Hyllos about the funeral pyre.

In view of this turn in the story – although Herakles has been onstage, as a character, for some time, he speaks now almost as a *deus ex machina* – and in terms of the philosophical logic which Aristotle demanded in the organisation of a play, *Women of Trachis* can be seen as not a self-standing unit but part of some larger conceptual picture. Given that the play actually *is* self-standing – Sophocles did not write play sequences in the Aeschylean manner – this nimbus of overtones and resonances is one of its most striking features, similar to the 'absence' of the Greek dimension of the Persian War in Aeschylus' *Persians* which is so strongly implied by the 'presence' of the Persian dimension (see page 52). *Women of Trachis*, it can be argued, is as much about what is *not* presented as what we see.

# Euripides

## Life

Euripides was born in the 480s (traditionally in either 485 or 480), in the area of Phlye on the honey-producing slopes of Mount Hymettos some 5km south-east of Athens. His family owned a hereditary priesthood of the local shrine of Apollo, an honour which implies that they were middle or upper class; the fact that Aristophanes mocks him by calling his mother a 'greengrocer' suggests that they may have been *nouveaux riches* rather than old aristocracy. He seems to have been wealthy: he was challenged to *antidosis* (a custom where a rich person could be invited to undertake someone else's tax obligations for a given year or else exchange possessions), and he owned property on the island of Salamis. (Later legend said that this included a 'cave' where he wrote his plays, thus giving rise to the idea that he was a recluse. But the word translated as 'cave' also means any kind of 'retreat', for example a secluded villa.)

Euripides' career began in the heyday of Athenian grandeur, and by the outbreak of the Peloponnesian War he was in his fifties, with over twenty years of professional activity behind him. All his surviving plays except *Alkestis* and *Rhesos* belong to the period of the war, and many reflect wartime issues (the nature of generalship, say, or the duty conquerors owe the conquered) and climates of opinion (uncertainty about the gods, say, or the despair engendered by endless conflict). Euripides was also affected by the growing fifth-century movement towards abstract thought, towards rationalisation and objectivisation of opinion on every conceivable issue. He was temperamentally an intellectual, a book-reader (something almost unheard-of at the time, when books were luxuries) and a friend of philosophers and other radical thinkers.

As well as working in Athens, Euripides is thought to have spent time in Corinth and in Sicily, where his reputation stood high. In 408, when Athens' defeat in the Peloponnesian War was only months away, he retired to Macedonia, dying there some eighteen months later.

## Works

Euripides' first known play, *Pelias' Daughters* (about the children of Pelias, persuaded by Medea to 'rejuvenate' their aged father by boiling him alive), was produced in 455 when he was in his mid twenties or early thirties. It is now lost. He went on to write 91 other works, chiefly tragedies but a few satyr plays. Known titles (including *Antiope, Chrysippos, Kresphontes, Philoktetes, Telephos* and *Theseus*) show that – as in the extant plays – he took subjects from a wide range of myth-stories; the Trojan War and its aftermath, however, inspired over a third of his output. Nineteen plays survive: *Alkestis* (438), *Medea* (431), *Herakles' Children* (430–27), *Hippolytos* (428), *Andromache* (*c.* 425), *Elektra* (425–13), *Hekabe* (*c.* 424), *Suppliants* (*c.* 422), *Herakles* (?*c.* 417), *Women of Troy* (415), *Iphigeneia in Tauris* (*c.* 412), *Helen* (412), *Ion* (*c.* 412), *Phoenician Women* (*c.* 409), *Orestes* (408), *Bacchae* and *Iphigeneia at Aulis* (performed posthumously, *c.* 405), *Cyclops* (date unknown), *Rhesos* (date unknown; thought by some not to be by Euripides).

## Style and approach

Of the three Athenian tragic dramatists whose works survive, Euripides is the most firmly rooted in the religious and dramatic culture of his time, and has been most misunderstood by critics and scholars of later ages who judged religious drama in general, and Greek tragedy in particular, by the standards of their own Christian upbringing. If Euripides had written the surviving plays in an atmosphere of Christian belief and worship, if the Athenian dramatic festivals had been anything like the European festivals of later eras, if Olympianism had had even the smallest points of contact with the ideas and practice of Christianity, he might have deserved some of the obloquy which has come his way. But his art, its circumstances and the thinking which underlies it are so alien to later ideas that the critical tradition can hinder understanding rather than help it.

Part of the problem is the sheer number of surviving plays, something like one-fifth of Euripides' output. We have so small a proportion of the work of Aeschylus and Sophocles – if the same amount of Shakespeare's work had survived, we would be defining his art from one or at most two plays – that it is easy to pontificate, on practically no evidence, about the kind of drama they wrote, the nature of Athenian tragedy in general and their relationship to it. But enough of Euripides' plays survive – the equivalent of seven or eight by Shakespeare – to reveal artistic development, experiment and varied approaches to the structures and strategies of the drama of his time. In particular, they show him applying a sharply quizzical mind to every technique he chooses, every character he creates and every scene he writes. Nothing is sacrosanct. He writes formal tragedy (in the mode later approved by Aristotle), comedy, melodrama, rhetorical and philosophical debate. His verse style ranges from lyric to doggerel. His use of such conventions as choral odes, messenger's speeches and appearances of the *deus ex machina* confounds expectation as often as it confirms it. Above all, his work is consistently ironical, concerned with the contrast between 'reality' and the depiction of 'reality' – an approach which uses the dramatic form not to preach at its spectators or 'emend' them (goals of Christian drama), but to disturb, challenge and entertain. Some have objected that a religious festival was not the place to do this – but as Aristophanes' work also shows, not to mention the many 'Euripidean' moments in Aeschylus' and Sophocles' surviving plays, whatever happened in other sacred precincts and other parts of the festival rituals, this was *exactly* what people expected in the Theatre of Dionysos.

## Structure

Euripidean irony involves consistently playing against expectation – sometimes even, in a kind of double irony, confounding our expectation that this is what will happen. Nothing can be taken at face value. In many plays, a god or mortal opens the action by telling the audience directly what has occurred till now and what is to happen next – and this ironises the entire spectacle, as we watch the action confirming or confronting that prediction. At the end of many plays, a god or messenger from the gods appears and declares that the direction the action has taken is not that required by Fate, that the characters' stories must progress to a different conclusion – an alienation device which prises apart the 'meaning' of what we have just seen, forcing us to reassess both it and the assumptions, religious, political, ethical or otherwise, on which it seemed to be based. In the middle of some plays – *Elektra* and *Iphigeneia in Tauris* are examples – the chorus sing odes about obscure corners of the original stories, then turn to the audience and say 'All that's just myth'. At the heart of many plays, the arguments for and against a particular point of view are presented in a long rhetorical discussion, often in striking contrast with the tormented emotions and desperate situation of the characters who engage in it – as when Hekabe and Helen in *Women of Troy*, about to be shipped away as slaves after the fall of Troy, debate the extent of Helen's guilt and her behaviour throughout the Trojan War. Very little of all this conforms to Aristotle's views about unity of form in drama, but it is consistently and thrillingly dramatic.

One of the main areas in which all three tragic dramatists, but Euripides in particular, surprised and disappointed some later commentators was the way they blurred the supposed distinction between tragedy and comedy. This was claimed to downgrade the dignity of the tragic form, and of tragic characters. Herakles in *Alkestis*, about to work a transforming miracle, first plays a drunk scene. In *Bacchae* Kadmos and Teiresias, about to go to Mount Kithairon to take part in the sacred rituals of Dionysos, parade before us in doddering, self-delighted ecstasy and in fancy dress. The servant in *Hippolytos* fusses indignantly about the bother

Phaedra's mental distress is causing her (the servant), and then tells her bluntly that the best cure for her passion for Hippolytos is to have sex with him. Evadne, about to commit suicide in *Suppliants* by throwing herself from the battlements into the funeral pyres of the Seven Against Thebes, first has a petulant-teenager argument with her aged father. Similar instances occur in almost every surviving play, and some (*Helen, Ion, Iphigeneia in Tauris, Elektra*) indulge in such elaborate interplay between 'tragedy' and 'comedy' that there has been earnest debate about precisely what kind of plays they are. When Helen, at the start of *Helen*, confides in us that her problem is that she is a perfectly ordinary woman who just happens to be the most beautiful person in the world, do we laugh at her condition, enter into it, or do both at once? When the soldier-messenger describes Agave and her women playing catch with lumps of Pentheus' flesh in *Bacchae*, the horror of what he is saying is heightened, not lessened, by the absurdity of the metaphor he uses. The terrible is 'absurd' (in the sense that it defies logic and confounds expectation), but in Euripides' hands, as so often in everyday life, it is often also ludicrous, the surreal enhancing, extending and explaining what is real.

## Realism

It is a characteristic feature of Euripides' work, as of that of his younger contemporary (and possibly friend) Aristophanes, to play games with the nature of reality itself, to present the grand in terms of the mundane and to elevate the ordinary. Euripides belongs less to the tradition of Aeschylus and Sophocles who (in their extant plays at least) consistently make a distinction between their 'high' and 'low' characters, and more to that of Homer's epics, where 'high' and 'low' are aspects of the same character. Rulers, gods and heroes are constantly given 'ordinary' human feelings and preoccupations and are placed in the situations of everyday life, while servants, rank-and-file soldiers and farmworkers take part in 'great' events and share the ethical and moral feelings and concerns of their 'betters'.

To some extent, this democratisation was part of a growing philosophical and political climate of thought in the city itself. But that climate had, in part, been created by drama, by the way it admitted ordinary people (in the form of audiences) into a kind of dialogue with the ethical and moral issues being presented onstage, encouraging them to make judgements and hold opinions, and showing how those judgements and opinions could be articulated. By Euripides' heyday, no stage play was simply a 'show', a presentation. All drama was open-ended and speculative. Collaboration between writer, performer and spectator had become essential to the medium.

Euripides was a master at the balance between philosophical discussion on the one hand and psychological investigation (often of the same situations) on the other. He used the fact that drama is able simultaneously to show two or three quite different kinds of thing to refract the emotional and intellectual implications of each situation inextricably into one other. *Medea* is both about how supernatural powers and nature can be reconciled with mortal emotions and sensibilities, and the depiction of an individual driven by suffering to madness and murder. The Trojan captives and Greek conquerors in *Women of Troy* on the one hand articulate two sides of a debate about the duties and agonies of war, and on the other show what happens to ordinary people caught up in that situation. Theseus in *Suppliants* is a heroic king from myth who has to cope with the dilemmas of everyday politics. No actions, either of mortals or gods, take place in an emotional vacuum. Their consequences are debated, and worked out in blood and tears, before our eyes.

The importation of realism is not just a matter of what people think and say, but of the words they use to say it. Euripides seldom gives his characters 'grand' language as a matter of course – in fact quite the opposite. In Aeschylus a watchman grumbling during a night shift and a god outlining the future of the universe use similar language, syntactically elaborate and enhanced by music and metaphor. In Sophocles the 'ordinary' people imported into scenes borrow, for the most part, the high emotions and ethical concerns of the princes and heroes they are addressing. In Euripides no one, of any degree or condition, uses high style at all unless it is for specific, brief effect, as in ordinary life when someone might express an emotion, or utter an idea, with particular linguistic vehemence. His verse-rhythms are subtle and varied, but are for the most part closer to ordinary speech than to 'high' literature or drama – a characteristic they share with comedy. His syntax is plain and his poetry precise and blunt. An Aeschylean chorus might begin an ode on becoming birds and flying free from trouble with some grand invocation of 'the Aether which enfolds the Earth'; a Euripidean chorus says crisply, 'Seagulls, flocking on the shore. Gods, take us there'. The more racked the emotions, the more tortuous the intellectual issues, the simpler the language. Orestes, reflecting on the nature of virtue in *Elektra*, begins, 'It's hard to get this right'; Medea, having made up her mind to ease her soul by murder, says bluntly, 'No choice. I have to kill the children and escape to Corinth.' The servants who report terrible events use the gasping, graphic language of people giving eye-witness accounts of a street accident: 'they tore off his limbs and played catch with them'; 'flesh oozed from her face like resin when you gash a pine-tree'; 'as the toddler huddled down, his father took aim and fired at him'. Everything is stripped to its bones – an alienation technique which forces spectators to enter the experience and ponder it. It is impossible, offhand, to think of a single line, speech or scene in which Euripides cossets his audience.

The disconcerting nature of this kind of writing is felt most strongly by those who think of Greek tragedy as religious drama. God, to Euripides – as again to Homer before him – is neither an abstraction nor above the same kind of comment and criticism as any other phenomenon of existence. In Greek religion, the divine is splintered into a thousand refractions ('gods'), each given a specific name and characteristics. (The power of sex, for example, is named Aphrodite and given beautiful female form; the sunshaft is personalised as Apollo the archer.) In Euripides, an attribute so characterised can take human form and take part in the action just like any other character. Dionysos in *Bacchae*, for example, appears as a seductive and mysterious young man. When gods appear to set the scene of a play or round off the human action, they speak in the same clipped language and use the same everyday images and metaphors as the human characters.

Writing of this kind has nothing to do with atheism, a charge regularly made against Euripides. To explore God's nature, however critically, is not to deny his or her existence. Dionysos is not demeaned by the humanness of his behaviour in *Bacchae*; Apollo is not diminished by the way the human characters in *Ion* call him a rapist and a liar. On the contrary, the process enhances their mystery, the mysterious nature of the divine, and invites human spectators, often quite specifically, to consider their own role in the relationship between natural and supernatural. Euripides' consistent message is not that God is non-existent but that understanding God is hard, is a process which leads us to find out more about ourselves – and by humanising the gods in his plays, by making them as capricious and unprepossessing as we are ourselves, he gives that message characteristically sharp focus.

## Use of myth

The plays of all three surviving tragic dramatists take 'liberties' with myth. In every case, the myth-story is merely the starting-point, a platform for the kind of play the author wants to write. Aeschylus' importation of Ocean and Io into the Prometheus myth, Sophocles' all-but-invention of the plots of his *Ajax*, *Antigone*, *Oedipus at Kolonos* and *Philoktetes*, the utterly different way each dramatist handles the story of Orestes and Elektra – these suggest that 'Euripidean' deconstruction of the myths may have been less the exception than the norm. He seems to have chosen particular stories – sometimes minor myths from remote regions, or obscure corners of more familiar myths – to give himself the opportunity to show strong characters, especially women, in fraught situations, and to investigate (often in an ironical or elliptical way) current ethical, moral and political dilemmas. With the exceptions of *Rhesos* and *Cyclops*, his plays are not 'about' the stories which are their starting-points. They use myth to give specificity and human density to such areas of debate as the nature of the divine (*Bacchae, Herakles, Ion, Medea*), 'heroism' (*Helen, Herakles' Children, Medea, Suppliants*), human love (*Alkestis, Elektra, Helen, Herakles' Children, Hippolytos, Ion, Phoenician Women*), and war (*Hekabe, Phoenician Women, Suppliants, Women of Troy*). In many characters, and several entire plays (*Hekabe, Herakles, Hippolytos*), 'madness' and 'sanity' are important themes. Politics, not least between women and men and in families; the gods; the difference between 'reality' and the ways we perceive and talk about it – these are subjects touched on in every play. To place such agendas on myth-stories, in some cases pulling them apart to do so, strikes some commentators as bizarre. But myth-stories have always been used, and still are used, in this way in real life as well as in art: to give specific instances of general questions and general truths. Without this penumbra of association, myth dies.

Euripides' restless mind and theatrical expertise – he is technically as surefooted as he is inventive; every apparent 'strangeness' is a calculated effect – make his work some of the most challenging of all surviving drama until Shakespeare's. His plays define, and consistently redefine, both what 'serious' theatre does and how it does it.

# Alkestis

## Characters

APOLLO

DEATH

SERVANT

ADMETOS, *ruler of Pherai*

ALKESTIS, *his wife*

HER SON

PHERES, *Admetos' father*

HERAKLES

ATTENDANTS, SECOND SON (*silent parts*)

CHORUS OF TOWNSPEOPLE

## Synopsis

Outside Admetos' palace, Apollo argues with Death. Apollo has persuaded the Fates to let Admetos live if someone else agrees to take his place in the Underworld. All have refused except Admetos' beloved wife Alkestis, and today is the day when Death has come for her. Apollo tries, in vain, to persuade Death to grant her a few years' more life. The gods disappear, and a servant welcomes the grieving chorus, telling them of Alkestis' preparations to part from Admetos and her children and go with Death. In a tender scene, Alkestis bids farewell to Admetos and their sons, and dies. Attendants carry her body inside as the chorus weep for her.

Herakles interrupts the mourning. He is travelling to Thrace to carry out one of his Labours, and on the way has called to visit his friend Admetos. He is embarrassed to find the palace preparing for a funeral, but Admetos asks him to stay, refusing to tell him who has died. He goes inside, and the chorus sing of Admetos' hospitality. The funeral procession appears, and Admetos has an angry confrontation with his father Pheres, whose refusal to go to the Underworld for Admetos led to Alkestis' death. As the procession leaves, a servant complains to the audience about the way Herakles is drinking, singing and joking inside. Herakles comes out, drunk, but sobers quickly when the servant tells him why the palace is in mourning. He leaves, just before Admetos and the other mourners return from Alkestis' funeral, but comes back with a veiled companion. He tells Admetos to welcome the stranger into his palace, Admetos angrily refuses, and Herakles reveals that she is Alkestis: he has wrestled Death for her and won. Wife and husband fall into one another's arms.

## About the play

*Alkestis* was first performed in 438, when Euripides was in his forties and some twenty years into his professional career. It is his first surviving play. The (known) fact that it was performed fourth on its festival day has led to speculation that it might be some kind of pastoral or satyr play rather than a 'full-blown' tragedy. Arguments for or against this theory have sometimes drowned out appreciation of the play which Euripides actually wrote.

*Alkestis* is written in elegant, syntactically unornate language, much of it in lyric metres – possibly more music was used in performance than in most surviving plays. Its plot is simple and linear, and the main event (Herakles' bringing Alkestis back to life) is announced by Apollo right at the start. This has the effect of throwing interest less on what happens than *how* it happens, and on the characters and relationships involved.

It is impossible to overstate the play's unfussy grace. If ever a work of art achieved the elegance of Greek sculpture, this is it. Situations and thoughts are presented with utmost simplicity and refinement, whether the speaker is a servant describing Alkestis taking leave of the palace staff –

> Tears in the house, the slaves all tears. She spoke to us,
> Held our hands, spoke gently; we spoke to her,
> Each of us, the grandest, the humblest. So it was.
> Admetos' house is a house of tears ...

– or Alkestis herself talking to her husband about the children:

> All I ask is this. Do this for me. A small thing –
> What else could it be, compared with the life I give you? –
> But earned, deserved. Our children: love them
> As I would have loved them. Let them grow up happy . . .

or the chorus weeping for the palace deprived of its beloved mistress –

> Gods love this place, protect
> Its placid fields where cattle graze,
> Its water-pools. Fields, pastures, stretch
> West, where the setting Sun
> Stables his horses, east to the sea,
> Sharp cliffs, Mount Pelion.

> Admetos welcomes now
> This stranger-guest; hides tears and smiles
> To welcome him. Her Majesty
> Lies dead, still warm, inside.
> He's a king; he understands; accept.
> God smiles on him; accept.

But beauty also lies in the deployment of the characters and the central relationship. Like *Helen* some twenty-four years later, *Alkestis* movingly depicts that rarest of subjects for drama, love between long-married people. Although Alkestis herself is like a beacon of light for everyone in the story, beloved equally by her sons, her servants, the palace women, the riotous visitor, even her indignant father-in-law, her affection for Admetos and his for her seem to isolate them from all around them. Each fully exists only in the other. Admetos has been criticised as unheroic and selfish, because he is afraid of death and searches desperately for someone to die in his place. But that fear and that search are in the past; the action of the play shows how he comes to terms with what Alkestis means and is to him, with losing her and then being given her back again. When the chorus in *Agamemnon* describe Menelaos' longing for Helen they talk of him embracing her statues and finding only 'empty joy', the image is frigid. When Admetos in this play tells Alkestis that he will do exactly the same thing, our focus

ALKESTIS

is not on emptiness but the ache of it, on love and loss; the passage
is a declaration of living love:

> I'll have your image made, exact, some craftsman's hand;
> I'll lay it in our bed. I'll cradle it, kiss it,
> Murmur your name, your own dear name.
> Cold comfort, wife no-wife, but all I'll have.
> You'll visit me in dreams. We'll laugh, we'll talk,
> Charm night away, so long as darkness lasts.
> If I could sing like Orpheus, play like Orpheus,
> I'd charm their ears, the King and Queen of Hell.
> I'd bring you back . . .

The effect of this speech is enhanced because it is not described or
quoted (as the Menelaos equivalent is in *Agamemnon*): Alkestis is
there, living and breathing, to hear Admetos' words. The scene
also sets up the closing section of the play, in which Herakles, by
claiming to Admetos that his veiled companion is a surrogate for
Alkestis, compels him to declare his love for the real Alkestis. For
Admetos, the declaration is a moment of devastating self-discov-
ery, that he has nothing left of Alkestis but his love for her. For us,
however, it is suffused with irony, the characteristic Euripidean
contrast between perception and reality. The scene shows that
Admetos has changed because of what has happened – that he has
grown in moral stature and self-awareness and he is rewarded,
against expectation, when his wife holds out her arms to him.

This is a 'happy ending', and is routinely deplored by critics
who expect 'tragedy' to end unhappily. But the tears it evokes in us
are just as cathartic as any we shed for Antigone, say, or Hekabe in
other plays. It is true that, to judge at least by surviving plays, the
focus we find in *Alkestis* on relationships and emotional realism
seem less typical of fifth-century drama than of later 'New
Comedy'. The part played by the servant in the action of *Alkestis*,
and particularly her or his 'running entrance' to complain about
Herakles' behaviour and the scene in which he or she scolds the
drunken god, also have equivalents in comedy rather than
surviving tragedy. But none of this is the predominant impression
as we see or read the play. Its serenity, its grave emotional
sureness, is ideal for a drama showing the redemptive force of love,

and the picture it presents of someone learning and growing by suffering is characteristic of the way it addresses the seriousness of life.

# Andromache

## Characters

ANDROMACHE
MOLOSSOS, *her son, a child*
HER SERVANT
HERMIONE, *Queen of Phthia*
HER NURSE
MENELAOS, *King of Sparta*
PELEUS, *former King of Phthia*
ORESTES
NEOPTOLEMOS' SERVANT
THETIS, *sea goddess*
ATTENDANTS, SOLDIERS (*silent parts*)
CHORUS OF WOMEN

## Synopsis

After the fall of Troy Andromache, widow of Prince Hektor, was given as booty to Neoptolemos, son of Achilles (who killed Hektor). Neoptolemos took her to his kingdom, Phthia, and had a son with her, Molossos. As the play begins, Andromache, in refuge at the altar of Thetis outside the palace, explains how Neoptolemos' queen Hermione, unable to have children, has accused her of witchcraft and is plotting to kill both her and Molossos while Neoptolemos is away consulting the Delphic Oracle. Andromache sends her servant to ask help from Peleus, Neoptolemos' aged grandfather.

The chorus pity Andromache, but point out that she's a slave and must accept her fate. Hermione jeeringly repeats this advice and says that she knows just how to make Andromache leave sanctuary. She goes, and the chorus sing briefly of the Judgement of Paris. Then Menelaos, Hermione's father, brings in the child Molossos, and tells Andromache that if she leaves the altar and goes to her death, Molossos will be spared; if not, his throat will be cut. Andromache does as he asks, only to be told that it was a trick. Molossos must also die, on Hermione's orders. Before the sentence can be carried out, Peleus arrives and offers Andromache and Molossos protection.

The chorus sing of the quiet life, and Hermione comes out in despair, comforted by her old nurse. Hermione plans suicide before Neoptolemos hears how she plotted against Andromache and comes to punish her. But at this point Orestes of Argos unexpectedly appears. Before he murdered his mother, he had been promised to Hermione in marriage, but after the murder Menelaos gave her to Neoptolemos instead. Now Orestes plans to elope with her and for Neoptolemos to be murdered. He and Hermione leave, and the chorus sing an ode of mourning for the dead at Troy. Neoptolemos' servants bring Peleus his corpse, and one of them describes how he was assassinated by a mob in Delphi. The goddess Thetis appears to tell her husband Peleus and the chorus not to mourn. Peleus must bury Neoptolemos in Delphi; Andromache will marry happily at last, and her son will found a royal dynasty. Peleus will be given immortality in the palace of Thetis' father the sea-king. The chorus end the play by reminding us that the ways of the gods are mysterious to mortals.

## About the play

*Andromache* was first performed in about 425, some two years before *Hekabe*, to which it is remarkably similar in tone and mood: a savage play, blunt, swift and bleak. Its date – some five years into the Peloponnesian War – and the merciless depiction of its Spartan characters, has led some to take it for an anti-Spartan tract. But while duller-witted members of Euripides' audience may have cheered such sentiments as Andromache's speech to Menelaos, Prince of Sparta, beginning 'You conquer other men and you rule over them in crime./ Your government – betrayal' (Robert

Cannon's translation, ll.447ff )* and jeered Menelaos' surly comments before his exit, 'Too quick to lose your temper./ I came here
neither to make threats nor to be threatened . . . Your expostulations/
I ignore' (ll.727–47), the rest of the play is too elliptical, and
Euripides (at least in his other surviving work) is too subtle a
dramatist to support such a simplistic judgement. *Andromache*'s
Spartan characters are a blend of vanity, duplicity and ruthlessness,
but these qualities are their own, it is never suggested that they
belong to their people as a whole, and the most arrogant and ruth-
less person in the whole action is not a Spartan but an Argive,
Orestes. Bluntly, if Euripides had wanted to write jingoism, he had
sufficient technique and self-confidence to do it better than this.

Like *Hekabe*, and like *Orestes* some two decades later, *Andromache* is a study of anarchy, of the chaos in a society which has
abandoned ethics and morality or had them stripped away by
events. *Hekabe* is a study of the collapse of its central character's
mind, not under the stress of defeat – she is a noble and inspiring
leader to her defeated people – but because of the unexpected and
apparently unmotivated murder of her son. *Orestes* shows how
people come to terms with themselves and their surroundings
after committing a horrific crime which is also morally justified.
*Andromache* is about what happens in an ordered society when it
becomes abruptly leaderless, when the guarantor of its laws and
hierarchies is suddenly removed. Neoptolemos' absence is the
most important factor in the story. This, rather than insults spat at
Sparta, may have been the play's relevance for Athenian politics at
the first performance, some three years after the death of Pericles
who had spent a generation at the head of the city's affairs.

Euripides touches on another theme which recurs not only in
Athenian politics, but also in many of the myths used by tragic
dramatists – and in Aristophanes, whose heroes and choruses
constantly repeat it. This is that the older generation was greater or
nobler than the younger generation, that the children of great men
and women are no match for their parents. In Athens the city's

* Published in *Euripides Plays: Five* (Methuen, 1997).

failure to win the Peloponnesian War was already being put down to the fact that a generation of people brought up to argue and quibble, to settle things with words, lacked the moral self-discipline which had helped their elders defeat the Persians some fifty years before. In Aristophanic comedy elderly heroes regularly outsmart fast-talking, younger rivals. In the myths favoured by tragic dramatists, sons and daughters of heroes regularly fall short of their parents' standards. The older generation weighs on the younger: Telamon on Ajax, Agamemnon on Orestes, Oedipus on Polynikes and Eteokles, Theseus on Hippolytos.

In *Andromache*, the overshadowing figure is Achilles, noblest of the Greeks who fought at Troy. His son Neoptolemos is no match for him, and in this play even he is absent from the action. The nearest representative of Achillean leadership is the hero's old father Peleus, and although he sends Menelaos packing he is doddering, clamorous rather than regal, and finally heartbroken and pathetic until rescued from despair by his goddess wife. Hermione is a clone of her mother Helen for selfishness and viciousness, but has none of Helen's seductive charm. Orestes in this play is not the heroic son of his father we see in other parts of his myth, but a thug arranging murder in the shadows. Only two characters appear onstage of the heroic generation of Achilles, Agamemnon and the others, and they are forcefully contrasted: Menelaos, who adds duplicity and cruelty to the boneheaded vanity with which he is regularly characterised in myth, and Andromache, pivot of the play, the only character in the action to show the qualities of long-suffering nobility and fineness of spirit which, in the Trojan myth, belong both to her and her husband Hektor.

A quality shared by *Andromache*, *Hekabe* and *Orestes* is dramatic and constructional unpredictability. Each, in its own way, seems to deconstruct the conventions of the form it uses. All have prologues, rhetorical discussions and messenger's speeches – and give an impression of playing with them, of going through the motions of each structure rather than inhabiting it. In a world where chaos rules, all order – by definition – totters. In

*Andromache* the way the action centres first on one character and then another, the way people drop out of the action, the springing of major surprises such as Orestes' first entrance or the arrival of the messenger who reports Neoptolemos' death at Delphi, the way the choruses are rags or wraiths of the grander odes in other plays – all these factors contribute to mood and meaning, constantly tripping the audience's expectation and leaving an impression of disorientation rather than security. As so often in Euripides, style and form are tailored precisely to produce the effect and articulate the meaning he desires.

# Bacchae

## Characters

DIONYSOS

PENTHEUS, *ruler of Thebes*

KADMOS, *founder of Thebes, his grandfather*

TEIRESIAS, *prophet*

AGAVE, *Kadmos' daughter, Pentheus' mother*

GUARD COMMANDER

COWHERD

ATTENDANT

ATTENDANTS, GUARDS (*silent parts*)

CHORUS OF BACCHAE

CHORUS OF WOMEN

## Synopsis

Outside Pentheus' palace, Dionysos announces that he is bringing his worship to Greece and will begin in his birthplace, Thebes. Its people have dishonoured his mother, their princess Semele. Their leader Pentheus persecutes the Bacchae (ecstatic dancers) and must be punished. As Dionysos disappears, the chorus of Bacchae dance and sing in his honour. Two old men come in, on their way to the hills to dance: Kadmos, founder of Thebes and Teiresias the prophet. Pentheus, furious that a stranger is seducing the women of Thebes, scolds the old men for abetting the orgies, and they warn him not to challenge God.

After another ecstatic chorus, the Guard Commander brings in a young man: Dionysos in disguise. Pentheus has him locked in the stables, and sends guards to arrest the women. The chorus sing to Dionysos, who calls down a thunderbolt to destroy Pentheus' palace, escapes and appears in person. Before Pentheus can attack Dionysos a cowherd hurries to report miracles on Mount Kithairon: the women, dancing in ecstasy, striking springs of wine and water from the ground, tearing animals to pieces and running through the villages, unharmed by the spears and sticks people throw at them. Dionysos seduces Pentheus into agreeing to disguise himself as a woman and go to Kithairon to see for himself what is happening. After another chorus (praising 'true wisdom', that is respect for God), Pentheus comes out in a wig and dress, entranced. Dionysos leads him to Kithairon, and the chorus sing of the hounds of madness.

An attendant stumbles in. Encouraged by Dionysos, and led by Pentheus' mother Agave, the women have discovered Pentheus spying on them from the top of a pine-tree, pulled him to the ground and torn him to pieces under the impression that he is a lion. The women enter, led by Agave with her son's head on a pole. She still takes him for a lion, and it is not till Kadmos explains that her eyes are opened and she sees what she's done. Dionysos announces that what has happened is punishment for mortal presumption.

## About the play

*Bacchae* ('Women in Ecstasy' or 'Women Dancing for Dionysos') was first performed, and was possibly written, not in Athens but in Macedonia, where Euripides had retired towards the end of his life. Euripides died shortly before the first performance.

As Euripides wrote the play, the Peloponnesian War was moving towards its conclusion – war-conditions may have been among the reasons which prompted him to leave Athens for Macedonia – and a few months after the first performance of *Bacchae*, the Spartans finally overwhelmed Athens and imposed political and artistic censorship. Tragedy, especially of Euripides' intellectually open-ended and quizzical kind, never recovered: *Bacchae* is the genre's final masterpiece. Some see the play as a political allegory, in which a long-established state is engulfed by an outside force which changes or destroys all with whom it comes into contact. Although some of Euripides' Athenian admirers may have found such overtones at the time, there is no hint of them in the play itself. *Bacchae* is one of the most self-contained of his surviving works, focused exclusively on the issue at its heart and moving with an unblinking logic paralleled in extant Greek drama only in *Oedipus Tyrannos*.

*Bacchae* is Euripides' last and most powerful presentation of a theme which runs through many of his surviving plays, from *Hippolytos* to *Ion*, from *Medea* to *Hekabe*, from *Herakles* to *Iphigeneia in Aulis*. How do mortals come to terms with the presence of God in their lives – particularly when God is, or seems to them to be, capricious, dangerous and uncompromising? In this play Dionysos demands submission in exchange for unimaginable ecstasy. But his cult, at least in human terms, is blood-crazed and outlandish. In the trance which marks the transition from one state of being (mortal self-awareness) to another (a glimpse of immortal ecstasy), humans become wild animals, work miracles which turn Nature topsy-turvy and make other animals their prey, playing catch with their limbs in a macabre simulacrum of mortal games. Innocence is achieved – animals have no moral awareness – but it is sticky with blood, soaked in the death which the ecstatics have been seeking to escape. This grim paradox lies at the heart of Dionysos-worship, and God demands not that mortals understand it, but that they accept it. To submit is, briefly, to conquer death; to question is to die.

The implications for cult-worship of any kind are obvious – all religious practice can seem bizarre to outsiders – and Euripides presents the issues in a way which at first sight seems to weight them entirely in favour of Dionysos and his worshippers. There are few passages in Greek lyric poetry so filled with energy as the odes of *Bacchae*, as the ecstatics recount their god's miraculous adventures and dance and sing their joy in him. The joy of religious faith has seldom been so urgently expressed. Dionysos himself, in his manifestation as a young, handsome foreigner, seems charming, quizzical and entirely rational; his adversary Pentheus is presented as a kind of tyrant-clown. When the issue of submission is debated, Dionysos' arguments are put not by himself but by the all-knowing prophet Teiresias and Kadmos, founder of the Theban dynasty – as if Abraham and Aaron appeared in a biblical drama to urge belief in God. The deeds of Dionysos' worshippers, and of the god himself, are narrated by 'ordinary' people, a cowherd and a soldier, and their naivety gives their accounts a kind of objectivity, as if they were chance bystanders reporting miracles.

So far, so good. But Dionysos frames all this action in a way which gives it another aspect, far less like a fairy tale. At the start of the play he announces that he has come not only to set the Thebans dancing, but also to punish them for denying his divinity and insulting his mother Semele. (Although their own origins were extraordinary – their ancestors were warriors who grew from dragon's teeth sown in a field – they were so outraged by the bizarre nature of Dionysos' conception, when his mother was raped by Zeus' thunderbolt, that they rejected her, banished the god and tried to build a state founded on reason, not faith.) In modern terms, Dionysos comes to present them with the 'Other', the psychological double they have rejected – and at the end of the play, when Agave and Kadmos realise the horror of what their innocent, 'other' selves have done, he tells them bluntly that this was punishment. They beg him to reverse what has happened and he rejects them:

Too late ... I was yours, and you defied me. God.

This moment is the heart of the play, articulating the human emotion, loss and pain involved in the 'philosophical' dilemma underlying the action. In Euripides' dramatic scheme, Agave and Kadmos are pivotal characters. He is interested not only in what religious faith is like, but also in what happens to those who leave a cult and have to live both with the 'sacred' knowledge they have acquired and with the way that acquisition has for ever changed them. He leaves his audience to reflect on why God should choose to teach these lessons in this particular way, and to ponder the natures of guilt and innocence – who is responsible for what has happened?

# Cyclops

## Characters

SILENOS, *father of the satyrs*
ODYSSEUS
POLYPHEMOS, *the cyclops*
SLAVES, SAILORS (*silent parts*)
CHORUS OF SATYRS

## Synopsis

Silenos bewails his lot. He and his satyrs have been shipwrecked on Sicily and enslaved by the savage cyclops. The satyrs work as shepherds, while he tidies Polyphemos' cave after the monster's banquets of human flesh. The satyrs bring Polyphemos' sheep and goats home from pasture, and Silenos hushes their racket. A group of strangers is coming, Greeks who know nothing of Polyphemos' savage ways. Odysseus and his sailors come in, and Odysseus haggles with Silenos for supplies, finally bribing him with wine. Silenos goes into the cave to fetch food and water, and the satyrs advise Odysseus to escape before Polyphemos attacks his crew. Odysseus proudly refuses.

The satyrs scatter and the Greeks hide as Polyphemos arrives, demanding his dinner. He sees the Greeks, and Silenos, drunk, claims that they came to steal food, and that only his vigilance prevented them. Odysseus tells Polyphemos that he and his men are under Poseidon's protection. Polyphemos mocks the gods and drives the Greeks inside to eat them. The satyrs sing in horror of the slaughter inside. Odysseus comes out and describes how Polyphemos roasted and ate two sailors, but how he (Odysseus) then fuddled him with wine till he fell in a drunken sleep. He says that he has something else planned for him, and suggests that the satyrs escape while they can. They prefer to stay and help.

Polyphemos comes out, drunk, and Odysseus and the satyrs

128

cavort with him, seducing him with drink, dance and the promise of sex. He drags the protesting Silenos into the cave, and Odysseus hurries after him. The chorus dance and sing wildly until we hear screams from inside and Polyphemos staggers out, his single eye put out. He shrieks that he helped a man called Nobody, and that now Nobody has hurt him. The satyrs run about, mocking him as he tries to find the Greeks. Odysseus sneers at him, and he threatens to uproot Mount Etna and hurl it to crush Odysseus' ship. The Greeks leave for their ship, and the satyrs dance after them to join them.

## About the play

Some scholars say that *Cyclops* may have been performed in the same festival as *Hekabe*, that the blinding of Polyphemos parallels that of Polymestor and that the cyclops' musical entrance from his cave parodies Polymestor's appearance from Hekabe's tent. But there is no supporting evidence, and the play's date remains unknown. In a similar way, those scholars who find intellectual themes in *Cyclops* – for example, a contrast between the 'real' barbarism symbolised by Polyphemos, the 'barbarism of the civilised' symbolised by Odysseus, and 'true innocence' symbolised by the satyrs – are indulging in wishful thinking.

Apart from a substantial section of Sophocles' *Ichneutai* (chiefly known in modern times as the inspiration of Tony Harrison's *The Trackers of Oxyrhynchus*), *Cyclops* is the only surviving example of the satyr play, the entertainment which followed the tragedies and ended each drama day at the City Dionysia. Hundreds of vase pictures show satyrs enjoying wine, dance and sex, but literary evidence for the plays is all but non-existent. Aristotle's claim (in *Poetics*) that tragedy 'grew out of' satyr plays may mean simply that satyr plays were one of the oldest known forms of ancient drama, originating the idea of dialogue between individual actor(s) and the chorus.

There is nothing intellectual about *Cyclops*. It is less like surviving tragedy, or indeed comedy, than a precursor of the scripts of Renaissance *commedia dell'arte*, the knockabout farces of the European puppet tradition of which Kharaghiozis and Punch and Judy are eloquent surviving examples, or the vaudeville and music-hall sketches of the late nineteenth and early twentieth centuries. Its plot may be drawn from Homer – chiefly from the story of Odysseus and Polyphemos in Book Nine of the *Odyssey*, but with side-glances at a tale told in *Hymn to Dionysos*, of how pirates who captured Dionysos were transformed into dolphins – but the characters are pure farce-stock. Silenos is the cowardly buffoon who becomes the butt of all the slapstick, playing drunk scenes, getting beaten and – in a scene paralleled a thousand times in later farce of this kind – forced to impersonate a blushing bride. (He is the ancestor of the *pappasilenos*, or fall-guy, of later Greek folk theatre.) Odysseus is not Homer's resourceful hero but the trickster/jester of traditional comedy, ancestor of Anansi, Brer Rabbit and Charlie Chaplin. (The trick he plays on Polyphemos, pretending that his name is 'Nobody', recurs in folk tales from all over the world, many from places which can have had no contact of any kind with ancient Greek literature, myth or folklore.) Polyphemos is the braggart who rides for a fall, loud, stupid and barbarous. (Often such characters are, as here, not only barbarous but literally 'barbarian', aliens to the culture of everyone else onstage: the Thracian army officers in Roman comedy, the 'Mamelukes' in *commedia dell'arte* and puppet-plays, even such literary derivatives as the Scythian policeman in Aristophanes' *Festival Time*, Caliban in *The Tempest* or the Monster in *Frankenstein*.)

For such vigorous but stereotyped characters, the writer needs to provide a basic script full of cross-talk, opportunities for song and dance and an enormous amount of slapstick. All these are present in *Cyclops* – and as with all such scripts, its written text offers probably only a glimpse of the effect in performance. (It contains, for example, only half as many lines as the average surviving tragedy or comedy, much as *commedia* scripts are no more than half a dozen pages long.) The action may well have been spiced with overtones of more solemn matters: Homeric epic, current politics, lampoons of the serious dramas performed by the same company earlier in the day. But the text suggests that the predominant feeling may have been one of carnival, as the chorus of satyrs, 'Dionysos' children', racketed and cavorted in the god's own theatre. With their human bodies, horses' tails and enormous goats' phalluses, satyrs are half-animal, half-human – beings trapped in the moment of ecstasy in which worshippers of Dionysos thought that their nature was transformed, the moment when, briefly but unforgettably, they shed their mortality and entered the condition of the gods.

# Elektra

## Characters

FARMER

ELEKTRA, *Princess of Argos*

ORESTES, *her brother*

OLD MAN, *Orestes' former tutor*

KLYTEMNESTRA, *mother of Elektra and Orestes*

KASTOR, *god*

SERVANT

PYLADES, POLYDEUKES, ATTENDANTS (*silent parts*)

CHORUS OF WOMEN

## Synopsis

Outside a remote farmhouse, the farmer tells how Princess Elektra's mother Klytemnestra married her to him to prevent her bearing royal children who might challenge her rule. Elektra, on her way to fetch water, is accosted by two strangers: Orestes and Pylades, sent by Apollo to take revenge on Klytemnestra for murdering Orestes' father Agamemnon. Not recognising Orestes, Elektra tells him her grief and prays that her brother will come back and punish Klytemnestra by killing her. She invites the strangers into the farm and sends her husband to ask Orestes' former tutor to bring wine and food.

The chorus sing of the contrast between Agamemnon's triumph in the Trojan War and his sordid death at Klytemnestra's hands. Then Orestes' tutor comes in, recognises Orestes and tells Elektra who he is. Brother and sister fall into one another's arms, and the tutor helps them to plot the deaths of Klytemnestra and her paramour Aigisthos. Orestes and Pylades go to kill Aigisthos, the old man leaves to tell Klytemnestra the (false) story that Elektra has borne a son, and Elektra hurries inside to prepare her mother's death. The chorus sing of the quarrel between Atreus and

Thyestes, ancestors of the dynasty of Argos. They hear shouting and call Elektra. An attendant brings news that Orestes and Pylades have killed Aigisthos.

After a choral dance of joy, Orestes and Pylades bring in Aigisthos' head. Elektra mocks and insults the head. Hearing Klytemnestra's chariot, Orestes and Pylades go inside. Elektra pretends to beg Klytemnestra to allow Orestes home, and when Klytemnestra refuses she wheedles her inside 'to see the new baby'. The chorus sing how Klytemnestra murdered Agamemnon, and are interrupted by screams from the queen, inside. Orestes and Elektra come out, covered in their mother's blood and aghast at what they have done. The gods Kastor and Polydeukes appear and announce the future: Elektra is to marry Pylades and Orestes is to run from his mother's Furies to Athens, where Apollo will free him from the guilt of matricide.

## About the play

Euripides probably first presented *Elektra* some time between 425 and 413. There is dispute about the exact date. Some scholars think that the play parodies Sophocles' *Elektra*, presenting Elektra not as a suffering tragic heroine but a self-dramatising obsessive, and Orestes as a terrified adolescent rather than a freedom-fighting hero. But there is no evidence that Sophocles' play was written first.

*Elektra* takes further than any other surviving work Euripides' technique of using myth material as the basis not for philosophical tragedy but to explore realistic characters engulfed in mythical events. In the original Argive myth, Orestes' murder of Klytemnestra was merely one step in a sequence of death-for-death justice, repaying her murder of Agamemnon and involving Orestes himself in blood-guilt and the necessity of punishment. Aeschylus explores this progression in the *Oresteia*, and Sophocles' *Elektra* concentrates on one aspect of it: Elektra's anguish as she copes with Orestes' absence, Klytemnestra's flouting of the demands of destiny and her own inability to put matters right. In Euripides' play, the murders of Aigisthos and Klytemnestra are shown not as fated and inevitable but as the results of Orestes' naivety and Elektra's hatred of her mother and love for her father. They are human crimes, related to the demands of destiny only in the characters' self-justifications and in the take-it-or-leave-it assertions of the gods who appear *ex machina.*

In such a scenario, turning the traditional 'meaning' of Greek tragedy inside-out, realism is an essential alienation device. It allows attention to be focused less on issues than on the crimes themselves and the characters of the people who commit them. Euripides' play shows the conjunction of three factors of all-engulfing importance in human existence: power, sex and death. The underlying issue is legitimacy of rule in Argos. Whose claims are the greater – Agamemnon (a warlord who murdered his own daughter at the whim of the gods), his wife and her lover (who assassinated him but are otherwise shown to be generous and benign), Agamemnon's son Orestes (who has not been seen in the country since childhood), or the baby Elektra might bear to a foreign prince (a child who might grow up to avenge his grandfather)? Sex is ever-present in Elektra's mind: she is obsessive both about her own virginity and the bedtime pleasures she imagines for Klytemnestra and Aigisthos. Death, in the minds of the principals, is the cure for every evil and the punishment for all assumed guilt.

The three themes are brought magnificently together at the moment of Klytemnestra's murder. She has been enticed to the farmer's house because Elektra has falsely sent word that she (Elektra) has given birth to a son and heir. Confronted by her assassins, she bares to them first her breasts and then her vagina (as Orestes says, 'I saw where I was born'). At the moment of destiny he is suddenly struck impotent, unable to thrust the sword into his mother's body – and Elektra guides it for him. In both Aeschylus and Sophocles such details are replaced by a kind of ritualistic overlay, as if the deaths truly were (as Orestes claims in the *Oresteia*) 'necessary sacrifice'. Euripides' realism makes us confront the physical butchery, the effort and mess inseparable

from violent death. Klytemnestra's murder leaves the killers
stunned, reeling, drained as if by the act of sex:

ELEKTRA
    She was screaming,
    ~~Reaching, touching.~~
    'Don't hurt me.
    Don't hurt Mummy. Please.'
    She clung. She hugged me,
    Arms round my neck.
    I dropped the knife. She hung from me . . .

ORESTES
    I lifted my cloak, hid my eyes,
    Sacrifice, knife, cut throat, blood, mother . . .
    She gave us life. We killed her . . .

Such close focus on the principals leaves little room for others. The
farmer, the old man and Klytemnestra have powerful scenes with
Elektra, but the power comes chiefly from her and the way she
handles them. Pylades either says nothing at all, or (in some
editions) speaks merely the factual, brutal account of how Orestes
murdered Aigisthos. Aigisthos himself appears only as a head for
Elektra to insult, gloatingly and with a dark eroticism which may
remind modern audiences more of Renaissance revenge plays than
decorous Athenian tragedy. Apart from the ode about Klytemnestra's murder of Agamemnon – placed just before her own
execution – the choral songs have only remote relevance to the
stage action, and for the rest of the time the chorus are little more
than Elektra's backing group, her confidantes. Kastor (the *deus ex
machina* who speaks; Polydeukes is as taciturn as Pylades) is cool
to the point of disdain, pouring the outcome of the original myth-
story into the emotional deadlock as one might put jam in tea.
Cynical to the last, the play leaves its spectators not reflecting on
issues or relating what they have seen to their own real lives, but
aghast. This is hardly the 'purgation of pity and terror' which
Aristotle found in tragic drama, and yet *Elektra* remains one of the
most theatrically effective pieces in the entire surviving canon.

# Hekabe (Hecuba)

## Characters

GHOST OF POLYDOROS, *Hekabe's son*
HEKABE, *Queen of Troy*
POLYXENA, *her daughter*
ODYSSEUS, AGAMEMNON, *Greek commanders*
TALTHYBIOS, *Greek officer*
POLYMESTOR, *King of Thrace*
ATTENDANT
POLYMESTOR'S SONS, SOLDIERS, ATTENDANTS (*silent parts*)
CHORUS OF WOMEN

## Synopsis

Outside the walls of ruined Troy, Polydoros' ghost tells how he was treacherously murdered by King Polymestor who had been asked to bring him up safely during the Trojan War. As the ghost disappears, Hekabe and her women come out of the tents where they are being held as prisoners of war. They mourn the fall of Troy, and the chorus tell Hekabe that her daughter Polyxena is to be sacrificed to Achilles' ghost. Hekabe and Polyxena weep in each other's arms, as Hekabe begs Odysseus, in vain, to persuade the Greeks to kill her and spare Polyxena. As Odysseus takes Polyxena to her death, Hekabe prays that one day Polydoros will come and punish the Greeks. After a choral ode about the cities of Greece in which the chorus will live as slaves, Talthybios tells Hekabe how Polyxena died, nobly, bravely, admired by all the Greeks. Hekabe asks for her body to bury, and sends attendants to the shore for water.

After a choral ode about the Judgement of Paris and the fall of Troy, the attendants bring in Polydoros' body, confirmation of Hekabe's fearful dream of the night before. She asks Agamemnon to punish Polymestor who killed him, and when Agamemnon refuses she herself sends for Polymestor. The chorus sing of the destruction of Troy. Polymestor comes in with his young sons, greets Hekabe like an old friend and assures her that Polydoros is 'safe'. She takes him inside, we hear screaming, and Polymestor staggers back outside, blind. He howls to Agamemnon that Hekabe's women have killed his sons and put out his eyes, and demands revenge. Hekabe scornfully suggests that Agamemnon should instead obey the laws of heaven and punish a murderer who betrayed his friends. She and Polymestor snarl insults at one another, and Polymestor prophesies that Hekabe will go mad and Agamemnon's wife Klytemnestra will one day murder him. Agamemnon orders that Polymestor be banished and Hekabe taken to Odysseus' ship, and ends the play by praying to the gods to give the Greeks happy homecoming.

## About the play

*Hekabe* was first performed in about 424, when Euripides was in his late fifties. The Peloponnesian War had begun some half dozen years earlier, and *Hekabe* is one of three surviving plays from the same period to show the effects of war on both winners and losers. The others are *Andromache* and *Suppliants*.

The injustice and cruelty of war underlie everything which happens in the play, corrupting Greeks, Trojans, guilty and innocent alike. No one is exempt and there are no redeeming qualities apart from Polyxena's self-sacrificial heroism which crowns the first half of the action. That half centres on the way political necessity overrides human emotions such as love or pity and engulfs both those who make decisions and those who suffer them. The second half, centring on Hekabe's revenge on Polymestor, takes as its underlying theme a favourite idea of Euripides, and of Greek tragedy in general: the way crime breeds crime, in a downward spiral. The journey is never towards the resolution the perpetrators hope for, but always away from it – for example, even if ethical justification can be found for Hekabe's blinding of

Polymestor, her murder of his sons is no more than brutal tit-for-tat.

Themes of this kind can be extrapolated from the play. But its pleasures are primarily theatrical rather than conceptual. In performance it is a *tour de force*, the virtuosity of the central role spreading to all the supporting actors and demanding a kind of tip-of-the-toes bravura style not always apparent on the page. Performance similarly reveals the logic of the play's construction. In reading, *Hekabe* can seem broken-backed, presenting one idea and then abandoning it entirely for another. In performance, its logic is primarily musical. Each of its parts has its own themes, speed and articulation, but neither is sufficient without the other, they combine and complete one another to make the whole experience. The choral odes are set into the texture in a way which similarly follows music and emotion rather than thematic logic. At first glance, the way the chorus sing of their own concerns – wondering to which Greek states they will be taken, recounting the moments when the Wooden Horse was dragged into Troy and when Greeks poured into the sleeping city to rape and murder – seems to interrupt the flow of events in which the odes are placed. They are linked neither to what precedes them nor to what follows. But, in what the critic Kenneth Burke called 'perspective by incongruity', the 'point' of the odes is made by montage, by juxtaposition with the surrounding material. Their musical and emotional energy refocuses our thoughts and changes the direction and impetus of the play. This kind of 'block' construction is common in music – and is a favourite dramaturgical strategy of both Euripides and Aeschylus.

In the ancient theatre, it was not merely the play's overall movement which was organised by music. Articulation within the main sections followed a similar pattern. *Hekabe* is rich in lyric passages – they range from the set-piece display of mourning between Hekabe, the chorus and Polyxena to the scene of Polymestor's suffering 'inside' and his appearance on all fours from Hekabe's tent, singing his blindness and his agony. Metre determined the speed of the spoken lines, the *stichomythia* (rapid dialogue) using 'resolved' verse patterns (groups of three 'short' syllables replacing those of one 'long' and one 'short') and the longer speeches using 'unresolved' patterns to broaden and slow the pace. Of surviving plays, only Aeschylus' *Suppliants* and *Seven Against Thebes* match *Hekabe* for the artful way metre controls emotional ebb and flow, for musical virtuosity.

Strikingly, music is reserved largely for the non-Greek characters. Talthybios is the only Greek who uses lyric metres at all, and those moments are few, revealing his (controlled) sorrow at Polyxena's death. Odysseus and Agamemnon do not sing – an especially striking feature of the final scene, where Hekabe and Polymestor move in and out of lyric metres, and Agamemnon stays in spoken mode throughout. Instead, the Greeks speak in fast, concise iambics, rising to flights of extraordinary rhetoric as they justify themselves to Hekabe and face down her pleading and her fury. These confrontations are written with a formality we might nowadays associate more with French Golden Age tragedy (particularly the plays of Racine) than with the emotion-packed style Euripides usually deploys in arguments. The style has the effects of distancing what the Greeks say from the 'reality' of the situation and of contrasting their temporising and vanity with Hekabe's emotional desperation and exhaustion. The focus remains on her throughout, and the dislocation between dramatic style and emotional content creates an urgency in performance which prepares for the extraordinary *dénouement*, in which she flies free from all ethical or intellectual restraint. If, as some claim, the play is 'about' this movement from sanity to madness, that movement stands as a symbol of the flight from reality which happens to individuals and states alike in the trap of war.

# Helen

## Characters

HELEN
TEUKROS, *Prince of Salamis*
MENELAOS, *ruler of Sparta, Helen's husband*
DOORKEEPER (*originally* 'OLD WOMAN')
SAILOR
THEONOE, *Egyptian prophet*
THEOKLYMENOS, *her brother, the Pharaoh*
SERVANT
KASTOR
POLYDEUKES, GUARDS, ATTENDANTS (*silent parts*)
CHORUS OF GREEK WOMEN PRISONERS

## Synopsis

Sitting outside a palace beside the Nile, Helen tells how the gods made a phantom 'Helen' to entice the Greeks to Troy, and how she herself was left to languish in Egypt for years, hearing stories of the havoc wreaked by her double. A shipwrecked Greek, Teukros Prince of Salamis, tells her that the Trojan War is over and that Menelaos and the phantom 'Helen' have been lost in a storm on their way home to Sparta.

The chorus advise Helen to ask Theonoe the priestess if Menelaos is still alive. As soon as Helen goes into the palace, a bedraggled Menelaos arrives. He is turned away by the doorkeeper, who tells him in passing that the pharaoh Theoklymenos is planning to marry Helen. This confuses Menelaos, who thinks that 'Helen' sailed with him from Troy. The real Helen comes out and after some confusion persuades Menelaos that she is who she says she is. They embrace.

Menelaos wants to take Helen home, but first they must outwit Theoklymenos, find a ship and escape. Helen asks help from

Theonoe, and persuades her not to tell Theoklymenos what is happening. Helen arranges that Menelaos will pretend to Theoklymenos that he is a sailor bringing news that Menelaos has been drowned. She will then ask for a ship to hold a funeral ceremony far out to sea for him. After a choral ode about the disasters Helen's phantom brought to Troy, Theoklymenos comes back from hunting. Reluctantly he agrees to Helen's request for a ship – and after another choral ode (about Demeter's grief for lost Persephone), a sailor reports that Helen and Menelaos have escaped for Greece. Theoklymenos is about to sail after them with soldiers when Kastor and Polydeukes, Helen's half-brothers, appear and stop him, revealing that everything which has happened is heaven's will.

## About the play

Euripides presented *Helen* in 412, and the following year Aristophanes parodied it, and him, in *Festival Time*.

Like *Iphigeneia in Tauris*, possibly written at the same time, *Helen* takes as its starting-point one of the miraculous substitutions which feature in Greek myth. From time to time, for fun or for deeper reasons, the Olympians substituted appearance for reality and tricked mortals. Zeus turned himself into a phantom Amphitryon to have sex with Amphitryon's wife Alkmene and engender Herakles. When Ixion, invited to a banquet in Olympos, tried to rape Hera, Zeus distracted him by creating a phantom Hera, the cloud-goddess Nephele. Artemis, having tested Agamemnon's faith by ordering him to sacrifice his daughter Iphigeneia at Aulis, substituted a fawn at the last moment and spirited the real Iphigeneia away. Aphrodite bribed Prince Paris of Troy to declare her the most beautiful of all immortals by offering him Helen of Sparta, the most beautiful mortal in the world – and the gods sent a phantom Helen to Troy and carried the real Helen away to Egypt.

When the historian Herodotos was travelling in the Middle East to research his history of the causes and events of the Persian wars against Greece, priests in Egypt told him the story of Helen's double, and he published it some ten years before Euripides' play. Euripides may also have been influenced by two ideas currently in the air in Athens, much discussed in the circle led by Socrates. First is the method of argument perfected by the philosopher Zeno, who proved his opponents mistaken by paradox, arguing logically and irrefutably from the same starting-point as they did but reaching an opposite conclusion. Second is the 'theory of forms', which states that for everything in existence, both actual (say, a table) and abstract (say, 'beauty') there is an ideal form – the Greek word is *idea*, 'vision' – and that what we see or imagine approximates to this to a greater or lesser extent.

At one level, *Helen* is a straightforward, sunny comedy exploiting all these themes. The real Helen is the 'form' of goodness and long-suffering, just as her phantom is the 'form' of amoral seduction. Paradoxically, everyone takes each for the other. Much of the set-piece humour – for example, Helen's dialogue with Teukros, the scene with the bewildered sailor who reports that 'Helen' has vanished from the cave on the shore but then meets 'her' moments later outside the palace, or the scene where Menelaos pretends to be a messenger bringing news of his own death – is of this satisfying but simple kind. It foreshadows the 'New Comedy' of a century and more later, in which substitution and mistaken identity engender misunderstanding and confusion of all kinds, leading to happiness when truth is finally revealed. In European folklore, substitution and transformation of similar kinds are major themes.

*Helen* is, however, more than simple comedy or fairy tale. On the basic framework Euripides built a box-of-mirrors piece, a game of heart as well as intellect, about illusion and reality, the nature of identity and the power of love. Not only Helen, but all the main characters in the action, are not what they seem. Menelaos, at first apparently no more than a fool dressed in rags and humiliated by a doorkeeper, is transformed (by his discovery of the 'real' Helen) into a loving husband and resourceful warrior – the man he hoped but never quite managed to be in Troy.

Affection for Helen persuades Theonoe, guardian of truth, in the cause of happiness to be economical in how much truth she tells her brother. Theoklymenos, ostensibly an autocratic boor, shows signs of true humanity and love for Helen, and his dismay when she turns out not to be the woman he thought she was adds darkness and profundity to the intrigue that ends the play. Menelaos' 'funeral' is in fact an escape; Egypt, which has seemed a prison to Helen, becomes the scene of a greater liberation than she could ever have imagined; the Trojan War was all about illusion, not reality. And in a way captured later in Shakespeare's Viola in *Twelfth Night* or Helena in *All's Well That Ends Well*, the transforming power in the action is not a supernatural force but human love, unclouded, unfeigned and embodied in a radiant heroine. Helen's presence transfigures everyone she meets – and none more touchingly or satisfyingly than her long-lost, errant husband. Their reconciliation is the heart of the play, and shows Euripides' art at its peak. The scene is realistic, even domestic, and yet its events are made sublime and emblematic by the transmuting power of poetry:

MENELAOS
    Hold me.
    Ten thousand days
    Wandering, wandering –
    Then this! God gives us this:
    Out of pain, God gives us joy,
    Gives happiness.

HELEN
    Hold me. Lean your head,
    Here on my heart. Oh joy.

MENELAOS
    I thought you'd left me.
    I thought you'd gone to Troy.
    How could it happen? . . .
    It's incredible, a fairy tale.

HELEN
    I cried in it, cried in it.

# Herakles (Hercules)

## Characters

HERAKLES
AMPHITRYON, *his father*
MEGARA, *his wife*
LYKOS, *usurper of Thebes*
IRIS
MADNESS
THESEUS, *ruler of Athens*
SERVANT
HERAKLES' THREE YOUNG SONS, ATTENDANTS, SOLDIERS (*silent parts*)
CHORUS OF OLD MEN

## Synopsis

Herakles' old father Amphitryon, wife Megara and three young sons are suppliants at Zeus' altar outside the palace gates of Thebes. Lykos, dictator of the city, intends to kill them while Herakles is in the Underworld carrying out the last of his twelve Labours. The chorus try to protect them but flinch from Lykos, who orders the suppliants inside to prepare for death. The chorus sing of Herakles' Labours and pray that he will hurry home and help his family.

Megara and Amphitryon return, dressed for death, and Megara bids farewell to the children. But the chorus's prayer is answered, and Herakles returns, his final Labour completed. He takes Megara and the boys inside, and the chorus sing an ode of praise and joy. Lykos arrives for the sacrifice, and Amphitryon sends him inside, where we hear his cries as Herakles kills him. The choral dance of joy is interrupted by the arrival of Iris, messenger of the gods, and the demon Madness. Iris reminds Madness of Hera's orders, that she is to send Herakles insane, and Madness reluctantly agrees. We hear more cries from inside, and a servant runs out to describe how Herakles has gone mad and shot Megara and the children dead.

The palace gates are opened, and we see Amphitryon grieving over the bodies and Herakles chained to a pillar. He recovers from his fit and discovers what he has done. He rages at the gods' cruelty and wants to kill himself, but his old friend Theseus persuades him to accept the burden of destiny and offers him sanctuary in Athens. Amphitryon is left mourning the dead, and Herakles and Theseus leave the stage.

## About the play

Most authorities say that Euripides wrote *Herakles* in about 417, at the time of *Elektra* and *Women of Troy*. A few put it later, saying that its lyrical style is like that of his last plays, particularly *Orestes* and *Bacchae*. It was once called *Herakles Mainomenos* (or in Latin, *Hercules Furens*), *Herakles Mad*, to distinguish it from *Herakles' Children*, but this title is no longer used. *Herakles* and *Herakles' Children* are not connected.

*Herakles* shows Euripides at the peak of his powers. Its plot balances stunning surprise – the change starting with the Iris/Madness scene is a coup of theatrical and ironical imagination almost unmatched in ancient drama – with scenes in which audience expectation is satisfyingly fulfilled: the contrast between Lykos' villainy and the pathos of Megara and the children; the servant's virtuoso speech about the murder of the children; the sequence in which Herakles 'comes down' from his madness and realises what he has done. The lyricism in that scene and the choral odes (especially those dealing with Herakles' Labours and extolling youth and the service of the Muses) is rightly praised. The character-dualities are beautifully organised. Theseus' goodness and nobility mirror Lykos' cruelty and tyranny, and his steadfast common sense mirrors Herakles' psychological panic and disintegration. Amphitryon the dodderer is a more loving grandfather to Herakles' sons than Zeus his counterpart, whose indifference to their fate is made to seem as inexplicable, possibly as culpable, as

Hera's hostility to Herakles. That hostility, the unforgiving nature of both Hera and Iris her messenger, is set against the compassion and regret shown by Madness who is forced to do their bidding. All these tensions throw light on the duality between the two sides of Herakles' own nature – like all children of one mortal and one immortal parent in Greek myth, he is at war with himself.

That war, between the conflicting claims of mortality and immortality, is the heart of the play. In the traditional myth-story, Hera sent Herakles mad much earlier in his mortal existence: the Labours were his punishment for killing the children. Euripides significantly changes this, putting the madness and the children's murders after the Labours and making it clear that Herakles undertook the Labours for an altruistic reason, to win freedom from blood-guilt for his father Amphitryon. Euripides presents Herakles as the model of mortal heroism, the ideal person to fulfil Zeus' plan (also in the original myth) of ridding the world of monsters, an example to mortals of how to live a 'godly' life on earth. And then he sends him mad. The world's noblest hero and greatest benefactor commits the most heinous crime known to mortals, murder of blood relations. God on earth becomes the 'hurt hero' or 'lame king' so common in myth and folk tale. Polluted by his own mortality, he gives death to those he once gave life. The nonpareil of human honour is dishonoured before our eyes.

When a more earthbound hero, Ajax, loses his honour in Sophocles' play, he commits suicide. At first, when Herakles realises the depth of his guilt and degradation, he too plans to kill himself, to 'curse God and die' (as Job's comforters advise in the Bible story). Lost honour may be partially redeemed by a dignified, self-inflicted death. But this option is not in fact open to Herakles, because it cancels only part of his nature, the mortal half. Theseus shows him that although his suffering is real and his grief for his children fine and noble, they are not the whole of him. In Greek religious thought, the gods' immortality means that they are unaffected by mortal death. They turn from it, they are not polluted. Herakles' dual nature gives him immortal invulnerability as well as mortal pain. It enables him to triumph over the hostility both of death-bound beings (giants and monsters) and of an immortal (Hera), the first by superior strength, the god in the mortal, and the other by long-suffering, the mortal in the god. The way to achieve dignity and serenity when both gods and mortals seem to betray him is to look inside himself, to enter his own condition and accept it. He will cope with the blows of Fate not by denying them but by enduring and surviving.

With some difficulty, Herakles learns this lesson:

> I'll not kill myself, slink out of life.
> 'He faced every danger,
> But he couldn't face himself' –
> They won't say that. I'll endure to live.

He agrees to continue to shoulder the war bow which symbolises his heroic power and status ('It breaks my heart, but still I'll keep it'), leaves Amphitryon to bury the dead, a mortal weeping for mortals, and goes with Theseus. This abrupt, bleak ending leaves the chorus in tears:

> Weep, friends.
> Our saviour's gone.
> Weep tears.

– but it also focuses attention on the play's great themes, on the two questions which occur time and again in Euripides' work, from *Alkestis* to *Women of Troy*, from *Philoktetes* to *Bacchae*: 'How can mortals find a way to live in a universe controlled by gods who seem aloof or actively hostile?' and 'How can we cope with death?'

# Herakles' Children

## Characters

IOLAOS, *former companion of Herakles*
KOPREUS, *messenger from Argos*
DEMOPHON, *ruler of Marathon*
MAKARIA, *Herakles' daughter*
ALKMENE, *Herakles' mother*
SERVANT
EURYSTHEUS, *ruler of Argos*
AKAMAS, HERAKLES' SONS, SOLDIERS, ATTENDANTS (*silent parts*)
CHORUS OF OLD MEN

## Synopsis

Outside the temple of Zeus in the small Athenian dependency of Marathon, aged Iolaos and a group of boys huddle at an altar. Iolaos explains. He was Herakles' helper in his Labours, and the boys are Herakles' sons. When Herakles passed from earth to heaven, Eurystheus of Argos (the rival who set Herakles his Labours) sought to kill his children, and they fled, the boys led by Iolaos and the girls by Herakles' mother Alkmene. They have taken refuge in Marathon and begged sanctuary from Demophon and Akamas, sons of King Theseus of Athens and rulers of the city.

Kopreus arrives with soldiers from Argos, and tries to kidnap the suppliants. The chorus stop this, but when Demophon and Akamas come in Kopreus demands that they hand over the children and threatens war if they refuse. They send him packing. After a war-song from the chorus, Demophon reports that the Argives are besieging the city and that the priests say that only the sacrifice of a 'noble child' will save it. Herakles' daughter Makaria volunteers to die and goes to execution.

After a brief chorus praising Makaria, a servant brings news that Herakles' son Hyllos has brought an army to lift the siege. The servant is sharply questioned by Alkmene, Herakles' old mother, and persuaded by Iolaos to fetch him arms and take him to join the fighting. After another choral war-song, the servant reports that Iolaos has been miraculously rejuvenated on the battlefield and has captured the enemy commander Eurystheus. The chorus sing for joy, and guards bring Eurystheus in chains. In defiance of the citizens, who recommend mercy, Alkmene insists that he must die. Unexpectedly, he agrees, and says that if he is buried in Athenian soil he will for ever protect the people – particularly if, at some time in the future, enemies come from Sparta to attack them.

## About the play

*Herakles' Children* was first performed between 430 and 427, and was probably written either during the lead-up to the Peloponnesian War or in the first months of the fighting. The play has no connection with *Herakles*, written some ten years later. It is incomplete.

The story seems to have been largely Euripides' own, though it may draw on details of the Herakles myth-cycle known in Athens but lost to us. Herakles was popular in Athens, and his worship must have included hymns, praise-songs and a mass of 'miracle stories' similar to those told about Christian saints in Europe a millennium later. Any one of these could have provided the germ of the ideas of his children seeking sanctuary or Iolaos' rejuvenation. As the play survives, however, it is mainly realistic, touching on the mythical and miraculous only in passing. Even the gods who play such a key role do not appear but are merely discussed, characterised less in terms of their supernatural natures than by the morality of behaviour – Zeus, for example, as an absentee husband, Hera as a vengeful stepmother, Athene as a champion of justice. The most rounded divine character – again, discussed and invoked but never physically present, unless he appeared as *deus ex machina* in one of the parts of the play now lost – is Herakles himself, at once a god who took human form and the emblem of human heroism aspiring to godhead. (Euripides developed this idea more fully in *Herakles*.)

To the original audience, *Herakles' Children* may have seemed intensely patriotic, free from the ironies and equivocations usual in Euripidean praise of Athens and its institutions. The story involves an act of unforced generosity by the Athenian people, Athene is hymned as victor in battle and protector of the innocent, and the play rings with such passages as the chorus's proud lines when Kopreus is sent packing:

> All we ask is peace.
> But if madmen come,
> If they bind themselves in bronze,
> Swing swords, lift spears, we're waiting.

The war-choruses are blunt to the point of jingoism:

> Mother Earth, Moon above,
> Sun's light that brings life to mortals,
> Take good news,
> Shout it through the sky,
> Let it echo against her throne,
> Grey-eyed Athene's throne:
> Sharp swords we take,
> Enemy threats we slice,
> For our native land,
> Our friends who need our help . . .

Tellingly, Euripides sets the play not in Athens itself but in Marathon, site of the land-battle some sixty years before, when the Greeks routed a huge Persian invading force. The chorus are 'old men of Marathon', veterans, and the effect for Euripides' audience must have been an electric reminder of the greatest moment of military glory in Athens' past. For the purposes of the play, Euripides ignores the fact that Athens' co-leader against the Persians was her present enemy Sparta – unless there is irony we can no longer perceive. Throughout the action, he returns to one of his favourite themes, the challenge offered to the younger generation by the achievements of their elders. In several plays – *Andromache, Orestes, Suppliants* – the children of great heroes of myth are shown either matching or falling short of the distinction of their parents. In *Herakles' Children* Theseus' son Demophon is invited to emulate his father's bravery and generosity, to support the weak against the strong. Hyllos, Herakles' son, is a saviour whose coming in arms will defeat the enemy and rescue the oppressed. Herakles' daughter Makaria is a beacon of stoical heroism, of self-sacrifice for others:

> Men, I'm here. Take me.
> Prepare your victim. Kill me.
> Do it, and defeat your enemies. A willing sacrifice,
> For myself, my brothers, I offer myself to death.
> I surrender my life, and win, by that,
> A glittering prize, a noble death.

In a strikingly Euripidean moment, Alkmene even claims that her son outstrips his father for compassion and honourable behaviour – a Euripidean moment because her son is Herakles and his father Zeus.

The implications of such sentiments for the current generation can hardly be exaggerated in a city whose most respected elders were *marathonomachai*, 'those who fought at Marathon'. But the play is rescued from propaganda precisely because of the obscurity of its original myth. Euripides could easily have written *Theseus' Children*, making explicit comparisons between the generations and focusing on jingoism. Instead, he chose a central issue which was remote and arcane and whose outcome was already known. The victims in his play are not Athenian allies cowering from the Spartans but uninvolved strangers, the aggressor not a Spartan but Eurystheus, King of Argos. In the real war, the Argives were Athens' chief Peloponnesian allies, and Euripides gets round the problem that they are villains in this play by giving Eurystheus a spectacular change of character after his capture, making him repent his wickedness and pledge that his people will help the Athenians in any future wars, particularly those emanating from Sparta. This twist in the tale is deliberate – Euripides had no need to use a myth-story which needed such a wrench – and may make us wonder if the complete play was as free of ironical layering as the surviving lines suggest. One equivocal ode for the chorus, one more speech for Demophon (who disappears halfway through), one *deus ex machina* scene, and the job is done. There are spaces for any or all of these in the torso which remains.

# Hippolytos

## Characters

THESEUS, *King of Athens*

PHAEDRA, *his wife*

NURSE

HIPPOLYTOS, *son of Theseus and Hippolyta, Queen of the Amazons*

OLD MAN, *his servant*

GROOM

APHRODITE, ARTEMIS, *goddesses*

HUNTERS

ATTENDANTS, SOLDIERS (*silent parts*)

CHORUS OF TOWNSWOMEN

## Synopsis

Outside the royal palace of Trozen, Aphrodite announces that she intends to punish Hippolytos for scorning her. To this end she has made his stepmother Phaedra desire him. Hippolytos returns from hunting, and ignores his servant who warns him not to pick and choose among the gods. After the chorus has described how Phaedra is afflicted by a mysterious sickness, she comes out in a distressed and confused state and admits to her Nurse that she longs for sex with Hippolytos, her stepson. The Nurse recommends her to give way, and goes to fetch a soothing potion while the chorus sing of the power of Aphrodite.

Hippolytos bursts out of the palace. The Nurse has told him about Phaedra, and he shouts his disgust for the female sex. When he has gone, Phaedra says that the only way to save her honour is suicide. She goes inside, and the chorus sing of her misery and her coming death. Theseus arrives in time to hear that Phaedra has hanged herself. He weeps over the body, then finds a letter in Phaedra's hand claiming that Hippolytos has raped her. Despite

Hippolytos' claims of innocence, Theseus banishes him and prays to Poseidon to kill him. Hippolytos leaves as the chorus weep.

A groom brings news that Hippolytos' horses, startled by a supernatural tidal wave, have crashed his chariot and fatally injured him. Artemis tells Theseus that Hippolytos was innocent and that Theseus' impatient rage has killed the son who loved him. Servants bring in the injured Hippolytos, and he and Theseus are reconciled. But it is too late. Artemis says that she will avenge Hippolytos by killing one of Aphrodite's favourites. She disappears, Hippolytos dies, and Theseus and the chorus are left to weep.

## About the play

*Hippolytos* won first prize at the City Dionysia of 428 BC. With *Medea*, *Andromache* and *Hekabe* (written at approximately the same time) it is, in part, a study of characters and emotions which we nowadays might categorise as neurotic. In *Frogs*, Aristophanes mocked Euripides for writing about 'lewd women' and 'love-sick females'. Although this may have been no more than the lead-in to a joke about Euripides' own unhappy relationships with women, it may equally well have reflected a common view of his work.

The play which survives is Euripides' second treatment of the myth. What little is known about the earlier version, *Hippolytos Veiled*, suggests that a major difference may have been its portrayal of Phaedra as desperate, scheming and shameless, rather than, as here, an innocent victim of the goddess. Changing her character enriches Euripides' dramatic options, allowing him to show all kinds of variations in the 'guilt' or 'innocence' of his three main characters, Hippolytos, Phaedra, Theseus, and to set up, in each of them, the pull between two implacable Olympians, Aphrodite (standing for surrender to passion) and Artemis (standing for withdrawal from it).

In this scenario, Phaedra is no less a victim than Hippolytos. She is destroyed by inability to cope with the presence of Aphrodite in her life, he because he fails to understand the demands made on him by Artemis. Each also dies as a result of the actions of others. The nurse's garrulousness leaves Phaedra no option but suicide; Theseus' curse against Hippolytos, once uttered, is irrevocable. The sequence of events leading to Phaedra's death begins with Hippolytos' involvement with a goddess he cannot understand; the sequence leading to Hippolytos' death begins with a similar involvement on her part. Phaedra triggers the first sequence by 'female' passivity and withdrawal; Hippolytos triggers the second sequence by 'male' forcefulness and action.

In Sophocles, symmetries of this kind are common; in Euripides they are rare. A major difference between the two writers is the treatment of the chorus. In a Sophoclean *Hippolytos* they might have presented a view of the nature of the gods and the workings of destiny more comprehensive than that of any individual character, or drawn out the differences between the characters' perceptions. Although Euripides allows them emotional engagement with the action, he keeps them philosophically remote – and the effect is to isolate the pointlessness and bleakness of each character's suffering without offering emotional or philosophical closure. The process highlights another of the play's main themes: the inability of humans, with their limited moral understanding, to achieve or contribute to universal harmony. In a harmonious universe, respect and accommodation rule. Because Euripides' characters are torn (by lack of social status, by impulse, by partiality), these qualities lie elsewhere, beyond their scope. If the play has a moral and philosophical point, this is it – and it is never expressed (as it might have been in Sophocles) but left, in a final ironical flourish, for the spectators to work out for themselves.

Philosophical layering, overt or ironical, is aided by the play's extraordinary structural formality. At its heart is Theseus, the only human character with any real power. Round him gravitate Phaedra and Hippolytos, twinned in distress and destiny. Beyond them are the two servants, and beyond them, framing the action, the goddesses. The chorus sing of Phaedra's affliction at the start of the action, and of Hippolytos' plight at the end; in between they have contrasting odes, one hymning the power of love and the other balancing a longing to fly like birds to safety with a reflection on Phaedra's fate when she 'flew' from Crete to Athens. The play's outer portions are predominantly male, a factor which throws into high relief the appearances in them of Aphrodite and Artemis. The inner part of the play is predominantly female, a factor which highlights the placing at its heart of Hippolytos' outburst against women. The action moves from rhetoric (in the scenes between Hippolytos and Phaedra and their servants) to emotion (in the scenes between Theseus and Hippolytos); this movement is balanced by a structural shift in the opposite direction, from the fast dialogue of the opening scenes to the narrative formality of the groom's account of Hippolytos' accident. Musical balance is similarly meticulous, the deployment of solo arias, choruses and multi-voiced musical scenes being organised with especial care.

Formal symmetry is set against the extraordinary volatility and dramatic intensity of the characters. The play is a sequence of outbursts; no characters except the goddesses are immune from a hysteria which is as much intellectual as emotional. Philosophically rudderless, they rage and flail; even the chorus is in a state of intellectual panic, replacing reflection with hand-wringing pity for this character or that, or with unfocused reflections on the power of the gods and prayers to be immune from suffering.

Several times in his surviving plays, Euripides creates similar tension and similar moods, but never in such a tightly organised formal structure. The impression is almost that the characters are trying to break out of their own story – the chorus, indeed, pray to do so – a deconstruction of the whole method of ancient tragedy equalled only in *Orestes* or *Herakles*.

# Ion

## Characters

HERMES

ION

KREUSA, *Princess of Athens*

XOUTHOS, *her husband*

OLD MAN, *her servant*

SLAVE

PRIESTESS *of Apollo*

ATHENE

ATTENDANTS (*silent parts*)

CHORUS OF WOMEN

## Synopsis

At the sanctuary at Delphi, Hermes tells how Apollo long ago fathered a son (Ion) on Princess Kreusa of Athens and brought him up as a temple foundling. Now Kreusa and her husband Xouthos are coming to Delphi to ask for children, and Kreusa and Ion will be reunited. Hermes hides as Ion comes out to brush the temple steps and welcome visitors. Pretending that it happened to 'a friend', Kreusa tells Ion the story of how she was (as she imagines) raped by Apollo and asks if the oracle will say what happened to the baby. Ion answers that God will not be accused in his own temple. Xouthos takes Kreusa inside to consult the oracle.

After a choral ode about the blessing of children and the horrors of rape, Xouthos runs out, claims to be Ion's father and insists that he return with him to Athens. When Kreusa hears of this from the chorus, she rages at Apollo for allowing Ion to usurp the princely position which should be her children's alone (if she ever has children), and tells her servant to poison Ion at the banquet Xouthos has ordered to celebrate his good fortune.

After an anxious choral ode, a slave tells how Ion has been saved at the banquet – the poison was miraculously spilled – and is looking for Kreusa to kill her. Kreusa and Ion confront each other, but are interrupted when the priestess brings a basket of childhood keepsakes which will reveal Ion's true identity. Kreusa recognises the keepsakes and she and Ion fall into one another's arms. Athene appears and explains the whole story, and Kreusa and Ion leave for happy lives in Athens.

## About the play

Euripides wrote *Ion* at about the same time as *Helen* and *Iphigeneia in Tauris*. The play was first performed in about 412, when he was in his seventies. Its starting-point was an obscure legend which used Ion's name to make a connection between Athens and Ionia (the mainland and island states of the north-western Aegean). On that, and a bustling, romantic story of his own about a long-separated mother and son who plot to kill each other, Euripides constructed a luminous, multi-layered play about identity, the loss and recovery of happiness and the relationships between mortals and between God and mortals.

Read on the page, the play's wit, its delicacy of tone and the tumble of its events are readily apparent. Performance reveals another crucial feature: the constant tension, or balance, between realism and lyricism. What can seem whimsical or sentimental as we read – Ion's bird-scaring; Xouthos' attempts to hug his new-found son; the absurdities of the recognition scene – can onstage be revealed as imbued with the deepest human feelings and a resonant simplicity which is, in its way, as cathartic as the events of any ancient drama of the grimmer kind. Euripides achieves this by ironising everything we see or hear. In the prologue, Hermes not only tells us the story to come, but also, by the playfulness and slyness of his language, makes us look quizzically at what happens even as it happens. Typical is his jokey description of the priestess discovering Ion on the temple doorstep, with its unexpected and radiant insertion in the fourth line quoted:

'Tut, tut, a baby. Some local girl, how impertinent,
Dumping her responsibilities here on us. Tut, tut.'
Then she looked at the child. Heart melted. Smiled –
Apollo had something to do with that – took him in,
Brought him up. She has no idea who his father was,
Or his mother – and he knows less than she does.

Such moments encourage a response which untethers the action
from reality. Events and characters pass before us with the logic
not of everyday life but dreams. Nothing is what it seems. Death
happens only to a pigeon. Rape is not rape, loss is not loss,
childlessness not childlessness.

If that were all, *Ion* would be no more than a sophisticated but
insubstantial game between author and audience. The interplay
between illusion and reality affects more than just the plot. *Ion* is
also about the way mortals perceive and come to terms with God –
and Euripides shows that, for everyone in the play, this relationship is never what it seems. The chorus's faith is simple, a matter
of big buildings, heartfelt prayers and exciting myth-stories, and
they have no way to cope when events seem to challenge it.
Xouthos thinks that he understands what Apollo tells him in the
shrine – and, in a double irony, what we are led to believe is
buffoonish misinterpretation is proved right after all. The central
characters take very different attitudes to God, and the action
shows how their discovery of one another leads them to develop
and change those attitudes. At first, Ion loves Apollo uncondition-
ally. He is fulfilled by the relationship – and then the play's events
challenge and remake it. Nothing Apollo does or says ever changes;
Ion's understanding changes, and the experience brings him to a
new, mature happiness of which, at the start of the play, he never
so much as dreamed. Kreusa, for her part, comes to the shrine
with a mixture of rage and anguish, expressed in railing at Apollo
and futile attempts at violence. As the action proceeds she is
calmed and shown the truth of what happened to her (and what
Apollo meant by it), and her new understanding is rewarded when
she is reunited with her son. Apollo – God – never appears
onstage, never justifies or explains, sends others to speak his words
or express his will, and yet he is the focus of the action. The

Euripidean 'message' may be stated more obliquely in *Ion* than in other plays, but it is still the same: what mortals are, what we know about ourselves and how we change are direct consequences of the way we think about God.

Irony affects the play's form as well as its events. Every traditional component of 'Greek tragedy' is present (prologue, messenger's speech, recognition scene, *deus ex machina*), but each is deconstructed as it happens – and happens anyway. Hermes' light-heartedness deflates the prologue, the slave spends more time describing a marquee than the solemn events she has come to tell, the recognition scene trembles between farce and lyricism. Euripides plays similar games with form in another play from the same period, *Orestes*. There, it is almost as if traditional structures are used distractedly, automatically, as if their remnants in the play's structure reflect the rags of social order which Orestes' matricide has replaced with anarchy. In *Ion* the effect is rather of reinforcement: a reiteration of the familiar which produces in adults a sophisticated version of the satisfaction children get from hearing nursery stories told and retold in undeviating detail.

The final element in the play's elusive power is lyricism. High points are Ion's song at dawn, the choral odes expressing faith in God and the recognition scene, whose distracted speech-rhythms gradually soften into radiant, shared song. Of later dramatists, only Calderón in *Life is a Dream* and Shakespeare in the late 'romances' have a similar power to make happiness seem transcendental by the quality of the poetry in which it is expressed.

# Iphigeneia at Aulis

## Characters

AGAMEMNON, *Grand-Admiral of Greece*
MENELAOS, *his brother*
KLYTEMNESTRA, *Agamemnon's wife*
IPHIGENEIA, *their daughter*
ACHILLES
SERVANT
SOLDIER
SOLDIERS, ATTENDANTS (*silent parts*)
CHORUS OF WOMEN

## Synopsis

At dawn, outside the admiral's quarters at Aulis, Agamemnon summons his servant and gives him a letter. The gods have told Agamemnon that if he wanted winds to carry the Greek fleet to Troy, he must sacrifice his daughter Iphigeneia. But he can't bring himself to do it, and now sends the old man to Argos with a letter for Klytemnestra, countermanding his earlier order that Iphigeneia be brought to Aulis to marry Achilles.

The chorus come in, girls on a trip to the mainland to see the famous Greek heroes before they go to war. Menelaos hurries in. He has intercepted the letter and accuses Agamemnon of betraying Greece. A soldier interrupts the brothers' argument to tell them that Iphigeneia has arrived. Agamemnon reluctantly agrees to return to the original plan, to sacrifice her, and he and Menelaos go to make preparations.

The chorus sing of the disastrous affair between Paris of Troy and Helen of Sparta. Klytemnestra and Iphigeneia arrive, and Agamemnon sends Iphigeneia to make ready and then Klytemnestra, in vain, to go home. The chorus sing of the grief the destruction of Troy will bring. Klytemnestra welcomes Achilles as

161

her future son-in-law – to his astonishment, as he has no idea what Agamemnon was planning. The old servant tells them the true situation, Klytemnestra begs Achilles to stop the sacrifice, and he agrees.

The chorus contrast the wedding-day of Achilles' parents Thetis and Peleus with the day of suffering now planned for Iphigeneia. Iphigeneia and Klytemnestra confront Agamemnon, but he refuses to change his mind. Achilles says that if he tries to rescue Iphigeneia the whole Greek army will mutiny. To prevent Greek killing Greek, Iphigeneia agrees to die. She is taken out, and the chorus sing her praise. A soldier brings news of a miracle: at the moment of sacrifice, Artemis has replaced Iphigeneia by a deer and carried her from mortal sight. Agamemnon bids Klytemnestra farewell and leaves for Troy.

## About the play

*Iphigeneia at Aulis* was first performed in 405, some time after Euripides' death, in a production supervised by his son or nephew. The surviving script gives the impression that Euripides left the play incomplete, and that parts of it were revised or added by others.

In the way that Wagner's *Rhinegold* stands as a kind of self-contained prologue to the other three parts of his *Ring of the Nibelung*, *Iphigeneia at Aulis* deals with events earlier in time than Euripides' other surviving 'Trojan' plays. *Rhesos* shows an episode from the war itself. *Women of Troy* and *Hekabe* are set immediately after the city's fall, and *Andromache, Elektra, Helen, Iphigeneia in Tauris* and *Orestes* show the cancerous effects of the war on the survivors and the children of those who took part. By comparison with the exhausted, experience-laden tone in several of these plays, the world of *Iphigeneia at Aulis* can seem morally uncomplicated, almost innocent. The characters, undeformed by war, are confronted with the first serious moral challenges of their lives, and grow, or fail to grow, as they deal with them. Agamemnon is not yet the pragmatic, devious politician we see as the war continues. Menelaos is hot-headed and vacillating, but the malice and vanity of his later character are here no more than sketched. There is no hint of Klytemnestra's hatred for Agamemnon or of her lust equally for power and for Aigisthos. Achilles in this play is an unformed youth. The action and experience of the play are ironised from start to finish precisely because the audience relates all this innocence to what they know will follow in the myth-sequence, events to which decisions made now, in this play, give birth. In a manner reminiscent of Aeschylus in *Agamemnon*, Euripides uses the chorus to reinforce this irony, giving them a series of odes which widen the perspective and place present events in a past and future context.

So far, *Iphigeneia at Aulis* inhabits tragic form and style. Its 'eminent' characters (Achilles, Agamemnon, Klytemnestra and Menelaos), whatever glimpses we see in them of human sentiment or motivation, remain within the boundaries not so much of myth as of myth-based tragedy or epic. But into this stylised world Euripides inserts two characters from an entirely different dramatic tradition, the old servant and Iphigeneia. Their everyday realism challenges myth-stereotyping and the 'meaning' of all the myth-bound characters. The old man scolds Agamemnon and blurts the truth to Klytemnestra in a 'dramatic' way quite unlike the stylised realism of (say) the guard in *Antigone* or Kilissa in *Libation-Bearers*. Iphigeneia, similarly, is characterised as a perfectly normal person, joking with her mother, excited about her coming wedding, affectionate with her father – and then wrenched from this easy domesticity into a myth-world where she must be sacrificed to a heartless god by the father she adores.

In *Poetics*, Aristotle condemned Iphigeneia's apparent change of character in the play, from terror to heroic resignation. In terms of abstract logic this 'change' may seem unmotivated. But in the dramatic picture offered by Euripides, it is simultaneously unexpected and inevitable, elevating the play from melodrama to genuine human tragedy. The stereotyped characterisation of Agamemnon, Klytemnestra and the others is a frame for the Iphigeneia Euripides shows us, and the stylistic confrontation between the characters throws ironical light on the 'meaning' of this myth, these events and these people. In *Henry VI Part One* Shakespeare performs similar sleight-of-hand with the character of La Pucelle (Joan of Arc), displaying her as a warm human being surrounded by stiff-jointed stereotypes from a medieval tapestry. After she is captured by the English and condemned to death at the stake, La Pucelle collapses psychologically, begging to live and claiming that she is pregnant – only to gather herself and accept her martyr's death for the glory of God and the honour of France. Iphigeneia's evolution in *Iphigeneia at Aulis* from 'ordinary' girl to tragic heroine is exactly similar.

*Iphigeneia at Aulis'* existing ending brings into the picture for the first time the variant myth-tradition that Iphigeneia was miraculously abducted by Artemis. As the scene stands, it is so baldly written that it destroys the mood and meaning of everything which has gone before, not refocusing but eliminating the moral argument. Writing some six centuries after the first production, the Roman-Greek author Aelian quoted a handful of lines in which Artemis appears as *dea ex machina*, stops the human action and announces what is actually to happen to Iphigeneia. If this was how Euripides himself ended the play – and the lines Aelian quotes are even less stylistically convincing than the soldier's speech from the existing script – then the irony of the whole piece, the 'meaning' of the events depicted and the relationship between mortals and the supernatural may well have been reinforced in a way typical of his most enigmatic and thought-provoking work. As it stands, *Iphigeneia at Aulis* hints at that quality but never quite achieves it.

# Iphigeneia in Tauris

## Characters

IPHIGENEIA, *priestess of Artemis*
ORESTES, *her brother*
PYLADES, *his friend*
HERDSMAN
THOAS, *King of Tauris*
ATTENDANT
ATHENE
GUARDS, ATTENDANTS (*silent parts*)
CHORUS OF GREEK WOMEN, *prisoners-of-war*

## Synopsis

Outside Artemis' temple in Tauris, on the Black Sea shore, Iphigeneia tells how she was not sacrificed by Agamemnon at Aulis, as everyone assumed, but was rescued by Artemis and made priestess of a shrine where all visitors are sacrificed to the goddess. As she goes inside, Orestes and Pylades arrive: Apollo has sent them to Tauris to steal Artemis' statue and take it back to Greece. Anxious not to be seen by Iphigeneia and the chorus, they go back to their ship. The women weep for their captivity in a harsh foreign land, and then a herdsman brings news that strangers have been captured. Iphigeneia tells him to fetch them, and she and the chorus sing of the death that awaits all visitors.

Orestes and Pylades are brought in under guard, and Iphigeneia questions them. Finding that they're Greeks, she asks if one of them, in exchange for his life, will take a letter to her relatives in Argos to say that she's still alive. While she goes inside to write the letter, Orestes and Pylades argue about which of them should be spared. Iphigeneia returns and asks Pylades to deliver the letter to her long-lost brother Orestes. To her astonishment, he does so before her eyes. Brother and sister fall into one another's arms.

165

Pylades interrupts their rapture by pointing out that they're all bound by the savage laws of Tauris. Orestes must be sacrificed, and Iphigeneia must order it. They make a plan for escape, and Iphigeneia begs the chorus not to tell King Thoas. The chorus sing how they long one day to fly free, like seagulls.

Iphigeneia persuades Thoas that Orestes and Pylades are murderers whose presence has polluted the shrine and the holy statue. She takes them and the statue to the shore for purification. After a choral ode in praise of Apollo, an attendant brings news that Orestes, Pylades and Iphigeneia have escaped, taking the statue. Thoas is about to send his men to fetch them back, when Athene appears. She says that everything which has happened is by the will of heaven and must be respected. Thoas accepts, and arranges to send the chorus, too, home to Greece.

## About the play

*Iphigeneia in Tauris* was first performed in *c.* 413, when Euripides was in his late sixties or early seventies. Its mood and style partly resemble those of two other plays from the same time, *Helen* and *Ion*, and scholars sometimes group them together as Euripides' 'romances'.

Unlike Euripides' other surviving works based on the Argive myth-cycle, *Iphigeneia in Tauris* is a busy, sunny play, full of intrigue and with a happy ending. Like *Helen*, it takes as its starting-point a small, all-but-overlooked incident from the basic myth, in this case the tradition that Iphigeneia was not sacrificed by her father at Aulis but miraculously replaced at the last moment and carried away by a god. Like Helen in *Helen*, she has lived her life far from the intrigues of the Trojan War and its aftermath, until the time comes – as the action of the play begins – for her to be rescued and return home. The rescue itself – in what is probably Euripides' own invented plot – involves coincidences, surprise and human ingenuity, on a level quite unlike the god-inspired machinations and anguish of the rest of the Argive cycle. It is as if Iphigeneia's physical separation from Argos amputates her, so to speak, from the mythic dimension, allowing Euripides to give her, and anyone who comes into contact with her, human warmth and verisimilitude. As a character, she is more reminiscent of the people in later 'New Comedy' than of the destiny-racked figures of most surviving tragedy.

This 'ordinariness' in the characterisation is one of the factors which give the play its atmosphere of almost breathless excitement. Iphigeneia, Orestes and Pylades may be facing issues of life and death, but they are also, predominantly, taking part in an adventure. The story is wonderfully melodramatic, hinging on a letter whose delivery will pull the scales from everyone's eyes, a statue taken to the shore to be washed, an escape-ship hidden in a cove and a fairy-godmother-like appearance by a god (Athene) who sorts out all problems and lets everyone live happily ever after. The custom of human sacrifice which edges the plot with danger is only lightly shaded in: there are none of the resonances Aeschylus (say) might have found between Artemis' gory demands and Agamemnon's attempted sacrifice of Iphigeneia, and none of the blood-crazed explicitness Euripides himself deploys in other plays. Thoas, potentially the most 'dangerous' character in the action, is actually kind-hearted and pliable. He is outwitted with ludicrous ease – he believes immediately in Iphigeneia's farcical invented 'custom' of washing the sacred statue – and he does the 'good' thing, the 'right' thing, as readily as the ogre who is transformed into the long-lost father in fairy tale. This characterisation is entirely appropriate for the ruler of such a magical place as Tauris, presented as a country outside normal time whose 'otherness' colours the play's whole atmosphere and action – a foretaste of the Bohemias and enchanted islands of Shakespeare's late 'romances'.

Because Euripides keeps the characters 'human', he is able to explore another of his most frequent and most plangent themes, the nature of love. The play is a prismatic presentation of affection: between friends (Orestes and Pylades), siblings (Iphigeneia and Orestes), fellow-dignitaries (Iphigeneia and Thoas), mistress and servants (Iphigeneia and the chorus). A key element in the emotional landscape is the nostalgia Iphigeneia and the chorus feel for Greece, a yearning satisfied at the end when their wishes come true and they can go back home. Their longing is expressed in some of the most lyrical, and emotionally most profound, passages in Euripides' surviving output, for example the ode in which the chorus, hearing that Iphigeneia is to leave Tauris, mingle happiness for her and tears for their own continuing imprisonment in a way which can break the heart:

> Seagulls, mewing,
> Sharp cliffs, harsh cries,
> Lovers' cries, lost love –
> We weep with you,
> Weep with you.
> Flightless, lost here,
> For Greece we cry,
> For our Lady in Greece we cry,
> Palm fringes, laurel,
> Grey-green olive,
> Water of rippling lake,
> Swans singing, singing.

We can only imagine the effect of such emotional directness and simple beauty on Euripides' Peloponnesian-War audiences. *Iphigeneia in Tauris* has sometimes been dismissed as 'unprofound' by scholars unmoved by its gentleness and embarrassed by its openheartedness. But like Anouilh twenty-five centuries later, Euripides wrote both '*pièces noires*' and '*pièces roses*' – and who is to pontificate about which genre, in its way, offers the more satisfying emotional and theatrical experience?

# Medea

## Characters

MEDEA

JASON

KREON, *ruler of Corinth*

AEGEUS, *ruler of Athens*

NURSE

TUTOR

SERVANT

CHILDREN *of Medea and Jason,* ATTENDANTS, SOLDIERS (silent parts)

CHORUS OF WOMEN


## Synopsis

Outside Jason's palace in Corinth, the Nurse tells how Jason is planning to discard Medea and marry Glauke, daughter of Kreon who rules the city. Hearing Medea inside, crying to the gods, she hustles Medea's sons and their tutor out of the way. The chorus ask anxiously what is happening, and Medea appears and pours out her frustration and fury at the way men treat women. Her talk of revenge is interrupted when Kreon comes and announces that she and her sons are banished. She persuades him to allow them one more day in Corinth, and tells the chorus that she will use it to kill Glauke. The chorus sing their horror.

In a heated scene, Jason tells Medea that she should be grateful to him for bringing her from a barbarian land to civilised Greece and giving their sons the chance of a royal upbringing, and she rages at him for deserting her. When he goes, the chorus sing of the agonies of exile. Aegeus, ruler of Athens, arrives and asks Medea to explain an oracle telling him how to end his childlessness. She persuades him that if he offers her sanctuary in Athens, she will restore his potency by magic. When he has gone she tells the horrified chorus that as well as poisoning Glauke she will stab the children. The chorus beg her to reconsider. Jason and the children come in, and Medea, pretending reconciliation, sends the boys to take Glauke wedding gifts and beg her to revoke their exile. Jason and the boys go in, and the chorus sing their despair at what is about to happen.

The tutor brings news that the children's exile is revoked, and Medea weeps over her sons and the terrible deed she is planning. She sends them inside, the chorus sing of the agonies of parenthood, and a servant brings news that the poisoned gifts have killed Glauke and Kreon. Medea hurries inside, and we hear the children's cries as she stabs them. Jason brings soldiers, and Medea appears overhead, in a Sun-chariot. She says that she will bury the boys' bodies, and she and Jason exchange vituperative insults. The chorus end the play by declaring that existence is unpredictable and we must accept whatever comes.

## About the play

*Medea* was first produced in 431, during the last weeks of the 'phoney war' which preceded the formal outbreak of the Peloponnesian War in May, and the atmosphere among Euripides' spectators may well have matched the febrility and nerviness so characteristic of the play. In the centuries since that production, *Medea* has been one of the most influential of all Athenian tragedies, and has been reworked to reflect the values of each new audience. Seneca's Roman adaptation, for example, presents Medea as the archetype of demonic femininity; some twentieth-century versions, by contrast, make her an icon of suffering womankind and present Jason as the emblem of patriarchy at its most heedless and most arrogant.

Euripides' play is about how mortals cope with the supernatural and supernatural beings with mortality. He makes plain that, at every point in the underlying myth, Jason and Medea knew each other's nature exactly, and acted within that knowledge. Medea, grand-daughter of the Sun and follower of the witch-goddess

Hekate, belonged entirely to the supernatural world – until she saw Jason, gave way to mortal emotion (love) and helped him first to outwit supernatural adversaries and then to escape the consequences. She accepted every condition of mortal womanhood, even – as she says in the play – the pains of childbirth. She put aside her supernatural nature in order to wrap herself in loyalty to her husband and love of her children. And then Jason cheated her.

For his part, Jason was a mortal given a supernatural education by the centaur Cheiron. Labouring under a common grievance of mortal princes, the usurpation of his rightful kingdom by a wily relative, he chose to redeem his fortunes by magic, entering the supernatural world of Aietes, son of the Sun, and stealing the Golden Fleece which was the source of his power. He faced all kinds of danger, from clashing rocks to warriors growing from dragon's teeth, and his prize was not merely the Fleece, symbol of his victory over the supernatural, but an immortal wife and two half-immortal children. Then, at the peak of his triumph, he succumbed to his own mortal instincts. Desperate for security in the world of mortals, he betrayed Medea, and the supernatural world she represented, for a mortal marriage.

At this point, as irresistible force meets immovable object, the play begins. At first the action is entirely in human terms. Medea suffers, longs for revenge and recruits the nervous chorus as if she were exclusively a human wife and mother wronged. Jason justifies, pleads and cajoles in a slippery mortal way. And Medea plots to hurt him in purely mortal terms, by killing his new beloved.

Euripides now abruptly shifts the focus – and does so, typically, in a scene of calculated surprise, confounding received ideas of 'appropriateness' and 'tragic style'. A fool comes in – Aegeus, ancestral king of Athens, no less – and in a scene of knockabout bumble complains that he is childless and doesn't understand Apollo's instructions about what to do about it. Medea takes on the role of comedy vamp, explaining the riddling oracle and seducing Aegeus into offering her sanctuary. The tone is so flippant that some critics dismiss the scene out of hand. But Euripides, as always, knows exactly what he is doing. Aegeus' pain and bewilderment at being without an heir suggest to Medea precisely the punishment for Jason which will bite most sharply: amputating his future by killing their children. The farce in the scene is mortal – gods' farce, as we know from Homer, is literally on a different plane – and allows her to see the human world for what it is and to spin free of it.

The focus is now on the battle Medea has to fight between her immortal and mortal selves. Killing the children, the mirror-image of the secure future Jason wants for them, racks her in exactly the way we might expect from a 'mortal' mother. Indeed, throughout the account of the deaths of Glauke and Kreon, Medea's self-lacerating farewell to her children and the murder-scene itself, Euripides focuses on this pain so intensely that we forget that Medea is operating in anything but human terms. But after the boys' deaths, when Jason bursts in with soldiers, Medea appears with the bodies not on the expected human level, the *ekkuklema* or 'roll-out' used in the theatre to show those killed 'inside', but on the *theologeion* or 'god-speaking-place' high above his head. The scene is a stand-off, and it also articulates the póint of the whole play: that when immortals put on mortality or mortals try to embrace immortality, the outcome is suffering. Jason's pain is endemic to his mortal condition; Medea's, like that of all the seal-wives and other supernatural beings who take mortal husbands in folk tale, is self-inflicted.

# Orestes

## Characters

ELEKTRA
ORESTES, *her brother*
MENELAOS, *their uncle*
HELEN, *his wife*
HERMIONE, *their daughter*
TYNDAREOS, *Helen's father*
PYLADES, *Orestes friend*
OLD MAN
TROJAN (*dialect part*)
APOLLO
SOLDIERS, ATTENDANTS (*silent parts*)
CHORUS OF WOMEN

## Synopsis

Outside Agamemnon's former palace in Argos, Elektra tends her sick brother Orestes, who has been driven almost to madness by guilt after killing their mother Klytemnestra. The citizen assembly is to debate that day whether or not Orestes and Elektra should be executed for matricide, and Elektra can see no hope unless Helen and Menelaos, on their way home from Troy, protect them. Helen arrives and sends her daughter Hermione to make offerings at the tomb of Klytemnestra her sister. The chorus come in, and despite Elektra's efforts to stop them, they wake Orestes who sees a vision of Furies swarming from the Underworld to punish him. Elektra goes inside for medicine.

Menelaos arrives and Orestes begs him for help. They are interrupted by Tyndareos, Klytemnestra's old father. He rages at Orestes for killing her, and goes to stir the assembly against him. Orestes again begs Menelaos' help, and Menelaos silkily refuses. After he has gone, Orestes persuades his friend Pylades to take him to the assembly to plead his case. The chorus sing of the murder of Klytemnestra, and Elektra comes back. Horrified to find Orestes gone, she is even more dismayed when an old man comes and tells her that Tyndareos has persuaded the assembly to vote that she and Orestes must die. She cries her misery to the gods, and Orestes and Pylades return. The three of them plan to kill Helen and hold Hermione hostage until Menelaos lets them escape from Argos.

After praying to Agamemnon's ghost to help them, Orestes and Pylades go inside. Elektra and the chorus wait and watch, and Elektra tricks Hermione into going to the palace gate, where Orestes snatches her. There is confusion, and a terrified Trojan slave runs out and tells how Helen disappeared just as Orestes and Pylades were about to kill her. Menelaos arrives with soldiers, but before he can attack the palace Orestes, Pylades and Elektra appear on the roof with swords, blazing torches and Hermione. Orestes and Menelaos shout insults at one another, and the confusion ends only when Apollo appears, says that Helen has been taken from earth to join the gods and foretells Orestes' future suffering and eventual release from the guilt of matricide.

## About the play

*Orestes* was first performed in 408, at about the same time as *Phoenician Women.* Euripides was in his late seventies. Soon afterwards, he left Athens for Macedonia, where he died.

The tone and mood of *Orestes* are unlike those of any other surviving tragedy. The play anticipates much later dramatic worlds, for example those of such dark Jacobean offerings as *The Duchess of Malfi* or, late-twentieth-century black film farces like *Reservoir Dogs* or *Prizzi's Honor.* The tone is bitter, the wit harsh, the presentation of corruption and moral anarchy unremitting and the action fast and unexpected. It is as if both the underlying myth and the whole ethos and strategy of Greek tragedy are being heated to meltdown before our eyes.

In Aeschylus' *Oresteia,* Klytemnestra's murder of Agamemnon is presented as a monstrous tear in the fabric of universal order, and when Orestes kills her, although the deed has painful consequences for him personally, it is a healing and restoring act, leading to the establishment of a system of justice overseen by mortals but approved by gods. In Sophocles' *Elektra* (and to some extent in Euripides' own *Elektra*, written some ten years before this *Orestes*), Klytemnestra's murder is clearly signposted as happening in obedience to the will of God. Sophocles' play ends with Orestes' triumph; we are not invited to speculate about the aftermath. Euripides' play ends with an explicit promise (by Kastor as *deus ex machina*) that although Orestes will suffer, heaven will in the end allow him to find his happiness.

By contrast, from the very beginning of *Orestes* it is clear that murdering Klytemnestra was a straightforward crime, violating the laws of both cosmic order and human civilisation. Orestes' sickness is a physical representation of moral corruption, and as the play proceeds Euripides reveals how that corruption is endemic in Argos, in the royal dynasty and all who marry into it or come into contact with it. Some have seen an allegory in this for the state of Athens in the dying months of the Peloponnesian War. But the play itself gives no hint of this. Its world is closed and hermetic, giving readers and spectators the sensation almost of peering into a box of seething corruption. *Orestes'* baleful glitter may arouse such reactions as fascination and repulsion, but Aristotelian pity and terror, much less Brechtian engagement with the issues, form no part of its agenda.

In the moral vacuum of the play, every action exists by and for itself. If one course of action fails, another – any other – can take its place. The deeds chosen include kidnapping, murder and arson. There is little sense of the moral weight of any given course of behaviour, no feeling of long-term cause and effect. The immediate moment is all that matters. The play is full of confrontations which lead nowhere but end in the same impasse as when they started: the argument between Elektra and Helen, the rows between Orestes, Menelaos and Tyndareos, the tricking of Hermione, Orestes' bullying of the terrified Trojan. Such passages turn action into attitude; they are quite different from similar confrontations in other plays (*Hekabe* or *Bacchae*, for example) where moral cause and effect directly or ironically resonate in everything each character says or does. The play's characters, similarly, are stripped of moral resonance, as if the human ambitions and feelings which motivated them have long ago fossilised into obsession: Orestes' bloodlust, Elektra's and Pylades' pathological devotion, Tyndareos' fury, the Trojan's terror, the vacuous arrogance of Menelaos and Helen. The chorus are entirely reactive, Elektra's shadows; only Hermione shows any glimmer of human warmth.

At first glance, the play formally and stylistically follows the Greek tragic 'recipe'. It has a prologue, choral odes, a messenger's speech, a rhetorical debate, and a *deus ex machina* appearance. But Euripides invests each of them with such irony that he seems to be mocking the form even as he uses it. The prologue, so far from telling us the myth-background and the moral and ethical dilemmas of the coming play, is no more than first, a tour of Elektra's state of mind – what she tells us is story for its own sake – and second a squabble between her and Helen which is lively but irrelevant (sending Hermione to Klytemnestra's tomb could have been contrived without it). Elektra subverts the entry of the chorus by begging them not to sing in case they wake Orestes – a moment which is enjoyable but frivolous. The confrontation between Orestes and Tyndareos replaces philosophical energy with emotional rhetoric; its urgency is that of soap-opera rather than 'high' tragedy. The 'messenger' speech is a *tour de force* of dialect comedy, its farce darkened only by the violent events the Trojan is describing.

The final scene is the blackest, most nihilistic section of the play. The god who appears *ex machina* is not the dazzling Apollo familiar from other treatments of the myth, shining the light of immortal justice on confused humanity and indicating how cosmic order must be restored. He is a police officer directing traffic, and his chief attribute is disengagement from the dilemmas and events of the entire preceding action. The 'resolution' he offers, the traditional outcome of the Orestes myth, has hardly any point of contact with the events and characters we have been watching. Myth, normally the continuum from which the events of a specific tragedy arise, is here a kind of sticking plaster for a situation past all healing. In the symphony of enthralling discord which is *Orestes*, this ending-which-is-no-ending is the most flippant, most ironical and – this being Euripides – intellectually most challenging moment of them all.

# Phoenician Women

## Characters

OEDIPUS, *former ruler of Thebes*

JOKASTA, *his consort*

ETEOKLES, POLYNIKES, ANTIGONE, *their children*

KREON, *Jokasta's brother*

MENOIKEUS, *his son*

TEIRESIAS, *prophet*

SERVANT *of Antigone*

FIRST SOLDIER

SECOND SOLDIER

ATTENDANTS, SOLDIERS (*silent parts*)

CHORUS OF PHOENICIAN WOMEN

## Synopsis

In a courtyard inside the Theban royal palace, Jokasta tells how Oedipus unwittingly murdered his own father, Laios, how he blinded himself and how his sons Eteokles and Polynikes are squabbling for his throne. From the battlements above, Antigone and her servant watch Polynikes' army gathering on the plain. The chorus sing how, on their way from Phoenicia to Greece to serve Apollo, they were trapped in the siege of Thebes.

Polynikes and Eteokles confront one another. Despite Jokasta's attempts to reconcile them, they part in anger. The chorus sing how, long ago, Kadmos founded Thebes. Eteokles holds a council of war with Kreon, who tells him of the seven champions in Polynikes' army, each leading the attack on one of the city's seven gates. The chorus sing of the generations of war and discord which have tormented Thebes, and Teiresias tells Kreon that the city can be saved only by the sacrifice of his son Menoikeus. Kreon begs Menoikeus to flee for his life, but Menoikeus, after pretending to agree, goes to the battlements to take his own life and rescue his city.

After a choral ode centring on the story of Oedipus and the Sphinx, a soldier brings news of the battle, the deaths of six of the seven champions, and Eteokles' and Polynikes' preparations to fight in single combat. The chorus sing of their foreboding, and Kreon brings Menoikeus' body and weeps for him. A second soldier reports that Eteokles and Polynikes have killed one another and that Jokasta has stabbed herself. Kreon decrees that Eteokles should be buried with honour while Polynikes is left to rot. He passes a sentence of exile on Oedipus, whose curse on his sons began their quarrel. Oedipus finally appears. Antigone, alone with her father, announces that she will bury Polynikes, and she and Oedipus sorrowfully part from one another.

## About the play

Euripides wrote *Phoenician Women* some time around 409, in the burst of late creativity which also saw *Helen, Iphigeneia in Tauris, Ion* and *Orestes*. He was in his middle seventies. The play is unconnected with the earlier *Suppliants*.

*Phoenician Women*, alone of Euripides' works, depicts an entirely godless society, a world of chaos in which people are left to sort out – or play out – their own destinies: the only 'heavenly' guidance comes from the doddery prophet Teiresias and is as bleakly unaffected by moral or ethical considerations as a weather forecast. Secondly, like its companion-pieces, the play takes the style of Greek tragedy in an entirely new direction – one, perhaps, as surprising to those who think of the genre in terms of (say) *Oedipus Tyrannos* or *Medea* as Shakespeare's *Pericles* might be to anyone who knew his art chiefly from (say) *Romeo and Juliet* or *Macbeth*. The organisation of *Phoenician Women* is not linear, focused on a single dilemma and a single sequence of events. It is more a pageant-like assemblage of self-contained scenes separated by sung interludes and written less to tease out character and philosophical meaning than to show colour, brightness and incessant variety. Instead of dealing with one section of the myth of Oedipus and his children, the play draws on all of it. Time is not sequential but impressionistic, past events continually interrupting present action. In addition, the play pays homage to earlier treatments of the Theban saga, notably Aeschylus' *Seven Against Thebes* and Sophocles' *Oedipus Tyrannos* and *Antigone* – *Oedipus at Kolonos* was not yet written – descanting on them in an ironical way verging at times on parody. All Greek tragedies are knowing about the myths they use; *Phoenician Women* engages with the theatrical tradition in the same quizzical and playful way.

In drama of this kind, surprise is the motor of the spectacle. In earlier plays based on the Theban saga, Jokasta killed herself when she learned the truth about Oedipus. In *Phoenician Women* she is the first person onstage, large as life, and sets the scene for us. As the play progresses, Euripides takes scenes of every traditional kind (except the *deus ex machina*) and alters them almost beyond recognition. There is a formal debate, of the kind common in his plays, as Polynikes and Eteokles argue their conflicting claims to the throne. But it is subverted even as it happens by the fact that it involves three people instead of two – all their arguments are addressed to and through Jokasta – and because Jokasta preempted its conclusion before it started by emotionally welcoming her 'beloved' Polynikes back to 'his' city and inviting Eteokles to state *his* side of the argument only as a matter of cold courtesy. Instead of one messenger scene there are two, and each contains two speeches – it is as if the messenger has so much to say that he keeps having to catch his breath and start again.

Euripides plays similar games with 'traditional' characterisation. Eteokles, normally the 'good' brother, is here peremptory and harsh, so that his character darkens his arguments for political discipline even as he makes them. Polynikes is not the swooping bird of prey from *Antigone* or the unbending warlord of *Seven Against Thebes* but a charming, all-too-human scamp. Teiresias the prophet is not the august figure of earlier plays but a fussy old man, ruining what he has to say by apocalyptic over-emphasis on the one hand ('on both sides, dungheaps of dead . . .'; 'there will be

wailing and shrieking throughout the land . . .') and on the other
by fretful complaints about rheumatism and the fact that it's hard
to be a prophet when no one listens. Antigone, in one of Greek
drama's most astonishing outbursts, plays against her stereotype to
such an extent that we wonder, for a moment, if we've actually
heard her right. Looking out over the plain of Troy, she glimpses
Polynikes and exclaims (in David Thompson's translation\*) with
almost sexual, incestuous rapture:

> Oh, could I fly to him, race down the wind to him,
> To my own dear brother, and fling my arms
> Round his neck, and kiss away all that time
> Of exile and suffering. Isn't he glorious
> In his golden war-gear? He dazzles like the sun
> In the morning!

That passage illustrates another of the play's most striking features,
the quality of the verse. Throughout *Phoenician Women*, without
taking a single step towards either Aeschylean grandeur or
Sophoclean precision, Euripides pours out a stream of poetry,
richer in images, emotionally more eloquent and rhythmically
livelier than anything in his surviving output except the choral
odes in *Bacchae*. There is something of the set piece about each of
the choral sections – they tell selected episodes from the Theban
myth-cycle with a flamboyant energy and musical richness more
reminiscent of Homer or Pindar than of other extant Greek
tragedy – and the feeling is enhanced by the chorus's own
exoticism: they are not women of Thebes but foreigners, from
Phoenicia or Phoenician settlements in North Africa. In addition
to the chorus, character after character fills our ears with a dance
of language. 'Mother, you are the only one/To unravel this web of
disaster,/To knit us in love again, as we were born . . .' (Polynikes);
'What sort of weakness would it be/To let the great thing slip and
settle/For a smaller?' (Jokasta); 'On, daughter, lead on. You are the
eye/For my blind steps like a star is to sailors . . .' (Teiresias);
'There was a sudden rally/And bloodied heads began hitting the

* Published in *Euripides Plays: One* (Methuen, 1988).

dust in hundreds ...' (Messenger) – Euripides' phrases (here in David Thompson's translation) unfailingly snag the ear and enrich the mind.

# Rhesos

## Characters

HEKTOR, *Prince of Troy*
AENEAS, PARIS (*also known as Alexander*), *his brothers*
ODYSSEUS, DIOMEDES, *Greek princes*
DOLON, *Trojan soldier*
RHESOS, *Prince of Thrace*
HIS DRIVER
MESSENGER
ATHENE
TERPSICHORE, *Muse of Dance, Rhesos' mother*
SOLDIERS, ATTENDANTS (*silent parts*)
CHORUS OF TROJAN SOLDIERS

## Synopsis

In the middle of the night a group of Trojan soldiers, the guard on watch, wakens Hektor with news that the Greeks are massing by their ships. Assuming that they are about to set sail, Hektor wants to attack them, but Aeneas persuades him that it might be a trick. Hektor sends Dolon to spy on them; his reward is to be Achilles' immortal horses, and he also plans to bring back the head of either Odysseus or Diomedes. As he leaves on his mission the chorus sing his praise.

A shepherd from Mount Ida brings news that Prince Rhesos of Thrace has arrived with soldiers to join the Trojans. The chorus sing a welcome-song as Rhesos swaggers in. He brushes aside Hektor's complaint that he is far too late for the fighting, brags that he will rout the Greeks single-handed and suggests that when the Greek lords are dead he and Hektor should lead an invasion to pillage Greece. Hektor takes him out to the part of the camp reserved for him and his soldiers.

After a brief chorus grumbling about night duty, Odysseus and

Diomedes creep in. They have caught Dolon, tortured the Trojan password out of him and now intend to murder Hektor in his bed. Athene persuades them instead to kill Rhesos and steal his horses, and tricks Paris (who has been alerted by the noise) by pretending that she is Aphrodite his protector and that all is well. In the darkness, the chorus come upon Odysseus and Diomedes, but let them go when Odysseus gives the password. Rhesos' Thracian driver staggers in, wounded. He reports that Rhesos has been murdered, and blames Hektor for lax security. The Muse Terpsichore, Rhesos' mother, appears with his body in her arms. She says that she is taking him to be mourned by her sister Muses, and that the next subject for their grief will be Achilles, who is doomed to die. She reminds us that tears are the end of all mortal lives – and Hektor ignores the warning, ordering the Trojans to gather for an assault on the Greek camp.

## About the play

Nothing is known of the date or circumstances of *Rhesos*. The play is unlike any other in the surviving canon, and some authorities think that it may not be Euripides' work at all. Others find many of his stylistic fingerprints, but are divided about whether it is early in his output (as its pageant-like organisation suggests) or late (as its verse style suggests).

In Book Ten of Homer's *Iliad*, Odysseus and Diomedes slip at night into the Trojan camp, on the way intercepting the Trojan spy Dolon. They kill Prince Rhesos of Thrace and steal the fabulous chariot-horses given him by his father the river-god Strymon. The adventure is told from the Greek point of view, and its main features are banter between Odysseus and Diomedes and long descriptions of their interrogation of Dolon and their escape with the horses from Rhesos' camp. The play *Rhesos* rotates this perspective through one hundred and eighty degrees. The action is set in the Trojan camp, its focus is the Trojan commander Hektor, the killing of Dolon and the stealing of the horses are reported not enacted, and characters not in Homer at all (for example, Rhesos' driver) play crucial parts. The play replaces Homer's style of ironical narrative with vivid theatrical articulation, offering lively scenes between Hektor and Aeneas, Hektor and Dolon, Hektor and the driver, and making outstanding use of such conventions as a messenger's speech, a *deus ex machina* scene and a busy chorus. In short, *Rhesos* is a skilful and original piece of literary adaptation – and if this means that it has the two-dimensional characterisation and over-concentration on incident which typify such work, it makes up for it by its exploitation of drama's ability to 'cast' its audience, ironically in the scenes between Hektor and Rhesos, and Hektor and the driver, and emotionally throughout by the immediacy and physicality of its depiction of an army edgy in the night.

*Rhesos* is the most democratic of all extant tragedies; indeed, its social politics at times foreshadow Brecht's. The chorus, for example, are not a single, cohesive group but a collection of individuals. They mutter about their commanders, argue about what should be done, come together and divide again, exhibit a dozen viewpoints and attitudes. And as the following passages (in Michael Walton's translation*) show, they engulf the theatre space each time they perform:

> Whose watch is next?
> Who's my relief?
> The evening stars are down,
> The seven Pleiades rising ...
> Come on. What's keeping you?
> . . .
> There they are.
> After them. After them.
> Get after them. Cut them down.
> Who's that? Who is it? ...
> They've woken the whole camp.
> Here they are. I've got them.
> Over here. Everyone, over here.
> They're caught.

* Published in *Euripides Plays: Six* (Methuen, 1997).

The articulation of such scenes in performance – at one point the chorus leave the theatre entirely, only to come creeping back, on guard in the darkness, and bump into Odysseus and Diomedes who are going the other way – seems likely to have involved a style of action and choreography reminiscent more of the satyrs in *Cyclops* than of the decorous choruses in more formal tragedy.

The chorus's vigorous realism is shared by the other 'ordinary' characters. Dolon the spy (who may step out of the chorus to volunteer, a piece of physical action unique in surviving tragedy), the shepherd who refuses to be browbeaten by Hektor, the wounded driver – all are drawn with a 'common man' decency which sharply contrasts with the vacillation, vanity and games-manship of the 'noble' characters in the play. Such 'ordinary' characters are a feature of Greek tragedy – the range is from the watchman in *Agamemnon* to the guard in *Antigone* or the bawdy old nurse in *Hippolytos* – but no other play uses so many or makes them so central to its meaning. The ironical gloss their involve-ment gives to the presentation of the heroism and glory of war is one of the most Euripidean features of the play. *Rhesos* can seem a patchwork, its dramatic and poetic quality varying from scene to scene, almost from line to line. But such conceptual strokes as these – and the play is full of them – suggest that even if Euripides was not the author, or the sole author, he was certainly a major influence.

# Suppliants

## Characters

AITHRA, *Theseus' mother*
THESEUS, *ruler of Athens*
ADRASTOS, *ruler of Argos*
THEBAN HERALD
MESSENGER
EVADNE, *Kapaneus' widow*
IPHIS, *her father-in-law*
ATHENE
SONS OF THE SEVEN
ATHENIAN HERALD, SOLDIERS, ATTENDANTS (*silent parts*)
CHORUS OF WOMEN (*mothers of Argive soldiers killed at Thebes*)

## Synopsis

In Demeter's shrine near Athens, Adrastos of Argos and the widows of his soldiers who died attacking Thebes beg Theseus to make the Thebans hand over the dead for burial. Theseus, at first reluctant, is persuaded by his mother Aithra to do as they ask. After arguing with an arrogant Theban herald, he leads his army against the Thebans. The chorus sing of their grief and apprehension. A messenger reports that Thebes has capitulated and the Argive dead are being brought for funeral rites in Athens. While the chorus mourn, attendants bring the bodies. Adrastos and Theseus speak eulogies, and the bodies are carried to their funeral pyres.

Evadne, wife of the dead hero Kapaneus, appears in a wedding-dress on a rock above the pyres, and hurls herself into the flames despite the attempts of her father-in-law Iphis to stop her. Iphis mourns his loss, and the chorus sing sadly as the sons of the Argive heroes bring urns with the ashes of their fathers. Adrastos asks Theseus to send the urns to Argos for burial, but Athene appears *ex machina* and says that before this happens the Argives must swear alliance with Athens and the sons of the Seven must promise to destroy Thebes as soon as they are old enough.

## About the play

*Suppliants* was first performed in about 422, when Euripides was in his late fifties or early sixties. By then, the Peloponnesian War had continued for a decade, and the first optimistic glow had long disappeared. Aristophanes' war-comedies, from about this time, picture Athens almost as a medical patient, literally sick of war. In 425 the Spartans offered peace-terms, and the Athenian war party rejected them. A year later the Athenians were defeated in an attempt to overrun the farming area of Boiotia, loyal to Sparta, and to destroy Thebes, its capital. The Thebans refused to return the Athenian dead for burial – a humiliation which may have been in many spectators' minds as they watched this play. Early in 422 Kleon, the most virulent of the Athenian war-leaders, was killed in battle, as was the Spartan general Brasidas, and peace was made. But it lasted only months, and did little to lighten the mood of weariness and cynicism which marked this period of the war.

Such is the background to *Suppliants*. Of all Euripides' surviving works, it seems most closely related to the condition of its audience. There is patriotic sentiment in plenty – the dialogue rings with praise of Athens, its gods, people, politics and leaders. But the prevailing tone, set not in the spoken scenes but in the choruses, is one of unrelieved sadness for those killed in war and those who weep. The elegiac quality of the choral odes is unmatched in Euripides; not even *Women of Troy* comes close:

> How happy we were!
> We'd children, sons,
> We danced with the mothers of Argos.
> No more. We're childless.
> Artemis, lady of childbirth,
> Won't smile for us.
> In misery we wander,

Aimless, unhappy,
Clouds scudding in a storm ...

The play's starting-point is a detail from the myth of the Seven
Against Thebes, already known to Athenian theatregoers from
Aeschylus' play of that name and Sophocles' *Antigone*. The myth
tells how Eteokles and Polynikes, sons of Oedipus of Thebes,
fought for power, Polynikes leading an army from Argos to attack
Thebes and Eteokles defending it. The Argive army was led by
seven champions and all were killed. Kreon, the new ruler of
Thebes, refused to release their bodies for burial until Theseus of
Athens went with an army and compelled him. Euripides' story,
almost certainly his own invention, centres on this last episode,
and his concerns are first, to contrast Athenian justice with the
vainglory and cowardice of Thebes, and second and most
important, to make his points about the folly and pain of war.

In the story, the most calamitous fool is Adrastos of Argos. In
obedience to an oracle he misunderstood, he married his
daughters to two strangers, Polynikes and Eteokles, and when the
brothers quarrelled he gathered an expedition to support Polynikes and led it to destruction. Now, in Athens ostensibly to ask
help in getting the bodies released for burial, he tries to persuade
Theseus to make him co-leader in a second expedition, to sack
Thebes once and for all. In his inept way he is a twin for
braggadocio of the Theban herald who lectures Theseus on the
correct way to rule, and is treated with comparable scorn. But his
is not the only folly in the play. In the final scene no less a person
than Athene appears *ex machina* and orders the young sons of the
Seven, standing before her with their fathers' urns in their hands,
to mount an expedition as soon as they grow up and topple
Thebes. War is endemic to the human condition, and gods make
no attempt to stop it. As the Theban herald says, in some of the
play's most pungent lines:

Put the question 'Peace or war?'
To an assembly of democrats,
You'll get your answer, 'War' – all think
They're immortal, it's someone else who'll die.

It's not as if we're stupid:
We can tell right from wrong,
We know the cost of war,
The benefits of peace,
Peace, mother of the arts,
Who smiles on families, turns her face
From vengeance, cherishes good living –
We know all that, and choose to ignore it.
We're fools, we fawn on war:
Individuals, cities, strong pounce on weak.

This is the play's grim rationale, discussed in the dialogue scenes, worked out in the action and triggering the mourning which engulfs that action. As the Athenians attack Thebes and win the bodies for burial, a messenger reports the futile dazzle of battle. A botched eulogy is spoken over the glorious dead (so flat a reminiscence of Aeschylus' description of the champions in *Seven Against Thebes* that some take it for parody, others say that Euripides cannot possibly have written it). A widow throws herself into her husband's funeral pyre. Children weep for parents and parents for children. As the play starts Aithra prays God to help the mothers of the Seven, and as it ends that prayer is savagely answered (by Athene) with an exhortation to still more distrust and yet more war. As Evadne's father-in-law Iphis puts it, speaking for all who mourn:

Mortal misery! Why can't we live our lives
Twice over, twice young then old again?
In everyday matters, if you get things wrong
One day you can put them right the next.
Not so with life. If we could only be young again,
Reflect in old age on the mistakes we made,
Then be young a second time to put them right!
I saw other people with children, I envied them,
Loved children – and it came to this.
If I'd known how it feels for a father to lose
His child, I'd have escaped today. What am I to do?

# Women of Troy

## Characters

POSEIDON

ATHENE

HEKABE, *Queen of Troy*

KASSANDRA, ANDROMACHE, *her daughters*

TALTHYBIOS, *Greek officer*

MENELAOS, *King of Sparta*

HELEN, *his wife*

ASTYANAX, *Andromache's small son*, SOLDIERS (*silent parts*)

CHORUS OF WOMEN


## Synopsis

On the day after the Greeks take Troy, two gods, Poseidon and
Athene, agree to give them dangerous homeward journeys, their
punishment for desecrating Athene's shrine. As the gods disappear, a bundle of rags stirs at the foot of the city walls: Hekabe,
Queen of Troy. She and her women weep for the destruction of
the city. A Greek officer, Talthybios, tells them the names of the
Greeks whose war-booty. they have become. Kassandra runs in,
dressed as a bride and carrying blazing torches. She prophesies
Agamemnon's death and sings the glory of all those who died
defending Troy. Talthybios leads her away, and Hekabe weeps for
her husband and children, slaughtered by Greeks.

The chorus sing of how the Greeks sacked the city. Andromache, widow of Hekabe's son Hektor, is dragged in with her baby
son Astyanax, on a cart loaded with war spoils. She talks of her
future as slave to Telemachos, son of Achilles who killed her
husband. Talthybios brings orders from the Greek commanders:
Astyanax is to be thrown to his death from the battlements. He
takes the child, and Hekabe and the chorus mourn the glory that
was Troy. Menelaos swaggers in, demanding Helen. She pleads her

innocence, and Hekabe savagely proves her guilt. Menelaos takes Helen to his ship, and Talthybios asks Hekabe to bury Astyanax's body with what ceremony she can find. She wraps the body and cradles it on Hektor's war-shield. Fire blazes in the city: the Greeks are torching Troy. Hekabe rushes towards the flames, but Talthybios' soldiers stop her and lead her and her women to the ships.

## About the play

*Women of Troy* was first presented in 415. Its companion-plays dealt with other stories from the Trojan myth-cycle, *Alexandros* with the way Hekabe and Priam ignored an oracle that unless they killed the child (Paris) in Hekabe's womb, he would grow up to set all Troy ablaze, and *Palamedes* about the son of King Nauplios of Euboia who was executed for insulting Odysseus at Troy. The satyr play was about the trickster-king Sisyphos. But there is no evidence that Euripides conceived the plays as a sequence, in the manner of Aeschylus' *Oresteia*, and *Women of Troy* stands well on its own.

Two contemporary events would have resonated in the minds of the play's first audience. A couple of years before *Women of Troy*, the Athenians sacked the island of Melos, killed the males and took the females as concubines and house-slaves. Many of Euripides' audience must have owned, or been aware of, Melian slaves, and although the play never hints at 'the Melian affair', the topical resonance of a tragedy set among women of a captured city, brutalised by their conquerors, seems unlikely to have gone unnoticed. Additionally, in 416, in the fifteenth year of the Peloponnesian War, the Athenians sent a war fleet to sack the Sicilian city of Syracuse. At the time of its departure, it was hyperbolically compared to the legendary Greek fleet which sailed for Troy – and *Women of Troy* specifically refers to the destruction of that fleet on the way home, destruction caused by overweening arrogance and insults to the gods. Euripides' audience cannot have known that their own fleet, pride of their city, was to be defeated some time after the production of the play, but the link with arrogance was there for those who wanted to make it.

*Women of Troy* could be seen as a tragedy of *hubris*. In their arrogance, the Greeks challenge the gods, specifically by desecrating Athene's shrine and generally by the whole endeavour of the Trojan War. The play shows them plunging ever deeper into self-destructive blindness, ignoring the claims of morality, justice, mercy and even political expediency. In particular, the slaughter of Polyxena and Astyanax, standing for the destruction of every innocent woman or child in Troy, carries them to the point where universal order can be restored only by their own punishment and suffering. Their guilt and the certainty of punishment are set out by the gods in the prologue, and later in the play Kassandra gives specific details, talking about the difference between the Greek and Trojan dead and outlining the gory ends awaiting the Greek commanders.

The play's form is unusual in surviving tragedy. The play is a continuum of lyrical sorrow for Troy (and by implication, for the horror of all wars everywhere). No hope is found or offered; the lyrical beauty of the language intensifies rather than soothes the pain. The scenes which arise from this continuum, part spoken and part lyrical, are ordered so as to provide both dramatic variety and a sense of mounting climax. Talthybios tells Hekabe of Polyxena's murder and the enslavement of the women. Kassandra capers in an insane parody of a wedding-dance, then contrasts the pain-which-is-joy of those who died for Troy and the triumph-which-is-misery of those who conquered them. Andromache cradles Astyanax, last hope of Troy, and Talthybios takes him away to die. Helen and Menelaos confront one another in a black-farce 'trial scene'. Hekabe and her women perform a ceremony of burial and mourning. The sorrow of the opening scene between Hekabe and the chorus is balanced by this final ritual, and in between them two scenes of enormous stage energy (Kassandra's prophecy and the argument between Helen and Menelaos) frame the Andromache sequence, the apex of the play's dramatic arch. That sequence is expressed not in heightened language but with the utmost austerity, not in shrieks and rants but in a kind of exhausted, toneless whisper:

> I'm to serve as slave in the house of the man
> Who killed my husband. What shall I do?
> Blot out my Hektor's face, fling wide my heart
> To a second husband – and betray the dead?
> Or scorn Achilles' son, pull down my master's rage
> About my head? One night of love unstrings
> A woman's hate, men say. Men say . . .

When Astyanax is taken from his mother, language fails entirely: the action is performed in silence.

*Women of Troy* challenges several of Aristotle's theories of tragedy. Its protagonist is not an individual but a whole city and people, its *hubris* not personal but a kind of national insanity. The experience it offers is not *drama* (performed action) but *stasis* (absence of action). At key moments, comedy and tragedy are inextricably entwined – for example, when Hekabe, faced with Andromache's despair as she is shipped away to slavery, can find no comfort and is reduced to musing

> I've never been on a ship.
> I've seen them in paintings,
> I've heard people talk of them . . .

– or when Menelaos, warned not to risk taking Helen on board his home-bound ship, brutally jokes

> Why not? She's put on weight?

Throughout the play, Euripides' formal artfulness and the quality of his verse – its intensity rivals anything that survives from Aeschylus – triumphantly avoids the problem that if you write about emptiness, you end up with empty writing. For all its un-Aristotelian procedures, *Women of Troy* produces true Aristotelian catharsis.

# Aristophanes

## Life

The only facts known about Aristophanes' life are the dates and production details of some of his plays. Everything else is inference from remarks in his own or other people's work. (He is, for example, a character in Plato's *Symposium*.) Particularly in his early plays, he gives the impression of being a confessional artist: remarks to the audience like the claim in *Acharnians* that because Aigina is his home the island should not be surrendered to the Spartans, or the instruction to bald men in *Peace* to clap especially loudly and 'win Baldy the prize' are typical. But, as with such remarks by all apparently confessional comedians, care is needed. If I call myself Baldy and have no hair, that is one kind of joke; if I call myself Baldy and have long, luxuriant locks, that is another. I can claim to live on Aigina although, or *because*, everyone knows that I detest the place.

With this proviso, the facts seem to be that Aristophanes was born some time in the 440s, perhaps about 448, the son of Philippos. He may have come from the nut-growing island of Aigina, not far from Athens, or owned estates there later in life. His first play, *Banqueters* (a satire on education, now lost), was produced in 427 by someone else, since (he claims) he felt too young and inexperienced to mount it himself. His second play, *Babylonians* (a year later, also now lost), satirised the demagogue Kleon, who sued him unsuccessfully for 'slandering the state in the presence of foreigners', so making Aristophanes' reputation. Thereafter, Aristophanes produced some forty more plays and consistently won high prizes.

Aristophanes' most productive years were spent in the shadow of the Peloponnesian War. His plays were watched by audiences under siege or who had taken refuge in Athens from enemy invasions, and the politics and effects of the war on ordinary people provided consistent inspiration. The heroes of many of his comedies take extreme, often surreal, steps to improve their situation: making a private peace treaty with Sparta (*Acharnians*), flying to heaven to rescue Peace (*Peace*), initiating a sex-strike so that men will hand state affairs to women (*Lysistrata*). Subsidiary characters include every kind of fraud and upstart who thrived in the chaos of war: Aristophanes flays corrupt politicians, place-serving generals, fake priests, spies, diplomats, lawyers, profiteers, con artists and perverts – and several were real individuals, pilloried under their own names.

After Athens' surrender in 404, when Aristophanes was in his mid or late forties, he seems to have slowed down his dramatic activity. The gaps between his plays grew longer, and he may have spent his time on his estates and furthering the careers of his three sons, particularly Araros who followed him as a comic playwright and who produced Aristophanes' last two plays. This change of pace was probably not due to the censorious régime imposed on Athens by the victorious Spartans – fear of officialdom had never muzzled Aristophanes in the past. The cause may have been adverse theatrical conditions – few new plays of any kind were produced – or that relaxation of intensity, that mellowing, which often gives comedy writers shorter creative lives than their tragic counterparts. (Plautus, Molière and Feydeau, for example, all slowed their creative activity at a similar stage in their careers.) Certainly Aristophanes' last two surviving plays, *Women in Power* and *Wealth*, though stylistically different from their predecessors, show no falling-off in originality or vitality.

Evidence from the plays suggests that Aristophanes was temper-amentally on the wavelength of two groups of people in particular. He portrays with warmth and sympathy the everyday lives and concerns of the *bourgeoisie*, particularly independent businessmen and small landowners. He is scathing about aristocrats and those who try to ape their betters, and his slaves and other working-class characters are less fully imagined than their employers. And he is in sympathy with intellectuals, or at least the Athenian 'chattering classes', interested in the arts and philosophy not with the magpie mockery common to all comedians but with enthusiasm for and knowledge of what at the time must have been arcane and avant-garde ideas. He was probably a friend of Socrates – Plato's *Symposium* shows them talking till dawn after the first-night party for a play by the tragedian Agathon – and he shared professional interests with Euripides (possibly another friend) to the point where a fellow-writer dramatist (Krateinos) coined the word 'euripidaristophanising' to lampoon the pretentious intellectualism he claimed was overwhelming drama. Not unnaturally for someone who spent his life satirising those in power, Aristophanes' political interests seem objective rather than subjective; no evidence survives that he took any active part in politics outside the theatre.

## Works

Eleven plays survive, about one quarter of Aristophanes' output: *Acharnians* (425), *Knights* (424), *Clouds* (423), *Wasps* (422), *Peace* (421), *Birds* (414), *Lysistrata* (411), *Festival Time* (*Thesmophoriazousai*, 411), *Frogs* (405), *Women in Power* (*Ekklesiazousai, c.*392), *Wealth* (*c.*380).

## Style and approach

The kind of surreal, satirical, musically extravagant comedy evolved in fifth-century Athens and perfected by Aristophanes is often called 'Old Comedy', in contrast to the more realistic, more character-based 'New Comedy' of such later writers as Menander. In the history of Western theatre, literary comedy has chiefly been influenced by New Comedy, while Old Comedy routines and practices have passed into the traditions of oral and physical comedy. Aristophanes' exuberant satire, the whirl of song and dance in his plays, and his explicit sexual and scatological jokes also tended to marginalise him in Christian Europe during the last two millennia. Proper understanding of the nature of his genius began to return only in the second half of the twentieth century, and despite his enormous exuberance and influence – virtually all current comedy techniques, from slapstick *lazzi* to impersonation, from funny accents to double acts, can be traced back to his work – he is still underperformed.

The essential event of each Aristophanes play, what the hero of *Acharnians* calls a 'strange and mighty deed', is an escape from reality into fantasy. People go to live as birds, visit the Under-world, take the blind god of Wealth to be cured at a healing shrine. Once the escape from reality is made, the 'heroes' treat the surreal world they have engineered as if it is entirely natural and everyday – with the result that when characters from the real world enter it, with 'real' preconceptions or concerns, they seem foolish and grotesque. This reversal of the rules of 'reality' colours all Aristophanes' satire. People from real Athenian life (say, Socrates, Euripides, police informers, whores or generals) are drawn into the action, and the behaviour Aristophanes imputes to them (an ironical 'take' on their real-life behaviour, already known to the theatre audience) is displayed as alien to the play's new 'reality' (which is, by implication, morally superior to that of life itself). Gods, frogs, characters from myth and tragedy, corpses and fairy-story monsters appear onstage, talk as equals with Aristophanes' own characters, and make 'reality' their plaything.

The fact that, in the Aristophanic world, the serious is made ludicrous and the ludicrous serious affects not only the content but the style of the drama. The plays are studded with quotations from tragedy – several hundred from Euripides' plays alone – and their context, a whirl of parody and mockery, makes them seem outrageous and preposterous. The following passage from *Festival Time*, drawing on Euripides' *Helen*, is typical:

EURIPIDES (*in dripping rags, as Menelaos*).
    Who lords it here, in this stupendous pile?
    And will he welcome wanderers, I wonder,
    Storm-tossed, ship-shattered, saved from salty sea?

MNESILOCHOS (*in a dress, as Helen*).
This place is Proteus' palace ...

WOMAN
Don't listen to a word he says. Such lies!
This isn't Proteus' place, it's somewhere else.

EURIPIDES
Say whither, whither have we steered our course?

MNESILOCHOS
To Egypt ...

WOMAN
He's doing it again. Don't you be taken in.
This is Athens, the temple of the Twain.

EURIPIDES
You mean, not Proteus' place? Not *Proteus*' place?

WOMAN
You've been too long at sea, darling.

By contrast, when clouds sing of the joys of Socratic education, or farmers who have gone up to heaven to rescue Peace hymn the satisfactions of ending war, or Lysistrata compares the management of state affairs with the spinning and carding of wool, we are seduced by an appearance of beauty, reason and harmony. In one play, *Knights*, the issue of how a political leader should rise to power is turned into a Punch-and-Judy-like contest between two outrageous, buffoonish blackguards – and Aristophanes' satirical point is made by style alone.

Even more disconcerting (at least, perhaps, for readers or spectators weaned on the conventions of Western literary drama), it is a feature of Aristophanes' style that characters refuse to stay within the confines of their own stage 'reality'. They turn to the audience, make jokes about the weather, the hardness of the theatre seats, lunch, the real-life toy-boys and placemen strutting just down the road – and then turn back into the action as if nothing had happened. In several plays, an entire choral section (the *parabasis*, 'stepping-aside') is devoted to some urgent contemporary issue, often lateral to the main action of the play, and the chorus talk or sing to the audience in terms modern spectators might associate more with a newspaper leader than with stage comedy. This passage, in which the wasp-costumed chorus of ancient jurymen in *Wasps* complain that the Athens they created in the good old days is being pillaged and ruined by the upstart young, is typical:

> We made you free.
> It was our exertions
> That walloped the Persians
> By land and sea.
> We'd no time for talking,
> Rhetorical tightrope-walking:
> Our work was real.
> We won the empire, the tribute, the riches
> That these yuppie young crooks, sons of bitches,
> Now snaffle and steal.

Moving in and out of the 'reality' of the character is particularly the province of the leading actor, whose relationship with the audience is crucial to the play. In a way largely lost in 'literary' comedy nowadays, but still the norm in comedy performances of all other kinds, from stand-up to clowning, from music hall to eccentric dance, the leading actor assumes from the start a kind of ironical complicity with the audience, a shared attitude not merely to the butts and ideas mocked in the story, but also to the situation and events of the performance itself, even as it happens. Dikaiopolis in *Acharnians* imagines that the spectators are as bored as he is with the bad tragedies they have been forced to witness. The flute player Chairis, a member of Aristophanes' company, is mocked in *Acharnians* and in *Birds* – in the latter case just as he comes on to take part in a slapstick scene. Trygaios in *Peace* invites farmers in the audience to come up and help in rescuing Peace, and later passes the nubile goddess of Holiday along the front row 'for the old men to ogle'. The dialogue is constantly peppered with asides and comments which rupture the stage illusion, and the energy of performance becomes the energy of the play. Slapstick *lazzi*, for example (comic routines such as those involved in knocking on a door, fighting, kissing, playing confidence tricks, cooking, dancing), are given an added appeal by audience complicity with the performers. We watch them indulgently, as if a friend or relative were playing tricks for us, and the performers ironically trump that indulgence by their professional expertise and flourish.

The fact that the leading actor, and the comic hero he plays, sit as it were on the hinge of the action, the point where the play moves from reality to fantasy, from frustration to wish-fulfilment, and back again, is vital to Aristophanes' purpose. If the satirist's new, invented reality is to persuade us, it is essential that we admire the character who creates it – and Aristophanes goes further, making that character our confidant and friend. In his last two surviving plays, where this dallying with the nature of illusion is sporadic (as in New Comedy, where it is almost entirely absent, so that characters retain their illusory roles throughout), the effect is of distance, of presentation of the situation rather than complicity.

Since Aristophanes' time, the 'stepping-aside' in his plays has sometimes been misinterpreted, by both scholars and theatre-directors. Scholars occasionally take the political and social comments (not to mention views on such people as Socrates or Pericles) for genuine revelations of Aristophanes' real opinions about his time – something as likely as assuming that what a modern comedian said about a modern head of state was intended to be serious rather than calculated for precise, hilarious effect. Modern theatre-directors sometimes interpolate contemporary political and social references and jokes, disrupting the dramatic flow in a way quite different from Aristophanes' own. In all his work, the stepping backwards and forwards from reality to surreality is as deliberate and as precisely manipulated as any other dramatic effect.

## Aristophanes' reputation

The change of fashion, towards the end of Aristophanes' life, from Old towards New Comedy, meant that by the time he died his work had already begun to be marginalised. (The survival of eleven plays is due not so much to continuing performance as to the work of third-century scholars at the Library of Alexandria, doggedly assembling a complete collection of extant Greek literature.) It was not until the Renaissance that his plays began to be rediscovered and read, and even then, his specifically Athenian political references created a barrier, and for three centuries he was mined by classical scholars for arcane words and for evidence of Athenian daily life rather than by theatre-lovers looking for comedy. His work hardly deserves such a fate. The 'line' of each play is clear and the incidents, however bizarre, are in context perfectly understandable and inevitable. His humour asserts the vigour and vitality of life; he accentuates the anarchic, optimistic side of human nature. Of all the 'submerged' geniuses of Western theatre, he is one of those most needing rediscovery.

# Acharnians

## Characters

DIKAIOPOLIS

SERGEANT

AMPHITHEOS, *a god*

AMBASSADORS

PSEUDARTABAS, *Persian envoy*

HIS EXCELLENCY

DIKAIOPOLIS' DAUGHTERS

KEPHISOPHON, *Euripides' slave*

EURIPIDES

LAMACHOS, *general*

MEGARIAN

HIS DAUGHTERS

THEBAN

LAMACHOS' AIDE DE CAMP

NIKARCHOS, *informer*

TOWN CRIER

YOKEL

BEST MAN

AMBASSADORS, BAGPIPERS, BRIDESMAID, CITIZENS, DANCING-
GIRLS, DIKAIOPOLIS' WIFE, EUNUCHS, THE FEARSOME FIRM,
ISMENIAS (*the Theban's slave*), OFFICIALS, ORDERLIES, POLICE
OFFICERS, SLAVES, XANTHIAS (*Dikaiopolis' slave*) (*silent parts*)
CHORUS OF CHARCOAL BURNERS

## Synopsis

Bored and fed up, Dikaiopolis waits for the assembly to debate
peace terms with Sparta. But when the officials finally arrive,
attention is given to frauds and cheats, and he decides on a
'strange and mighty deed': to make a private peace treaty of his
own with Sparta. He sends the demigod Amphitheos to fetch the

treaty, and then defends his actions to the chorus of hostile charcoal burners, first borrowing a costume and some props from Euripides to make his case more tragic.

After an interlude in which the chorus praise the older generation, Dikaiopolis comes out to sacrifice in honour of peace. He is interrupted by liars and con-men of every kind, and drives them away. A town crier arrives and summons Dikaiopolis' next-door neighbour, General Lamachos, to battle in Thrace. Dikaiopolis himself celebrates his private peace with two nubile dancing-girls as the play ends in a ceremonial procession.

## About the play

*Acharnians*, the earliest of Aristophanes' extant plays, won first prize at the Lenaia in January 425. It was presented under the name of Kalistratos, its producer, since it wasn't until *Knights*, performed the following year, that Aristophanes' work was staged under his own name. The play appears to have required three doorways and the use of the *ekkuklema*, a device whose function is clear even if its form is not. It was used for discoveries such as that of Euripides in this play. It appears that Lenaia plays had greater latitude to be politically trenchant than Dionysia plays, partly because the dates of each festival meant that there would be fewer foreigners present at the Lenaia.

There had been a brief pause in the Peloponnesian War, already six years old, as an earthquake had prevented what had become the virtually routine Spartan invasions of Athenian territory and the consequent flights of country dwellers into the city itself. Aristophanes used the plight of the displaced countrymen and that of various disgraced allies to explore the implications of the war. The Acharnians of the title are inhabitants of Acharnai, a town close to Athens that had been an early victim of the war. It was a centre of the charcoal industry, which explains the consistent references to fire, burning, coal and charcoal as well as the chorus's fiery tempers and their reluctance to make peace with Sparta. The Megarian is from Megara, a city widely regarded by the Athenians as being responsible for starting the war, and the Theban is another enemy of Athens. It is not clear how many actors were used in comedy but clearly doubling was routine: in *Acharnians* it would make sense for Lamachos and Euripides (the bombastic mock-tragic soldier and the tragic dramatist) to be doubled and for the Megarian and the Theban (both dialect parts) to be doubled since each doubling, if recognised by the audience, would increase their understanding of the issues being debated.

*Acharnians* is the first extant example of Aristophanes' characteristic mixture of personal invective aimed at named individuals with generic attacks on the kinds of bureaucrats and jobsworths who profit from the machinery of the state. Lamachos, who commanded naval forces in expeditions to the Black Sea in 436 and 424 and was killed in the campaign in Sicily in 414, may have been presented as the first theatrical braggart soldier as much because of the martial connotations of his name and its contrast with the name Antimachos as because of any great personal animus. On the other hand, Aristophanes' persistent attacks on the politician Kleon seem to be rooted in a deep and genuine hostility. Aristophanes' quarrel with Kleon apparently started with the lost play *Babylonians* since *Acharnians* refers to Kleon beginning some kind of legal action against the author for slandering the state in the presence of foreigners. Aristophanes' aversion to Kleon's policies is a notable feature of many of his plays, and Thucydides offers a vivid portrait of Kleon though little is known about him from other sources. Aristophanes presents him as an upstart warmonger. Dramatists were allowed and expected to be political in ways that some commentators have preferred to ignore and on the strength of those parts of the plays where political comment was encouraged (particularly the *parabasis*) it does seem that Aristophanes was politically conservative, favouring those sections of Athenian society that had traditionally held political power. One of the paradoxes of Aristophanes' theatrical success with plays full of virulent attacks on Kleon is that the Athenians continued to elect the object of those attacks to political office: the workings of Athenian democracy were clearly complex and sophisticated.

*Acharnians* establishes a pattern that typifies Aristophanes' plays: someone is dissatisfied with the current state of affairs and attempts to rectify it, usually by appropriate legal methods, and then, when that fails, pursues a more idiosyncratic course. At the beginning of the play Dikaiopolis is waiting for a meeting of the assembly to put his case for making peace but when that is frustrated he embarks on his own private peace-making efforts. In *Acharnians* Aristophanes is careful to establish that the hero is not simply an eccentric: he prepares the context from the opening lines in which the hero is waiting for the assembly to begin, through the frustrations of a meeting to the eventual conclusion that the only way out is through direct individual action. This action then moves us into a fantasy world where private treaties take the form of wineskins and the state is powerless against the individual. The preparation for this is crucial since it should align the spectator with the hero's position rather than dismissing it, since we have joined in the hero's journey. There is some debate about how we are to regard Dikaiopolis' private peace. Some would argue that he is essentially selfish. However, this view ignores the trajectory of the hero, who has been presented to us as someone trying to get the state to see sense before rejection leads him to his personal plan. It also ignores the fact that we spend far more time watching him than we do watching Lamachos, so that we are much more likely to sympathise with him than with the bombastic Lamachos.

For the sequence in which Dikaiopolis seeks Euripides' help, Aristophanes draws heavily on *Telephos*, a now lost play by Euripides which had been staged in 438. Although the play was old and may not have been familiar in detail to the original audience, they would, presumably, have been familiar with the myth and may have known speeches from Euripides' play through private recital or in manuscript form. In *Telephos*, Achilles wounded Telephos while defending his kingdom, and his wound failed to heal. An oracle said that he could only be saved by 'the wounder' so he went to seek help from Achilles. Disguised as a beggar, he defended himself by telling the Achaeans they would have done what he did. Eventually, after taking the baby Orestes hostage, he was recognised as Greek rather than a barbarian (he was actually the son of Herakles and Auge), cured by Achilles' sword, and became the Greeks' guide to Troy.

Aristophanes draws on this material directly with verbal quotations and parodies and in costuming and action (the hostage-taking is parodied in the threat to the Acharnians' coals). Even Lamachos' injury probably relates to part of the myth in which Dionysos tangled Telephos' foot in a vine. The allusions are partly designed to reinforce Aristophanes' attempt to gain acceptance for what is after all an outrageous viewpoint, by locating it within an acceptable tragic-mythic matrix, linking the dramatist, the comic character and the mythic king in order to get a hearing for an unpopular view against war.

# Birds

## Characters

PEITHETAIROS

EUELPIDES, *his friend*

AIDE

TEREUS, *king of the birds*

PRIEST

POET

ORACLE-SELLER

METON, *surveyor*

INSPECTOR-GENERAL

LAW-SELLER

WATCHMAN

MESSENGER

IRIS, *messenger of the gods*

YOB

KINESIAS, *lyric poet*

INFORMER

PROMETHEUS, POSEIDON, HERAKLES, BIGGUN, *gods*

BIRDS, CHAIRIS (*flute player*), SLAVES (MANES, MANODOROS, XANTHIAS *and others unnamed*), SOVEREIGNTY, WITNESS (*silent parts*)

CHORUS OF BIRDS

## Synopsis

Peithetairos and Euelpides, tired of the fuss and fret of life in Athens, leave to find a more congenial country. Lost in the desert, they stumble on the kingdom of the birds, ruled by Tereus the hoopoe. They persuade him to let them grow wings and join the birds, and then to build a wall across the sky, prevent sacrifices getting through and force the gods to hand over rule of all the universe. The chorus are initially hostile, but Peithetairos convinces them. While the Athenians are inside growing wings, the chorus sing of the birds' ancient power and glory and the benefits they will bring the human race if that power is restored (and if Aristophanes' play wins first prize).

The building work begins, and Peithetairos prepares to sacrifice for good omens. But word has reached mortals, and a succession of cheats and frauds arrives, trying to join Cloudcuckooland (the birds' new state). Peithetairos unmasks and beats them all. The wall is built, the blockade begins, and the gods send Poseidon, Herakles and Biggun (a deity 'from beyond the stars') to make peace. Peithetairos insists that they give up their rule and symbolise it by letting him marry Sovereignty, the beautiful woman who previously sat at Zeus' right hand and polished his thunderbolts. The play ends with a wedding procession and a peal of heavenly thunder, as Peithetairos and his bird-subjects take over the universe.

## About the play

Aristophanes presented *Birds* at the City Dionysia of 414, when he was in his thirties.

Like *Frogs* a decade later, *Birds* avoids topicality almost throughout. It may have contemporary overtones we no longer notice or understand – some commentators link it with the Sicilian Expedition, whose issue was still unknown in 414, or with the kind of utopian speculation which led, later, to Plato's *Republic* – but for the most part its comedy is general, taking place in a fantasy world unconnected to 'reality' of any kind. The king of the birds is a being from fairy tale, the new city is built on clouds, the chief sufferers from Peithetairos' ambitions are gods in their most mythical, most untranscendental forms. The only 'satirical' components in the action are that the mortals who try to enter Cloudcuckooland and bounce off the new ethics of fantasyland are the (comparatively minor) impostors familiar from Aristophanes' other plays, and the way in which the birds' blockade of heaven may satirise the Athenian blockade of the island of Melos some three years earlier (a matter of which Euripides made more pungent use in *Women of Troy*, produced one year before *Birds*). These apart, and ignoring brief passing references to such real-life individuals as Theagenes and Chairephon, *Birds* is timeless, a *jeu d'esprit* whose only purpose seems to be to entertain. (In an edgier version, for example, Peithetairos and Euelpides might have left Athens because of some political scandal or to right some monstrous wrong; in *Birds* they go because they are tired of *polypragmosune*, 'busybodying', the incessant need of Athenians to stick their noses in other people's affairs.)

One of the main factors contributing to this happy atmosphere is the play's linguistic dance. The birdsong which several times appears (*kikkabau; tiou tiou tiou tioutinx; epopoee popopopopopopoee*, perhaps musical indications for the actor or the flautist) seems to have seeped into both language and philosophy, making them insubstantial and charming. After the chorus have demanded attention from

> You down there. Mortals. Leaves. Dreams.
> Shadow-creatures. Mud puppets . . .

they claim sovereignty for the birds not for grand cosmological reasons but because the lark was the oldest creature in the universe, so old that when her father died she had nowhere to dig him a grave and had to imagine a tomb for him, complete with 'headstone'. When Peithetairos affects Aeschylean grandiloquence to send Zeus a defiant message, it has all the fire and fury of a canary displaying in a cage:

> Tell Zeus to put a sock in it –
> Unless he wants his palace purged
> With eaglefire, a fearsome force
> Of firecrests, zooming up with zest
> To kindle chaos and dish out doom.
> I've got six hundred here on standby,
> Tawny as leopards, grim as giants –
> That's right, giant trouble, just like he had before . . .

The final apotheosis, in which thunder rolls to add solemnity to the wedding procession of Peithetairos and Sovereignty, reduces the symbol of universal domination to a flash of pyrotechnics in the 'walkdown' which ends a pantomime. Such insubstantiality entirely suits a plot whose 'strange and mighty deed' is to starve the gods into submission by stopping smoke with a wall – and the ironical point is that the birds' new 'reality' does succeed and does change the universe.

In form, *Birds* is itself a kind of apotheosis, taking to unprecedented lengths the 'hierarchical' dramatic structure of Aristophanes' earlier surviving plays. (Each of his later extant works is structurally different and structurally unique.) Peithetairos, the leading character, is pivotal to the action. His is the 'strange and mighty deed', he controls the new reality, he deals with the impostors who invade it, his is the wedding which ends the play. Like Lysistrata, he is predominantly a 'serious' character, driving the story forward and keeping steady the dramatic line from the initial search for a new country 'more comfortable than Athens' to usurpation of Zeus' universal rule. Round him the other actors provide a whirl of verbal and physical slapstick like that in other Aristophanes plays in every respect except quantity. Usually there are four or five impostors, in *Birds* there are seventeen. Part of the audience's pleasure must have been the spectacle of actors appearing in a multitude of roles, vanishing offstage only to return almost instantly in another mask and another absurd persona. The action slows down only towards the end, with the arrivals of Prometheus, Iris and the delegation of gods. Purposeful plotting replaces the sequence of 'turns' as the story moves towards conclusion – and Peithetairos, who has with the earlier impostors been something like the still centre of a whirlwind, suddenly takes back control and dominates proceedings as he did in the first third of the play.

This arch of comedy action, from plot to slapstick 'turns' and back to plot, is itself presented in the context provided by the chorus. *Birds* offers more space for spectacle than any other surviving comedy, and one can only imagine the richness of the costumes, music and dance provided. If the Sicilian Expedition represented Athenian hopes and self-image at their highest (some would say most hubristic) point in the Peloponnesian War, *Birds* is that spirit transformed into comic theatre: self-indulgent, insubstantial and gloriously presumptuous. Perhaps, given the circumstances of the first performance, that was precisely what made it topical.

# Clouds

## Characters

---

STREPSIADES

PHEIDIPPIDES, *his son*

SLAVE

STUDENT

SOCRATES

RIGHT *and* WRONG, *philosophical wrestlers*

PASIAS *and* AMYNIAS, *creditors*

PASIAS' FRIEND

STREPSIADES' SLAVES, SOCRATES' STUDENTS (*silent parts*)

CHORUS OF CLOUDS

## Synopsis

Driven to desperation by the cost of his son Pheidippides' addiction to horse-riding, Strepsiades tries to persuade him to enrol in Socrates' school, the Thinkery, in order to learn how to balk his creditors. When Pheidippides refuses, Strepsiades enrols himself. He is so amazed by the sights he sees – Socrates making metaphysical observations from a swing, the students peering at the ground to discern its hidden secrets, the gigantic mathematical and scientific instruments – and so overwhelmed by the chorus of clouds who float in, that he fails to notice their warning that his attempts at self-betterment may end in tears.

Socrates takes Strepsiades inside to begin the course, and the Clouds tell the audience about Aristophanes' merits and the benefits they (the Clouds) will bring the judges if the play wins a prize. Socrates bursts out of the Thinkery, exasperated by Strepsiades' stupidity – which we then see proved as he rejects every effort to improve his mind. Strepsiades thinks that he has completed the course and hurries home to show off his new knowledge. Pheidippides is so embarrassed by his father that he agrees to go to the Thinkery himself. Two philosophical wrestlers, Right and Wrong, stage a contest to demonstrate the difference between Old Ways and New. Two creditors of Strepsiades, Pasias and Amynias, demand repayment of their loans, so he brings Pheidippides out to bamboozle them. Strepsiades scolds Pheidippides for beating him and Pheidippides responds by using his newly acquired skills to prove that it is logical for children to thrash their parents. Outraged, Strepsiades burns down the Thinkery.

## About the play

A version of *Clouds* won third prize at the Dionysia in 423. In other words, it was a failure. Aristophanes later revised it and it is that version that survives today. According to one of the ancient commentators who had access to both versions, significant changes in the second version included the *parabasis*, the burning of Socrates' school and the argument between Right and Wrong. A surviving vase, depicting two figures in bird costumes apparently squaring up to one another, may show this scene, since an ancient commentator notes that the two characters 'are shown on stage in wicker cages, fighting it out like cocks'. Of course the commentator, if accurate, is conflating the way the characters were brought on stage and what they did subsequently, but it is a very nice image and could be seen as referring forward to some of the ideas in the play about the relationship between the natural world and the world of intellect.

The function of the Clouds who form the play's chorus and give it its name varies throughout the play, as they metaphorically change their moral identity like real clouds change their shapes. In some senses, as Douglas MacDowell suggests, the Clouds seem to be little more than hot air, but, as well as being what Socrates apparently worships as the true gods, they also sing praises of Zeus in the *parabasis* and it is left to them to restore order when they eventually reveal their function of punishing evildoers and making them respect the gods.

Unlike Aristophanes' earlier plays, *Clouds* is not directly engaged with major questions of war, peace and the civic good, although there are still references to Kleon, his now dead *bête noire*. Instead the play tackles a moral and social theme rather than a purely (party) political one. Education was a hot issue in fifth-century Athens because of new educational opportunities offered at what we would think of as tertiary level by teachers who have come to be known as 'Sophists'. Very little of their actual teaching was written down, so much of what we know about their ideas stems from critical attacks on them, including *Clouds*. The play portrays Socrates, now revered as one of the founders of Western Philosophy, as a charlatan and corrupter of the young. Even worse, Plato suggests in the *Apology* that the play played a significant part in creating Socrates' popular reputation and thus paved the way to his condemnation and death, albeit some twenty years later. It may be, however, that Socrates was simply a convenient name to target because he was the best known of these teachers and because he was so notoriously ugly that a character mask could have easily identified him to native Athenians. Moreover, the fact that the then trendy ideas associated with Socrates have become a staple of the Western tradition does not mean that they had to be perceived as right when they first appeared.

One of the reasons for Aristophanes' suspicion of the new learning was because of its stress on the power of rhetoric. He appears to have believed that political success had become a function of demagoguery and rhetorical persuasion, and that political debate had become more Sophist-icated and dependent on technique rather than content, medium rather than message, spin rather than substance, to adopt some more modern near-equivalents. In attacking Socrates, as in attacking Kleon, Aristophanes was apparently siding with conservative, anti-rhetorical arguments, but, paradoxically, he used all his rhetorical and theatrical skills to do so.

The breakdown of communication between the generations and the young taking up new ideas that seem scandalous to an older generation are staple comic themes but *Clouds* deals with an intergenerational conflict that is never fully resolved. Unlike Aristophanes' earlier anti-war plays, *Clouds* has no grand mad plan to bring peace in the face of wider political opposition. Instead there is a much more realistic situation conducted at a much more mundane level. Instead of undertaking a heroic quest for peace, Strepsiades is looking for a way to renege on paying his son's debts and instead of a trip to heaven he goes next door to Socrates' school. Whereas the crane is used in *Peace* for a comic journey to heaven, here it is used only to display Socrates floating above earthly concerns. The action stems from the conflict between the father's desire to deal with his son's debts and the son's unwillingness to do what his father wants. Of course when he does do his father's bidding by attending Socrates' school, he learns not only how to repudiate debts but also to justify further inversions of law and custom by justifying beating his father.

At the end Stepsiades' plan has fallen apart because his son has not only chased away the creditors, according to plan, but has also beaten him, which was not in the plan. Whereas in earlier plays Aristophanes had, through a kind of logic of the absurd, established the positive claims of peace, here he can do no more than burn down Socrates' school. In many of Aristophanes' plays the ending involves feasting after the triumph of the bizarre idea. In *Clouds* the farcical arson may be potentially spectacular, but it is negative and fails to progress beyond the joys of revenge. Perhaps we can see the destruction of the Thinkery as a restoration of the natural order, but the ending of *Clouds* lacks the spacious presentation of the positive joys of that order that characterises many of Aristophanes' other plays.

# Festival Time (*Thesmophoriazousai*)

## Characters

EURIPIDES

MNESILOCHOS, *his elderly relative*

AGATHON, *playwright*

HIS SECRETARY

HERALDESS

MIKKA, KRITYLLA, MYRTLE-SELLER, ORGANISER, *festival-goers*

KLEISTHENES, *poet*

CONSTABLE

DANCING-GIRL, MANIA, PHILISTA, THRATTA *(silent parts)*

CHORUS OF WOMEN

## Synopsis

Euripides drags his protesting relative Mnesilochos to Agathon's house. The women of Athens are going to censure him, at an all-female festival, for slandering them in his plays, and he wants Agathon to dress as a woman and plead his case. Agathon refuses but lends Euripides a dress, high-heeled shoes and a wig. They dress Mnesilochos as a woman and send him to the festival.

At the festival, the women make speeches attacking Euripides for revealing their feminine secrets, and Mnesilochos defends him on the grounds that there's a great deal more he *hasn't* told. The effeminate poet Kleisthenes reports that one of the 'women' is a man in disguise, and Mnesilochos is unveiled. He kidnaps a 'baby', but when he holds it to ransom he discovers that it's a wineskin and drinks it dry. The women go for the police, and Mnesilochos desperately sends word to Euripides to rescue him.

Time passes, filled by a chorus about the way men disparage women. Mnesilochos impersonates Helen in Euripides' play, longing for her husband Menelaos to come to Egypt and rescue her. Euripides duly arrives as Menelaos, and the two play as much as they can remember of the rescue scene from Euripides' play, much to the annoyance of Kritylla who has been left on guard. Euripides hurries out as the festival organiser arrives with a policeman, and Mnesilochos is pilloried to await his punishment. The chorus sing in honour of Demeter and Persephone, whose festival this is. Euripides flies overhead on the theatre crane, attempting in vain to land as Perseus on the flying horse Pegasos, come to rescue Andromeda. The policeman goes for a whip. Euripides creeps in disguised as Echo, and tells the bemused Mnesilochos to pretend to be Andromeda. The policeman comes back and fends off Euripides/Perseus with his scimitar. Euripides goes offstage and returns as a brothel-keeper, with a pretty dancing-girl. While the policeman is chasing the dancing-girl, he and Mnesilochos escape at last.

## About the play

Aristophanes produced *Festival Time* in 411, the same year as *Lysistrata*. The play's Greek name, *Thesmophoriazousai*, 'Women Celebrating the Thesmophoria', refers to a three-day annual festival in honour of Demeter goddess of harvest and her daughter Persephone – a 'mystery' exclusive to women, about which Athenian men must have known as little as modern Western women might know about the meetings of Freemasons.

A striking feature of *Festival Time*, as of *Lysistrata*, is the variety of opportunity it offers male actors for performing effeminate or travesty roles. In *Festival Time* the leading actor, playing Mnesilochos, is given wonderful scope to parody femininity – the whole point is the ineptness of Mnesilochos' drag acting. The second actor parodies femininity more briefly, appearing as the nymph Echo and as a brothel-keeper, but otherwise plays the aggressively masculine Euripides, assuming heroic roles from his own tragedies. (If the theory is true that by this stage in his career Aristophanes had stopped playing principal roles and begun taking second-actor parts, in this play he would be playing the writer who had for years been his principal artistic butt and possibly his friend

– a delicious 'in joke'.) The actors, sharing the other roles, play the gamut from camp males (Agathon, his secretary and Kleisthenes) to women whose characters may be different – Mikka ('Spark'), the harassed myrtle-seller, the headmistressy organiser and the bemused but fierce Kritylla – but all of whom, like the members of the chorus, are expected to give no suggestion that they are played by males. The policeman veers from camp aggression towards Mnesilochos to lasciviousness when he sees the dancing-girl. This character may have been played by a (male) dancer, or – since you could hire a female slave for less than the price of dinner – by a real woman, the only genuine female in the production.

The similarity between this range of characterisation and that in *Lysistrata* raises interesting, if unanswerable, questions about Aristophanes' theatre-company in 411. Did the same actors appear in both plays? Was 411 a good year for that highly skilled activity, travesty acting? Were all or some of the costumes reused, as a wartime economy measure? Variety of travesty performance is an important factor in creating the shifting presentation of illusion and reality throughout the play. The actors are men playing women. The audience is all male (or may have had a small number of women in it) watching the comic simulacrum of an all-female festival. Two of the main characters are playwrights, creators of illusion, and one of them (Agathon) is both renowned for writing and appearing in travesty roles, and markedly effeminate in 'real' life. To escape from the 'reality' of his imprisonment, the leading character impersonates trapped heroines in plays, and escapes when his guard is tricked by a playwright playing not a character from one of his own fictions but a bawd invented *ad hoc*, Dunabunka. The chorus end the play by jeering at this guard as he runs frantically from the stage in search of a shadow woman – not the least of the 'in jokes' about Euripides' *Helen* which permeate the play.

In *Festival Time*, as in *Lysistrata*, Aristophanes replaces the 'hierarchical' style of the acting company found in his earlier surviving plays – one in which the leading actor plays the star role and gets the best lines – with a much more company-oriented allocation of initiative. (Unlike in *Lysistrata*, where the chorus take a major part in the dramatic action, here their role is reduced and fairly serious, leaving comedy to the professionals.) Each actor gets his chance to lead scenes and take the comic initiative, and the third actor in particular (playing Agathon, one of the women and possibly the policeman) is given a challenging and satisfying range of parts. At the heart of the whole enterprise Euripides and Mnesilochos, like all great double acts, give the impression that they are indissolubly linked and with a joint identity separate from all the other characters, indeed from the general 'reality' of the play. This feeling is established at the very opening, when we seem to be eavesdropping on an ongoing grumble which involves the participants alone and has nothing to do with the main action. Laurel and Hardy, Abbott and Costello, Burns and Allen, Morecambe and Wise – any of the twentieth century's great double acts could have played this scene with hardly a word or inflexion changed – and the feeling of complicity against the world, the continuum of comfortable mutual affection and aggression, affects everything which subsequently happens. The balance between the two characters, established in this scene, is maintained throughout – so successfully that one wonders whether this double act was created by Aristophanes or developed from real-life complicity, in this case a long-standing relationship between the author-performer and his leading actor Kallippides.

MNESILOCHOS
Zeus almighty! Talk about early birds and worms.
He'll be the death of me. He's been lugging me round
Since breakfast time. Oi! Before I collapse entirely,
I'd like to hear where you're taking me, Euripides.

EURIPIDES
You can't. You mustn't. You can't say *hear*
When what you mean is *see.*

MNESILOCHOS
Pardon? Say that again.
I can't say *hear* –

**EURIPIDES**

For *see*. Not *hear* for *see*.

**MNESILOCHOS**

What about *see* for *hear*?

**EURIPIDES**

*See* for *hear*? See, hear? No, no.

**MNESILOCHOS**

You put it so well. But what does it mean?
Are you saying I mustn't see *or* hear?

**EURIPIDES**

They're entirely disjunct phenomena.

**MNESILOCHOS**

Not seeing and not hearing?

**EURIPIDES**

Precisely.

**MNESILOCHOS**

How d'you mean, disjunct?

**EURIPIDES**

Like this ... (*etc.*)

# Frogs

## Characters

DIONYSOS, *god of drama*
XANTHIAS, *his slave*
HERAKLES
CORPSE
CHARON, *ferryman of the Underworld*
AIAKOS, *gate-guard of the Underworld*
SERVANT GIRL
LANDLADY
PLATHANE, *her friend*
EURIPIDES
AESCHYLUS
PLUTO, *ruler of the Underworld*
CORPSE-BEARERS, EURIPIDES' MUSE, MUSICIANS, SLAVES (*silent parts*)
CHORUS OF FROGS
CHORUS OF HOLY ONES

## Synopsis

Aeschylus, Sophocles and Euripides are all dead, their successors are worthless, and Dionysos is in despair. He decides to visit the Underworld, disguised as Herakles the hero, to bring back Euripides. After rowing across the river Styx (battling a chorus of frogs who keep throwing out his rhythm) he knocks on the gate of the Underworld. Aiakos the gate-guard doesn't recognise him, and tests his identity by beating him. Then he says that Dionysos is just the person to adjudicate in an argument between Aeschylus and Euripides for the Throne of Poetry.

After a choral ode about the way Athens is letting politics get in the way of self-preservation, Euripides and Aeschylus appear before Dionysos to present their cases. They examine each other's works play by play, scene by scene, line by line, testing themes, style, prologues, vocabulary and music. No test is conclusive, even when Dionysos insists that the playwrights see who is weightier by climbing into the pans of a pair of scales. Dionysos asks them to advise the Athenians what to do about Alcibiades, but doesn't understand a word they say. Pluto insists on a decision, and Dionysos chooses Aeschylus and leads him to the Upper World as Euripides sulks and the chorus sing a hymn of praise.

## About the play

*Frogs* was first produced in 405, in the last months of the Peloponnesian War. Aristophanes was in his forties.

The heart of the play is not slapstick or literary criticism (though both are brilliantly effective), but rebirth. The chorus are initiates of Iacchos, Dionysos in his most mysterious aspect, lord of the moment when we shed one form of being and enter another. Their first appearance, in a torchlight procession some fifth of the way through the action, must have been one of the most spine-tingling moments in surviving ancient theatre:

Iacchos,
Here in this holy place,
Iacchos, O Iacchos,
Dance with us,
Sing with us,
Toss your head,
Flower-crowned,
In the holy dance ...
Shine in our darkness, lord.
Iacchos, O Iacchos,
Morning star,
End night for us,
Shine for us ...

– and their later advice to the audience, not to neglect long-serving soldiers who favoured the 'wrong' general in the political in-fighting which marked this period of the war, has an edge of desperation which sets it apart from the advice handed out in his other surviving plays. Perhaps significantly in the political context of the first production, when Dionysos imposes his last test on Aeschylus and Euripides – the question about Alcibiades – to see who is fit to return to the upper world, to be reborn, their answers are purest gibberish:

> What you trust, distrust, and start to trust
> What you distrusted heretofore. (Euripides)

and

> Make enemy land your own, your land their land.
> Make taxes ships. Who sails on silver coins? (Aeschylus)

For modern audiences, darkness of this kind can be less apparent than the flow of comic invention which makes *Frogs* one of Aristophanes' most enjoyable works despite its arcane subject matter. From start to finish, the jokes and routines have a feeling of aptness, inevitability, rare even in his work – the range is from the surly corpse who refuses to carry Dionysos' baggage down to Hell to the scales which weigh the dramatists at the end, from Dionysos' Euripidean musings on which gods are responsible for the monster Empousa ('Air, Zeus' garden shed? The foot of time?') to Euripides' Muse, dancing 'in the Lesbian mode'. The scene in which Aiakos tries to determine which of his visitors, Dionysos or the slave Xanthias, is the 'real' god by thrashing them is topped only by Dionysos' invocation, at the height of his terror, of his own (real) priest, sitting in a throne of honour in the front row of the audience. Nothing is extraneous and nothing is wasted. *Frogs* is one of the most economical comedies in literature.

Over the years, scholars have mined the play's last third for literary criticism, with mixed results. We learn that Aeschylus is long-winded but magnificent, Euripides innovative but 'slippery'. We hear a couple of dozen authentic lines, wrenched out of context, and enjoy parodies of style. A moment's reflection on similar treatment, by modern comedians, of literary figures, should make it clear how close such material is likely to lie to the red meat of literary comment. When a modern jokester, soliciting laughter from a large and heterogeneous audience, claims to be subjecting 'modern art' to close examination, the last thing we expect is academic rigour. The Aeschylus and Euripides in this play are probably no nearer their real-life equivalents than are Aristophanes' Kleon or Theramenes or Socrates. Aeschylus represents the 'good old days' and Euripides the avant-garde, and that is enough. Aristophanes' parodies are brilliant, but that does not make them accurate:

> O clamorous clanchief, the warfare is woeful –
> Drub, drub the doom-drum, rush to the rescue.
> We lake-lovers clamour for Hermes our helpmeet –
> Drub, drub the doom-drum, rush to the rescue ...
>
> (Aeschylus)

or

> Kingfishers, diving, arriving
> At the salt sea spray at the water's edge,
> Chattering, spattering
> Their wings with watery wetness,
> Then flying high where spiders spin
> Spi-i-i-i-i-i-in
> Webs woven under roof-rafters ...   (Euripides)

The relationship of such lines to the 'reality' of what they mock is tenuous.

In common with Aristophanes' later surviving plays, *Frogs* is formally innovative. All three main actors share the comic initiative, passing it between them from scene to scene. The beating scene shows this virtuoso dramatic construction at peak: a 'three-hander' or triple-act in which every partner is equal. Aristophanes reinvents the 'impostors' of earlier plays so thoroughly that they lose 'impostor' status entirely: the corpse, the landlady and Plathane, Aiakos, Pluto. The formal argument, displaced from its keystone position in earlier plays, now leads the plot to climax. Above all, the choral *parabasis* (in which Aristophanes advises the audience about soldiers who have followed the 'wrong' leader) is highlighted by incongruity, standing proud from the hilarity all round it. Academic commentators in the past sometimes attacked the play for 'tiredness', ignoring or relegating its comic effervescence and over-emphasising the 'irrelevance to real life' of the poetic contest. This is nonsense. Modern audiences have little trouble understanding what Aeschylus, Euripides and Dionysos are talking about, and the gusto of the earlier scenes carries all before it. The play still lives.

# Knights

## Characters

DEMOSTHENES

NIKIAS

AGORAKRITOS

PAPHLAGON

DEMOS

SLAVES, DECKCHAIR ATTENDANT, TWO GORGEOUS GIRLS (*silent parts*)

CHORUS OF KNIGHTS

## Synopsis

Two slaves, Demosthenes and Nikias, complain that Paphlagon, a newly purchased slave, is exerting too much control over their elderly master Demos. They steal Paphlagon's prophecies which reveal that he can only be defeated by someone who is even worse than he is. They enlist the sausage-seller Agorakritos as their champion. After a series of farcical contests, he eventually defeats Paphlagon and rejuvenates the decrepit Demos.

## About the play

*Knights* was staged at the Lenaia in 424, winning first prize. *Knights*, like *Acharnians*, operates on a domestic scale appropriate to the Lenaia both in terms of its specifically Athenian political undertones and in terms of its staging demands, which are the most modest of the extant plays. It requires no machinery, only one door and the costumes only have to represent recognisable types: slaves and knights rather than frogs or birds. The play is an attack on Kleon, a politician who was the consistent target of Aristophanes' satire. The Knights who form the chorus are

Athenian citizens who performed their military service as cavalry-men rather than foot soldiers. They were therefore wealthy, since they could afford to maintain their own horses. There is some evidence to suggest that there was some kind of extra-dramatic conflict between Kleon and the Knights prior to the play.

In this play the upstart slave Paphlagon (Kleon) is defeated by the sausage-seller in a popularity contest for the favours of Demos, who, as his name suggests, represents the People. The text alludes to the possibility that a Kleon-like mask might have been created for Paphlagon, but the mask-makers were too timid. Aristophanes does not name the two slaves who open the play complaining about the antics of Paphlagon, but it is clear from the textual references (and possibly from their masks and costuming) that they are meant to be identified with the Athenian generals Demosthenes and Nikias. Part of the play re-enacts in comic parody the political situation of the preceding year, 425. Demosthenes was the general besieging Spartan troops on Sphakteria, Kleon had persuaded the Athenians to demand more concessions from the Spartans than they were willing to accept. When the siege dragged on, Kleon, under political pressure from Nikias, was forced to say he could raise the siege. Kleon made good his claim, but according to the historian Thucydides (c.460–400 BC), who is hostile to him, he took undue credit for work that had been done by other generals. Identifying the two slaves with the two generals explains some of the claims and counter-claims in the contest between the sausage-seller and Paphlagon for Demos' ear.

*Knights* is a free-wheeling comedy that adopts a significant number of strategies to attack Kleon. One of the accusations against Kleon was that he was a populist who adopted new rhetorical tricks to sway the assembly and that he courted the assemblymen by offering them rewards based on taxing the rich. At the level of allegory the play initially sets up Demos as the People, Kleon as Paphlagon, who tricks the people by pretending that his self-serving actually helps them, and the two displaced slaves who are the generals in trouble at Pylos. But the situation moves between the political and the domestic. Although the contest will eventually become one for Demos' favour it begins with the two slaves looking for someone who will fulfil a prophecy that Paphlagon can only be displaced by someone even more vulgar and venial than he is. Aristophanes is not concerned at all here with consistency of approach since he starts with the premise that the sausage-seller has to show his suitability for power by out-blaggarding the blaggard Paphlagon but then, in the actual contest for Demos' favours, the trick is to show who is the most altruistic. The sausage-seller makes his living from catering to people's basic needs for food but his products, with their phallic overtones, also reduce high-minded debate to the traditional comic staple of appetite. He tends to win arguments by asserting his basic understanding of appetite and his openness contrasts with the hypocritical approach of Paphlagon. Perhaps the key moment in the contest over Demos comes when the sausage-seller does what Aristophanes accuses Kleon of having done at Pylos, that is steal what someone else has prepared and claim it as his own. The comic theft of food defeats the Kleon figure whose triumph at Pylos was (allegedly) based on stealing another man's triumph. One of the ironies of Aristophanes' satire is that he uses precisely the same kinds of rhetorical tricks that he condemns Kleon for in order to persuade his audience against him. The Knights and Agorakritos the sausage-seller combine to defeat the demagogic Kleon in a process that reflects on the ways in which Aristophanes, an educated upper-class poet, uses the democratic medium of comedy to advance a political viewpoint that is anti-demagogic.

Aristophanes' concern with Kleon is matched throughout his career by dissatisfaction with what he regarded as an Athenian tendency to look to politicians for a quick fix and then discard them for someone offering novelty. However, there is something very direct in *Knights* in the way that the antagonism to Kleon is the structuring principle of confrontation. There is a lack of logic in the contest but that perhaps reflects Aristophanes' sense of the way that public debate turns on illogical and ephemeral issues rather than strict logic and dispassionate assessment of the public good. The politician is in a contest with other politicians for the favour of the public just as the poet is in competition with other poets. Thus the play's references to other dramatists in the *parabasis* also act as a reminder of the parallels between artistic and political discourse and, since the comedy itself is a civic act, it too has a role to play in cleansing the state. Aristophanes' political and theatrical projects are parallel: through his theatrical expulsion of the Kleon figure he rejuvenates the body politic as represented by Demos. Indeed the revitalised Demos reappears dressed in the fashionable garb of the heroic period of the struggles against the Persians. Aristophanes hopes his audience will recognise his poetic worth by giving him the prize but also hopes that his symbolic process of cleansing will result in a more heroic politics.

# Lysistrata

## Characters

LYSISTRATA

KALONIKE, MYRRHINE, *her neighbours*

LAMPITO, *a Spartan*

KINESIAS, *Myrrhine's husband*

ATHENIAN COMMISSIONER

SPARTAN MESSENGER

BABY

CITIZEN

DEFECTOR

DOORKEEPER

OLD MAN

OLD WOMAN

THEBAN WOMAN

CITIZENS, CONSTABLES, CORINTHIAN, ORDERLY, RECONCILIATION, SERGEANT, SLAVES, SPARTANS (*silent parts*)

CHORUS OF OLD MEN

CHORUS OF OLD WOMEN

## Synopsis

At the Acropolis entrance, Lysistrata waits impatiently. She has invited women from all over Greece to come and help her end the Peloponnesian War. One by one the women arrive, including Lysistrata's neighbours Kalonike and Myrrhine and the Spartan Lampito. They are eager to help until Lysistrata says that her plan involves refusing marital sex until peace is made. But she persuades them, and they reluctantly swear an oath using a phallic wineskin. They go into the Acropolis and barricade the gate.

The chorus of old men come to burn down the gate, but the old women douse their flames by throwing water from the battlements above. An Athenian commissioner argues with Lysistrata about whether or not women have the mental capacity to run state affairs and put an end to war. He refuses to listen 'to someone in a dress', and the women put him in female clothes and conduct a mock funeral.

After another standoff between the male and female choruses, Lysistrata has to stop some of the women slipping home for sex. Kinesias, Myrrhine's husband, arrives, and Myrrhine puts Lysistrata's plan into action, seducing him, offering him sex then and there in exchange for peace. As his frustration mounts, she fetches a bed, a pillow, a blanket, scented oil (in a phallic flask) – and then runs inside when he refuses to agree to peace. A Spartan delegation arrives, bent double with sexual frustration, and they and the commissioner agree to make peace if the terms are right. Lysistrata uses a pretty woman, Reconciliation, as a map of Greece, and the men drool over her. But terms are finally settled, and the play ends with a sequence of dances to welcome peace.

## About the play

*Lysistrata* was first performed in 411, the same year as *Festival Time.* Aristophanes was in his mid thirties, at the peak of his career.

Each of the plays was performed at a different festival, and there is argument about which was which. The traditional view is that *Lysistrata* was performed at the more domestic Lenaia, *Festival Time* at the City Dionysia. This seems to some to contradict the nature of the plays – *Festival Time* is a farce with specifically 'local' themes, *Lysistrata* a more serious affair with implications for international politics. But politics, precisely, may explain why the traditional placing is the right one. By 411 the Peloponnesian War had lasted for two decades, and there was no sign of its ending. Athenian morale had been devastated, some eighteen months previously, by the destruction of the glittering expedition sent to Sicily. In 411 there were stirrings of political revolt, culminating in a coup which replaced democratic rule with a puppet council ('the Four Hundred') controlled by Persia, the old adversary of eighty years before. The movement was short-lived and a failure, but it must have poisoned the air at the time of *Lysistrata*'s first performance, at whichever festival that took place. A play as controversial as this – not only bringing Spartans onstage and treating them like human beings, but also showing the Athenian authorities capitulating to a coup inside the city – may not have seemed ideal fare for a festival like the City Dionysia, visited by allies and other visitors from overseas.

For centuries Western commentators, brought up in the tradition of Christian attitudes to sex, tended to be shocked by what they claimed was *Lysistrata*'s 'licentiousness'. The Myrrhine-Kinesias scene and the scene when the women try to escape from the citadel for sexual relief were particularly deplored. But ancient Athenian attitudes to such matters were different, and to its original audience this aspect of *Lysistrata* may well have seemed genial and uncontroversial. In any case the play is about frustration, not licence, and sexual fulfilment is a metaphor for the release that will come with peace.

In fact the original spectators would probably have been startled by something else entirely. Each of Aristophanes' plays involves the hero doing a 'great and mighty deed' which replaces the unpleasant status quo. Most of these 'deeds' are as surreal as they are effective (for example, becoming birds or visiting the Under-world). In *Lysistrata*, written for a society where, as Lysistrata points out to the commissioner, women were expected to stay at home keeping their thoughts to themselves and leaving 'big issues' to 'their betters', the idea of women taking a political initiative and making it work may have seemed just as unreal to the (mainly male) theatre audience. Aristophanes trumps this expectation ironically, by making his women better than men at every 'male' activity they undertake. But he is not playing sexual politics so much as making far more serious points about peace and war. Like Euripides' *Women of Troy*, another war play centred on women, *Lysistrata* uses the convention of male actors playing female roles to ironise the spectacle, an alienation effect which adds pungency, by performance alone, to the over-riding theme.

Technically speaking, *Lysistrata* breaks with Aristophanes' earlier style to such an extent that it seems almost experimental. The chorus are divided, and utterances which might have been theirs in a more 'traditional' play are given to named individuals (Kalonike, Myrrhine), with distinct personal characters. The *alazon* scenes (see Glossary, p.293) are not clustered in the second half but scattered through the action – Aristophanes replaces random set-pieces with sequences integrated with the plot, for example the phantom pregnancy or the fire-and-water battle between the halves of the chorus. The finest *alazon* scene, between Myrrhine and Kinesias, unlike every other surviving *alazon* scene in Aristophanes, does not involve the play's leading character – a reflection of the 'company' performance articulation throughout *Lysistrata*, so different from the hierarchical structure of his earlier plays and foreshadowing even more radical later developments. The play demands from the chorus far more than the straightforward attitudinising found in such earlier comedies as *Acharnians* or *Peace*. They express a range of forceful and individual opinions, initiate slapstick, keep a delicate balance between lampoon and lyricism. We have no information about what the performers in comedy choruses were like, especially in wartime. But this chorus seem to require ability outside the usual range.

The fact that everything about *Lysistrata* – theme, political overtones, language, dramatic style – now seems subversive raises questions about the nature of the society for which it was written and the place of comic theatre, perhaps theatre in general, within that society. The play has regularly been banned by subsequent political and social régimes, on one ground or another, and its name on a theatre billboard still seems to some people to guarantee an evening which is 'risky' in every sense. If we project ourselves back to the situation of the original performance, there seem plenty of reasons why it should have pricked its spectators – not least, perhaps, its pervasive war-weariness and the political impotence so dazzlingly revealed by the controlling metaphor (in which the impotent, in the widest sense, become potent and the potent, in every sense, are made impotent). But if at the time there was outrage, or even comment, not a hint survives. Athens' politicians went on with their lives as if *Lysistrata* had never existed. And although Aristophanes went on to write political satire as part of other plays (not least *Frogs* and *Women in Power*), he seems never again to have tackled the political situation head-on. *Lysistrata* is the last in its genre, both among his surviving plays and those others about which anything is known, and the slowing down of his theatrical activity seems to have begun soon afterwards. Perhaps the situation in 411 was too desperate, or too cynical, for even his barbs and his common sense to influence people's attitudes. Or perhaps, as some commentators claim, comedy *is* principally a medium for entertainment rather than education, and no comedian has ever changed the world.

# Peace

## Characters

TRYGAIOS

TRYGAIOS' TWO SLAVES

TRYGAIOS' ELDEST CHILD

HERMES

WAR

QUARREL

HIEROKLES

SICKLE-MAKER

ARMOURER

TWO BOYS

TRYGAIOS' YOUNGER CHILDREN, CITIZEN, COMMANDOS, DUNG-
BEETLE, ARMOURER'S FRIENDS, HARVEST, HOLIDAY, LAMACHOS,
PEACE (*a statue*), SHEEP (*silent parts*)

CHORUS OF GREEKS

## Synopsis

Trygaios, a farmer, has decided to visit Zeus in heaven to demand
peace. He has fattened up a dung-beetle in order to make the
precarious journey. When he arrives in heaven he finds that all
the gods except Hermes, who remains as caretaker, have left,
disillusioned with the Greeks' quarrelling. They have leased heaven
to War (personified as a god) who has sealed Peace in a cavern and
is preparing to grind the Greek cities up into a meal. Trygaios
bribes Hermes to let Peace escape and with the help of the chorus
(representing a cross-section of Greece) they release her from
captivity. Peace, a statue, is accompanied by two nubile companions, Harvest and Holiday. Trygaios returns with them to Athens,
presents Holiday to the council men in the audience and marries
Harvest in a final section expressing the joys of peace and the
rhythms of nature.

## About the play

*Peace* won second prize at the Great Dionysia in 421. The Peloponnesian War had been continuing since 431 but negotiations that would lead to the Peace of Nikias were well under way when the play was performed. This may have contributed to its only gaining second prize, since the original idea was, presumably, that Trygaios' deed in getting peace back from heaven by direct action was a fantasy, whereas by the time the play was staged something that had seemed to demand a bizarre supernatural journey had been reduced to diplomatic negotiation.

The play itself makes exuberant use of the resources of the theatre. The emphasis is on the joys of peace, on festivity rather than on the grim realities of war. The goal of peace can only be achieved through the use of the lowest and stagiest means, a fact emphasised by the way that the play moves from a drama of dung and broad farce to one of feasts and marriage, from knockabout to lyrical celebratory comedy.

As in many of Aristophanes' plays the action derives from a combination of factors, using mythological frameworks, contemporary theatrical practices and contemporary politics to create its heady satirical-comic mix. Trygaios' quest to heaven is itself an inversion of a familiar literary theme involving the gods journeying to earth. Aristophanes' presentation of the idea of flying to heaven on a giant dung-beetle parodies more heroic flights such as Bellerophon's on the winged horse Pegasos (the subject of a lost play by Euripides), and his play also draws on one of Aesop's fables in which a dung-beetle avenges herself on Zeus' eagle by going to heaven and eating its eggs. The giant dung-beetle was, of course, a stage prop and the journey was accomplished by using the machine, a crane that could hoist an actor and the beetle and swing them from one place to another. The play itself parodies the action of the machine and draws attention to its inadequacies. Some critics have worried about the location of the scenes but while the stage may respresent a heaven that Trygaios had to fly to, it is also accessible to the chorus. It is also always a stage around which a very obvious machine trundles a very obvious prop on which an actor sits precariously, commenting both on his metaphorical journey and on his actual journey about the stage, even directing a remark to the actual crane operator.

There is a distinct contrast between the presentation of War and Peace in the play: Peace, when she appears, is a statue, becoming an important visual reference point throughout the play: a silent pervasive presence open to interpretation. War, on the other hand, is a braggart-soldier type, ineffectual but full of bluster. War's plans to grind up the cities are thwarted because he hasn't got a pestle, so he sends Quarrel first to Athens and then to Sparta to borrow theirs, but they have both lost them. This is a topical reference to the deaths of Kleon, the Athenian leader whom Aristophanes lampooned for his venality and war-mongering, and the Spartan general Brasidas. Both had been killed at the Battle of Amphipolis in 422. In the *parabasis* Aristophanes continues to heap dispraise on Kleon despite his death, but once the statue of Peace has been recovered Aristophanes can leave behind the beetle, the dung and Kleon to develop a Peace plot instead. Some critics have argued that the departure of War, never to return, is a dramatic weakness, since Trygaios does not defeat War within the scheme of the play, but Aristophanes simply chose to switch his focus from the negative to the positive by abandoning War to his pestle-making. Aristophanes not only celebrates peace, he banishes invocations to war gods and onstage sacrifice (with a theatrical joke about needing the property sheep again).

Once Peace is returned to earth, despite opposition from those who profit from war, the instruments of war are converted to more mundane use and Hierokles' pro-war oracles can be defeated both by counter-oracle and also by scraps of food. Ultimately the lyrical quality of the speeches delivered by Trygaios and the chorus when Peace is recovered and the chorus that begins significantly with 'Happiness! Happiness', not only suggest an appreciation of and longing for the benefits of peace but they also enact a desired state in a compelling fashion.

The final feast in the play is a mark of how far things have come since the beginning when we were presented with the ceremonious preparation of the dung-beetle's meal of rolled dung, a sharp contrast to the preparations for the concluding feast. Once Peace has been recovered, the play emphasises the positive pleasures of peace rather than threats to those pleasures, so that the relative absence of conflict in the later stages of the play challenges conventional notions of the necessity of dramatic conflict.

# Wasps

## Characters

BDELYKLEON

PHILOKLEON, *his father*

SOSIAS, XANTHIAS, *their slaves*

BOY

CITIZEN

BREAD-WOMAN

BOYS, CHAIREPHON, DARDANIS (*dancing-girl*), DOGS (SNITCH *and* SNATCH), DONKEY, DRUNKS, KITCHEN UTENSILS, PUPPIES, SLAVES, WITNESS (*silent parts*)

KARKINOS, *his sons* (*dancers*)

CHORUS OF AGED JURYMEN (*the* 'Wasps')

## Synopsis

The Wasps are veterans paid a dole to sit on juries. They wear striped coats and 'sting' their victims: hence the nickname. One old man, Philokleon, has an upwardly-mobile son, Bdelykleon, who locks him indoors and puts a net over the house to stop him slipping off to court. Philokleon tries to break out, and he and Bdelykleon argue their points of view before the chorus. Philokleon says that he likes being a juryman and enjoys the respect it brings him. Bdelykleon says that the Wasps are dupes of wily politicians, and that he will look after his father and see that he has work and respect at home.

Bdelykleon builds a domestic court in the garden, and Philokleon tries the case of the cheese-stealing dog Snatch. The witnesses are another dog, Snitch, and a collection of kitchen utensils. Bdelykleon tricks Philokleon into giving a 'Not guilty' verdict, the first in a lifetime. He takes his (now reformed) father indoors to prepare him for society, and the chorus sing of the good old days and the way Aristophanes has always stood up against cheating politicians. Philokleon comes out, complaining about the new clothes and shoes he has to wear, and goes off to a banquet after practising polite manners and dinner-table jokes. After a choral interlude lampooning notorious members of (real) society, Philokleon comes back, drunk, with a dancing-girl in tow and pursued by a citizen and a bread-woman he has insulted. Bdelykleon takes his father inside to sober him up, but Philokleon soon bursts out again and challenges the dancer Karkinos and his sons to a contest of dances which ends the play.

## About the play

*Wasps* first appeared at the Lenaia of 422, during the brief lull in the Peloponnesian War known as the 'Peace of Nikias'. Aristophanes was in his mid twenties.

*Wasps* is the third play in a group of four written in consecutive years and centring on the same kind of outrageous, anarchic comic hero. (The others are *Knights*, 424, centring on Agorakritos, *Clouds*, 423, centring on Strepsiades, and *Peace*, 421, centring on Trygaios.) Although, apart from similarities of comic style, there is no proof that the parts were all written for the same actor, perhaps Aristophanes himself, this remains a possibility. All four roles are scene-stealers, but none rivals Philokleon for sheer exuberance. He embodies the Dionysian spirit of subversion, of delight in contrariness for its own sake; he erupts through the bounds of convention and makes ordinariness his butt simply because it is there; he is a descendant of Silenos, the drunken old lecher who leads Dionysos' satyrs, and the ancestor of such later figures in European comedy as the Lord of Misrule, the Pantaloon of *commedia dell'arte*, Gargantua, Falstaff and Mr Punch.

Aristophanes' demands on the actor are commensurate with the part. The performer is onstage for four-fifths of the action, with strategically placed breaks to catch his breath or change his costume. He plays every conceivable kind of slapstick, including such *tours de force* as the domestic court scene and the drunk scene. He sings, in a variety of styles ranging from Euripidean parody to patter song. He has scenes of quickfire comic dialogue with the second actor, and takes part in a mock debate sending up schoolroom rhetoric. He plays a dozen impersonations including Odysseus escaping from Polyphemos, a learned judge and an upper-class dinner-guest expert at light conversation and 'fanny flaunt'. He ends the play by challenging four dancers to a competition in comic dancing culminating in the virtuoso *kordax* or 'twister'. It makes more virtuoso demands on the actor's skills than any other role in the surviving canon of Greek comedy.

As in *Knights* and *Clouds*, Aristophanes in *Wasps* turns his attention from issues of war and peace to more domestic matters. The background to this play is the system of *euthune* ('putting straight') which required every elected official in Athens, at the end of his term of office, to subject himself to public account, to have his decisions and his finances scrutinised by a jury of 'ordinary' citizens. These juries were chosen from a pool of 6,000 people, and were often several hundred strong. Instead of listening to objective evidence from professional lawyers and accountants, they heard the cases argued by politicians and orators, and their decisions – which could make or break a man's career – were influenced as much by rhetoric and sentiment as by the facts. At the time of the play Kleon, leader of the Athenian war-party, was notorious for the unscrupulous use he made of the *euthune* system to discredit rivals, and also because he ensured the jurors' loyalty by paying them three obols (half a drachma) a day, a kind of dole. Young, able-bodied men tended to be away from Athens on military service, and the pool of jurymen therefore consisted mainly of veterans, dependent for survival equally on handouts and on misty memories of their own 'glory days' at Marathon and Salamis – feelings of which Kleon and his cronies took full advantage.

The dodderiness of the Wasps in the play, coupled with the stately nature of the choral odes and the fact that Philokleon and a group of dancers perform most of the physical action, has suggested to some that the chorus of this play were themselves ex-servicemen, whose presence gave pungency to the generation conflict which is *Wasps*' main theme. There is no proof of this theory, but if true it would give the play an edge hard to appreciate today. In a similar way, topical satire must have added danger to the trial scene, already a piece of dazzling comic invention. Kleon was fond of calling himself 'watchdog of the state', he was nicknamed 'Dog' because of his ferocious, barking style of public speaking – and in this court scene the defendant is a dog accused by his crony of stealing a piece of Sicilian cheese. If the fact that the defendant was a dog would remind people of Kleon, the dog's name Labes, 'Snatch', would also suggest his aide-de-camp Laches, widely suspected of taking bribes while serving in Sicily. The trial scene is a kind of comic *euthune* of that accusation. Laches, 'Labes', 'Dog', Kleon – Aristophanes stirs the pot and then leaves his spectators, and the politicians involved, to make what they like of it.

Details of this kind, and the wealth of allusions to food, clothes, doors, window-frames, ladders and other details of everyday Athenian life, have over the years made *Wasps* a happy hunting-ground for scholars. Unfortunately they have also damaged its reputation with theatre managers and stage directors, so that in performance it is one of the most neglected of all Aristophanes' plays. Onstage, however, scholarly concerns disappear. The references are perfectly understandable in terms of the action alone, needing no notes and baffling no spectators. The jokes are funny and the play is a crescendo of slapstick action. Above all else, the gusto of the central role, the pleasure of watching a comic actor challenged to display, and exult in, every aspect of his professional skill, carries all before it.

# Wealth

## Characters

CHREMYLOS

KARION

BLEPSIDEMOS

POVERTY

CHREMYLOS' WIFE

CITIZEN

SECRET POLICEMAN

OLD WOMAN

YOUNG MAN

HERMES

PRIEST

SLAVE, WITNESS (*silent parts*)

CHORUS OF ELDERLY FARMERS

## Synopsis

Chremylos and his slave Karion are following a blind old man from the oracle at Delphi. He was the first person they saw after the oracle told them to take home the first person they saw. After some not so gentle persuasion, the man admits that he is Wealth, blinded by Zeus so that he would not be able to associate with deserving people. Chremylos and Karion persuade him that he is more powerful than Zeus and Chremylos sends Karion off to fetch his farmer friends (who will form the chorus). The task now is to restore Wealth's sight so that they can all become wealthy, and so they decide to take him to the shrine of the healing god Asklepios.

Poverty appears, like 'the Demon Queen/From some Greek tragedy', to put her counter-claim to be vital to human happiness. Although she puts up a spirited fight, Chremylos dismisses her. After a choral dance Karion reappears to tell Chremylos' wife how Wealth's sight has been restored at the shrine. Wealth and

Chremylos then arrive and Karion tells the audience how the house has been transformed with riches and abundance. A citizen who had been impoverished as a result of his generosity appears with gifts for Wealth to celebrate his restoration to riches. A secret policemen who had profited from the old dispensation tries to restore the old ways but Karion defeats him. An old woman complains that her toyboy has deserted her now that wealth is readily available elsewhere. When he arrives to thank Wealth, they go off with the issue between them unresolved. Hermes then appears, out of a job as no one is sacrificing to the gods any more since they have everything they need. Karion employs him as a menial servant. Finally the priest of Zeus arrives, asking to join in the new wealth. A procession then takes Wealth back to the treasury and the old woman is told the toyboy will still come round.

## About the play

*Wealth* dates from 388 but we don't know which festival it was performed at, nor what prize it won. Aristophanes had written an earlier *Wealth*, performed in 408, and the surviving play is probably a revision of that text. Most of Aristophanes' extant work dates from the darkest days of the Peloponnesian War, but by 388 Athens had undergone something of a recovery from the crushing defeat and there was no obvious topical reason for tackling the question of wealth.

There are some contemporary political references in the play but, like *Women in Power*, its subject is less overtly political than Aristophanes' earlier extant work. However, Chremylos has the familiar fantastic task to perform, in his case curing Wealth, even though his initial dissatisfaction, which is also typical, has little direct bearing on his ultimate project. He does, after all, start off by asking the oracle whether his son should behave well or badly (a question reminiscent of Strepsiades' attitude towards the problems with *his* son in *Clouds*). Chremylos may begin with selfish motives, but he soon becomes a genuine if muddled philanthropist. He is a straightman; Karion is the comic slave/servant who will become a staple of the new comic tradition.

Of course, one of the strengths of Aristophanes' comic method is his refusal to be too concerned about what we might now anachronistically call naturalism, or even probability. His treatment of the characterisation of Wealth is a good example of this: Wealth starts off as a decrepit old man, but he is also a god, money itself, and an allegorical abstraction according to the demands of the moment. Similarly, there is something of a dichotomy in attitudes to wealth: sometimes it is only to be available to the good who were previously poor, sometimes it seems more as though everyone is to be wealthy anyway. In the traditional *agon* or contest, Poverty doesn't take on Wealth himself but Chremylos. Poverty argues against everyone being equally well off, leading to counter-arguments on the same terms, thus partly subverting the idea that wealth will be distributed according to worth. In its turn, this is then subverted by streams of stereotypical comic visitors (Hermes, the priest, the secret policeman, the old woman) complaining about the change in the status quo. The quick succession of victories by 'our hero and slave' is what is likely to matter to an audience rather than the blurring of the logic that the good will be rewarded with riches, thereby causing the bad to become good so that everyone will become rich. As in *Women in Power*, it may be that the confusion about rewarding everyone or only the good represents a critique of the way that good intentions get sidetracked by the realities of situations.

*Wealth* appears to be moving towards the Middle/New Comedy of which Menander is the surviving example. It is not a spectacular play: the costumes only have to represent ordinary Athenians and there is nothing extraordinary about the chorus. Only Wealth, after his transformation, and Poverty might have spectacular costumes and Poverty's clearly comes from the stock of tragedy. The increased prominence of the slave character and the reduction in obscenity are quite marked even in comparison to *Women in Power* where the treatment of the motif of the old woman with a young lover is far more systematically obscene. Similarly both the direct address to the audience associated with the *parabasis* and the role of the chorus are reduced in comparison to Aristophanes' earlier works. Most of the chorus's songs are marked in a way that suggests they were not regarded as intrinsic to the work. This is much closer to Menander, where the chorus (simply marked by a stage direction *'chorou'*) seem to be something of an irrelevance to the actual plot.

These changes have sometimes been interpreted as a slackening of Aristophanes' powers, but it is more likely they represent him experimenting with new forms after a career of over thirty years. He may have felt that his older style was no longer as viable as social and political concerns changed and it may be that he was leading or reacting to changes in artistic practice from the other writers of the time whose work is no longer available to us.

# Women in Power
## (*Ekklesiazousai*, also known as *Assemblywomen*)

## Characters

PRAXAGORA

FIRST WOMAN

SECOND WOMAN

THIRD WOMAN

BLEPYROS

PHEIDOLOS

CHREMES

TOWN CRIERESS

PRETTY GIRL

EPIGENES

FIRST HAG

SECOND HAG

THIRD HAG

SLAVE (*silent part*)

CHORUS OF WOMEN

## Synopsis

Praxagora, disillusioned with the way men are running Athens, has had a cunning idea to improve the government of the city. Her plan is to trick the assembly into letting women rule by packing it with women disguised as men. The women of Athens arrive, dressed in male clothes, and practice speech-making and appropriate behaviour for the assembly. They then go off to the assembly. Blepyros, Praxagora's husband, arrives, dressed in her clothes because she has taken his, looking for a suitable place to defecate. His neighbour Pheidolos arrives, also dressed in his wife's clothes, and similarly baffled by the absence of both wife and clothes. Chremes, fresh from the assembly but unaware of the plot, reports that Praxagora's motion to let women govern has been carried.

After the men leave, the women arrive and change back into women's clothing.

Blepyros returns with Chremes and tells Praxagora about the assembly vote. She moves from explaining her absence to setting out her basically communist political programme. Although Chremes and Blepyros question some aspects of it, they are seduced by the idea of free food and free love. Chremes enthusiastically plans to take all his goods to be shared out, but Pheidolos hangs back.

After a choral interlude, a hag and a young woman argue over the sexual favours of a young man: the hag claims precedence since one of the regulations governing free love is that the less attractive have to be serviced before the attractive. Although the young woman defeats the first hag, her boyfriend Epigenes is then besieged by two even grosser hags. The town crieress comes looking for Blepyros to remind him of the feast that he is missing and he goes off to join in.


## About the play

The exact date and production details of *Women in Power* are unclear but it was probably written after 395 and before 390, more than a decade after *Frogs*. In that period the political context had changed considerably. Athens had been defeated in the Peloponnesian War, democracy had been forcibly replaced with experiments in oligarchy, which had been followed by a bloody restoration of democracy, a gradual recovery of external political power and renewed war with Sparta as an ally of Thebes. Compared to *Frogs*, *Women in Power* has a greatly diminished role for the chorus, the *parabasis* offers much less direct address to the audience compared to earlier comedies and the contemporary political references seem more sporadic, less integral and less biting than in earlier plays. Superficially it also seems as though the part of the play centred on Praxagora's political ambitions does not relate closely to the contest of the three hags, which is a grotesque parody of the Judgement of Paris.

Although, like *Lysistrata*, the play can be read from a feminist viewpoint as an affirmation of the waste of the potential of women, in its original context the political project is self-evidently absurd: women were not allowed to be politically active. Throughout his career Aristophanes was concerned with castigating what he, and others, saw as an Athenian tendency to demand quick political fixes, always looking for a new leader to solve a problem. Probably, therefore, we should read the assembly turning to women as a mark of its collective stupidity in being unable to see through the women's travesty of masculinity, rather than as a comment on the women's self-evident wisdom.

Praxagora herself is a serious character in the sense that she proposes a serious solution to a serious problem and she actually encounters little opposition. She suggests that her gynocracy will lead to a world without crime, hate, jealousy or theft. Unlike Lysistrata's her women are under control and well prepared; they encounter no onstage opposition to their plans; there is no counter speech to undercut Praxagora's plan; nor does the opposition from her husband and neighbour last for long. Unlike Lysistrata, who has to defend her plan throughout the play, or Trygaios in *Peace*, who returns from his perilous journey, she herself drops out of the play completely soon after the proclamation of her project and she plays no part in the finale.

This was probably one of those cases where the fact that male actors were playing women dressing as men had a significant effect on audience reaction. From the beginning of the play we see (men playing) women taking over both men's physical attributes (clothing, beards, sticks) and taking over their political power, feminising the men who lose both male clothes and male power. However, the net result of this, as seen in the play, is that the young man is forced to pleasure the old women against his will. This is not only an inversion of the natural order but also a disservice to his girlfriend, since the old women steal him from her: female solidarity is no defence against the demands of age. The text suggests that the hags may well have been played in a way that differentiated them from the 'normal' women, otherwise some of the comic horror would have been lost.

The final summons to the feast and the town crieress' *parabasis*-like demand for a prize have a perfunctory quality to them that suggests a mood of ironic dissatisfaction rather than a fully realised practical project: what had initially been seen as a positive development collapses under the weight of its internal contradictions. And perhaps this is where the play matches so much else in Aristophanes: yet another political idea cannot cope adequately with the unruliness of human existence. The lack of plot connection between the communist gynocracy and the hags' pursuit of the young man does not mean that there are not powerful underlying connections: as in so many utopias the system cannot cope with the realities of human intercourse.

# Menander

## Life

Menander, the son of Diopeithes and Hegestrate, came from a wealthy Athenian family. He was born in 342/1 and educated at the Lyceum by Theophrastos, Aristotle's successor. In 317 the kingdom of Macedon imposed Demetrios of Phaleron as ruler of Athens. Demetrios knew both Aristotle and Theophrastos, and Menander was friendly with him. Demetrios' ten-year rule of enlightened despotism brought Athens a degree of peace and relative prosperity but democratic activity was not welcomed, so it may not be entirely coincidental that Menander's plays focus only on the domestic sphere. He wrote some 105 plays but only won the prize at Athens eight times and came last in the Dionysia in 312 and 311. The number of plays he wrote suggests he had a wider Greek audience and his subsequent reputation was very substantial, so his relative lack of success in Athens may have had something to do with his political affiliation with Demetrios rather than the artistic merits of his work. Indeed when another Demetrios overthrew Demetrios of Phaleron in 307, Menander, like Theophrastos, came under political suspicion. He apparently drowned while swimming off Piraeus around 290.

## Works

Most of Menander's plays are lost. Until 1905 his work was known mainly through the Roman comedies of Plautus (c.254–184 BC) and Terence (c.190–159 BC) adapted from his plays, through quotations preserved by other ancient authors, or from papyrus fragments. These fragments vary from individual lines of unidentified plays to several hundred lines of others. In 1905 some of *The*

*Woman from Samos* (Greek *Samia*) as well as sections of several other plays were discovered during an excavation in Egypt, being used as a wrapper for legal documents. Other discoveries in Egypt resulted in the publication of *The Malcontent* (*Dyskolos*) in 1959 and a fuller version of *The Woman from Samos* (1969). Most astonishing of all, and highly appropriate for a comedy, substantial portions of a text of *Sikyonios* (*The Man from Sikyon*) that had been recycled to cover mummies were published in 1965.

## Reputation

Until the publication of the two virtually complete plays in the twentieth century, little was known directly about Menander's work. Although Plautus and Terence adapted many of his and his contemporaries' works in their plays, they tended to combine elements from different plays and dramatists into new works so that it is hard to determine the exact relationship between the new Roman works and the lost Greek originals. In antiquity Menander's reputation was very high. For example, Julius Caesar (*c.*102–44 BC) is reputed to have believed that Menander was twice as good a dramatist as Terence, and the biographer Plutarch (*c.*46–120 AD) wondered why any educated man would ever go to the theatre except to see Menander. The scholar Aristophanes of Byzantium (*c.*257–180 BC) said 'O Life and Menander! Which of you imitated the other?' Material evidence also points to Menander's popularity: an excavated house in Mytiline is known as the House of Menander because of the mosaics of scenes from his plays that decorate it.

Although Menander wrote at what has conventionally been regarded as a time of decline from the cultural and political high-water mark of the fifth century, his plays represent the beginning of crucial strands in theatrical comedy that permeate the European comic tradition, shown in writers from Plautus and Terence through Shakespeare, Molière, Wycherley, Congreve, Sheridan, Wilde, to Cooney and Ayckbourn.

## Approach

We do not know for certain how far Menander was a unique voice since no other comedies of his time have survived, other than in the translated adaptations and conflations of later Roman comedy. However, through his influence on Roman drama, he can legitimately be described as the originator of a major form of comedy that presents the concerns of a more or less realistically presented cross-section of ordinary people as they tackle significant life events (particularly marriage), get into muddles based on situations and character, and then resolve them as misunderstandings are cleared up and normality is restored. One ancient anecdote about Menander suggests that he placed great emphasis on situation and narrative: when asked if he had finished writing his new play he replied: 'Yes indeed, I have finished the comedy. The plot has been worked out. I have only to add the accompaniment of the verses.'

Compared to Aristophanes, Menander's comedy is much less overtly political, more character-centred, less dependent on the chorus, more realistic, more plot-centred, and (within the constraints of contemporary ideas about women) romantic. Whereas Aristophanes cast his audience as politically active citizens, Menander treated them much more as spectators watching a representation of a version of contemporary reality. Menander seems to adopt what are known as the Aristotelian unities of time, place and action: there are no independent plots, the setting is a simple one involving two adjacent houses and the action of the play takes place over one day.

The plays, like Greek politics, are organised around the males not the females. The underlying political issue may be what it means to be a citizen and how that may conflict with being human, but it is not the plays' prime concern. The key character is the young male citizen who moves from adolescent dependence to new maturity as he becomes the centre of a new family unit. The younger women in Menander's plays are basically ciphers, sometimes even without a name. This accurately reflects their subordinate position within society and the fact that they did not appear very much in public. In Menander's two complete plays there are basically two family groups in conflict and that conflict is resolved through the movement towards intermarriage between them. Wealth and poverty are issues in both plays: the poverty of one family is one obstacle to marriage, although ultimately generosity means that it is not a serious one. The conflict is also one of economic status, where attitudes between the classes are reconciled, as are differing male and female perspectives, antagonisms between town values and country values and between fathers and sons. Menander's characters appear to be lifelike: they have a past, we see their present and we can imagine their future of domestic bliss; there is a sense of an offstage world that continues the imagined real world represented onstage. In reading, therefore, it is relatively easy to ignore some aspects of the differences between our own conventions and those of Menander's theatre.

## Menander's theatre

The theatre in Athens had been rebuilt by the time of Menander and, although there is controversy about the exact nature of some of the changes, it is clear that it was now built of stone and it seems likely that the main acting area was a relatively narrow and high stage in front of a façade. The plays are set in the street with a house on each side so that domestic action that would normally be confined indoors bursts through into public scrutiny, although there are numerous references to a life within the various houses, partly in the form of the various messenger speeches or soliloquies evoking life offstage. The high shallow stage in the rebuilt theatre appears to have facilitated a theatrical style that utilised chases and processions. In *The Malcontent*, for example, Menander uses the 'running slave' routine that became a staple of the Roman theatre. Here the slave believes that his master, who has, in fact, given up, is still chasing him, but the narrow space of the stage literally offers no hiding place. The increasing importance of slave figures in later Aristophanes (Xanthias in *Frogs*, Karion in *Wealth*) points the way towards their pivotal role in Menander. The plays use a plethora of stage business that tends towards the frenetic activity of farce: the various festivals and the preparations for them form a very significant part. As the contemporary scholar David Wiles says, the cooks, their equipment, the fires, the ceremonial costumes, the animals and the musicians all contribute to a sense of comic bustle.

Menander used a verse form with much of the flexibility of the English iambic pentameter exploited so successfully by Shakespeare and his contemporaries. His basic metre is iambic trimeter with trochaic tetrameters for scenes that needed to be marked out from their context.

Menander's choric practice is markedly different from what happened with the tragic or Aristophanic choruses. Menander's plays operate within a five-act structure and at the end of each of the first four acts the chorus fills in some time in which the action of the play is taken forward in some way offstage. The chorus is far less central in the later plays of Aristophanes than it is in the earlier ones, but in Menander it has dwindled into the stage direction 'chorou', often preceded by a character's comment that a group of rowdies are just coming in. We have no idea what the chorus sang or danced and whether it related to the action of the play. This change partly reflects the way that drama had become more of a Greek than an Athenian phenomenon by Menander's time: political changes at Athens had reduced funding for choruses but Menander's plays appear to have been performed widely throughout the Greek world by professional companies who did not tour a chorus, presumably for logistical reasons.

Crucially, Menander's theatre was still a masked one. A wide variety of character masks were available for such types as shown in a list by the ancient writer Pollux, writing after Menander, who identified several different categories (old men, young men, slaves, old women, young women, each divided into sub-sets such as delicate, dark, and curly youths or withered, fat or sharp old women). Even more crucially (although there is significant disagreement on this point), it is possible that Menander's plays were written to be performed by only three actors. If this is true, then it follows that one actor played not only several roles within a play but also that several actors played the same role within a single performance of the play. That means that the crucial delimiter of character was the mask and costume, and not, as in many types of modern theatre, the individual actor identified with his or her role. For example, if only three actors were available in *The Woman from Samos* it would appear that all three would have had to play Parmenon at different times. This practice is so counter-intuitive to most modern approaches to characterisation that many scholars believe that Menander must have used more actors, particularly in *The Malcontent* where they believe that the large number of characters meeting an equally substantial number of others demands a larger cast. It is possible, however, that the breakneck precision required in switching roles might itself have been part of the theatrical pleasure of the event. After all, Alan Ayckbourn's kaleidoscopic *Intimate Exchanges* (1982) is written to be performed by two actors who each play several characters and at one point the woman plays two women fighting each other under a curtain, emerging into view sporadically as one or the other.

We know that the mask could be used for a metatheatrical comic effect, as in the case of Sostratos in *The Malcontent* who reappears after he has been working in the fields getting sunburnt. His slave Getas apparently doesn't recognise him and Knemon, meeting him for the first time, assumes he is a farmer, whereas others have described him as more of a city boy. This suggests that the character is now being represented by a different mask. Clearly the audience was capable of following the transitions in a character from mask to mask, so it is possible they could follow the same character being played by different actors.

Costuming will also have been a factor in aiding audience recognition since it too operated through a recognised set of conventions. In Aristophanic comedy the grotesque padded phalluses and the choruses of clouds and birds and frogs were a significant indication of the fantastic elements in drama, but the costuming in New Comedy was much more realistic and conventional in both colour and style, reflecting the more purely domestic subject matter. According to ancient sources, old men wore white and carried a 'hooked stick', old women wore quince or sky-coloured clothes, heiresses wore 'white with a fringe', young men wore purple but parasites wore black or grey (Pollux) and 'slaves wear a scanty costume, by virtue of their traditional poverty, or so that they can move more freely' (Donatus).

## Menander today

When his work was unknown in anything like its complete form, Menander's reputation was perhaps higher than it has been since the discovery of the two virtually complete plays. He was rightly acknowledged as the first known practitioner of what has come to be a major, sometimes dominant, form of comedy. Because his successors have ruthlessly exploited the frameworks he created, adding layers of complication and complexity to the material he explored, some critics have been disappointed that, viewed in retrospect, the work does not seem particularly sophisticated. Of course we cannot know to what extent Menander's was a lone voice, but the fact remains that his plays are not only the earliest extant versions of situation comedy, comedy of manners, and romantic comedy, they are also the earliest successful examples of those forms.

# The Malcontent

## Characters

PAN, *the god*

CHAEREAS, *a parasite*

SOSTRATOS, *a young man in love*

PYRRHIAS, *his slave*

KNEMON, *a malcontent*

HIS DAUGHTER

GORGIAS, *Knemon's stepson*

DAOS, *Gorgias' slave*

SIKON, *a cook*

GETAS, *a slave in Sostratos' family*

MOTHER OF SOSTRATOS

SIMICHE, *Knemon's slave*

KALLIPPIDES, *Sostratos' father*

PLANGON, *Sostratos' daughter,* MYRRHINE, *Knemon's former wife,*
   ATTENDANTS (*silent parts*)

CHORUS (*indicated in the text only by a stage-direction*)


## Synopsis

*The Malcontent* begins with Pan explaining the situation. Sostratos
(a city dweller) has fallen in love with the daughter of Knemon,
the country-dwelling malcontent of the title. Knemon is so
misanthropic that he has driven out his wife and Gorgias, her son
by a previous marriage. They now live in the house at the other
side of the stage with Pan's shrine separating them. Sostratos has
already sent his slave Pyrrhias to try to get Knemon's agreement to
his marriage. Sostratos arrives with Chaereas who he also hopes
will help him to secure the marriage. When Pyrrhias appears to
report his violent reception at Knemon's hands, the parasite
departs never to be seen again. Knemon appears and Sostratos
fails to mention why he is really there, deciding that he will have to

enlist the help of his father's slave Getas. He then meets the daughter, who has come to get water from the shrine because the old slave Simiche has dropped her bucket down the well in the house. Daos, Gorgias' slave, sees their encounter and reports back to Gorgias. Gorgias, protective of his half-sister's honour, confronts Sostratos. Convinced of Sostratos' bona fides, Gorgias agrees to broach the subject of marriage to Knemon and persuades Sostratos to join him working on the farm as part of the plan.

Sikon the cook and Getas then arrive to conduct a sacrifice at the behest of Sostratos' mother who has had a prophetic dream about his fate. Preparations for the sacrifice involve various unsuccessful attempts to borrow a pan from Knemon, who reacts in his usual misanthropic way. A sunburnt Sostratos eventually returns from his work with aching back. Simiche enters with news that the spade has now fallen down the well. Knemon chases her off and Sostratos invites Gorgias to the post-sacrifice dinner. Simiche then reappears to announce that Knemon has fallen down the well. Sikon, smarting from his rebuff when he tried to borrow cooking gear, abuses him but Gorgias and Sostratos go off to help Knemon. When Knemon reappears he is chastened enough by his experience to admit that he can't be a complete hermit, adopts Gorgias as his son and asks him to find his daughter a husband. Gorgias persuades him that Sostratos is a suitable potential son-in-law and Sostratos then persuades his father Kallippides who has just arrived for lunch. Sostratos also persuades his father to let Gorgias marry his sister Plangon. Knemon refuses to join the festivities but is musically tortured by Getas and Sikon into reluctantly joining the celebration.

## About the play

*Dyskolos* (dated to around 316 BC) has been variously translated as *The Grouch*, *Old Cantankerous*, *The Bad-Tempered Man* or, as here, *The Malcontent*. There are obvious parallels with the Timon story, which was already well known, and with later treatments, such as Molière's *Misanthrope*. Menander uses the five-act structure creatively so that the gaps filled by the stage direction '*chorou*' are also significant gaps in which events unfold. Between the first act and Act Two Sostratos goes to find Getas and Daos goes off to find Gorgias; between Two and Three Sostratos goes off to the fields and the cook prepares the sacrifice. Knemon falls down the well between Three and Four, while Gorgias and Sostratos have gone off to the sacrificial dinner. Between Four and Five Kallippides and Sostratos eat and the son persuades his father to let him marry.

Knemon's farm is in Phyle outside Athens, set conventionally on audience left to indicate that it is remote from Athens, both in location and in its owner's mindset. There is a strong thread of town versus country opposition, with Sostratos and company being regarded as slick townies whom the country dwellers treat with great caution. Chaereas is called a parasite in the papyrus but although that doesn't have all the negative connotations of the modern use of the term, he is also an example of a particular kind of urban lifestyle. Ultimately Sostratos is able to convince Gorgias, the girl's half-brother, of his honourable intentions in spite of being a city dweller and enlists him as a helper in his quest, while Daos the countryman suggests that Knemon appreciates hard work and so encourages Sostratos to do some work in Knemon's field. However, we are never encouraged to share any real romantic pain: Sostratos is not a romantic hero even in the mould of Lysander or Demetrius in *A Midsummer Night's Dream* who are at least allowed sustained interaction with the objects of their affections.

In *The Malcontent* Knemon's comic version of Timon's misanthropy is a useful comic tool since it provides structural opportunities for failed communication deriving from the protagonist's character traits. Although the fact that he has a child and was once married limits Knemon's misanthropic tendencies, he is deliberately distanced from us so that his misanthropy seems pervasive and omnipotent. Knemon is the key person around whom everything revolves since each plot strand (the would-be lovers, the slaves and the cook concerned with the sacrifice and the lost pot) has to deal with his recalcitrance. The characters' fear of Knemon means that they always have to take into consideration how best to approach him: Sostratos is clearly very scared of him, Chaereas and Pyrrhias appear to be terrified and the girl goes in just because she thinks he might be coming out. Some of Knemon's power also derives from the way that Menander introduces characters that appear for only one scene, apparently solely in order to be defeated by him.

Having established Knemon's misanthropy, Menander gradually sets up a contrast between the broad comic attacks associated with the cook and the more sympathetic attitudes of Sostratos and Gorgias. The interpenetration of the comic by the serious and vice versa is a key technique in Menander. The catalyst for Knemon's eventual change of heart is the incidents deriving from the problems with the pot and the well. Knemon's daughter, the object of Sostratos' affections, only has one scene but she is presented in a way calculated to establish her as an echo of tragedy: her situation and her diction are reminiscent of Elektra, specifically Euripides' version of her. She sets up the situation when she tells us about the nurse dropping the pot down the well. Simiche the nurse develops it later herself when she enters in Act Three like a tragic messenger with cries of disaster because she has now lost the spade down the well. The tragic atmosphere is, of course, undermined by the disparity between the portentous language of the speech and the triviality of the actual event, by Getas' reactions and by Knemon's immediate irate entrance. The plot is taken further when Simiche enters with another messenger speech to announce that Knemon himself has now fallen down the well. The repetition of the messenger speech is itself comic, but its comedic force is further enhanced by the unsympathetic reaction that Simiche gets from Sikon the cook. When Sostratos comically describes Knemon's rescue from the well, in yet another version of a messenger speech, the humour stems partly from the narrator's honest retelling of his own undistinguished role in the rescue.

Knemon's late entrance on the *ekkuklema*, a device most often associated with tragic discoveries, actually undercuts his potential tragic status. Yet Knemon's speech remains within a classic tragic pattern: he has had a catastrophe, caused by his character failings; he now recognises those failings and that in turn leads him to a partial recanting of his old views. Being trapped in the well provides the impetus towards self-recognition but not reform: Knemon does not become warm-hearted as a result of his ordeal and he is still tormented by the cook and the slave. He is forced to recognise the altruism of his rescuers and therefore that his blanket distrust of all humanity will have to be modified, but he also recognises that he cannot entirely give up his old ways so he enlists help to marry his daughter off.

Sikon the cook and Getas the slave are mainly concerned with the sacrifice plot but they also serve as a source of broad comedy with what were already stock characters, situations and jokes. Their attack on Knemon is moderated first of all by the fact that Knemon has been presented like a tragic hero on the *ekkuklema* and then by changes in metre and musical accompaniment. Then the scene gradually modulates from viciousness into the quasi-reconciliation that enables the play to end with an inclusive wedding celebration of the kind that was to become such a staple of the Western comic tradition.

# The Woman from Samos (Samia)

## Characters

MOSCHION, *adopted son of Demeas*

CHRYSIS, *the woman from Samos*

PARMENON, *Demeas' slave*

DEMEAS, *a well-to-do Athenian*

NIKERATOS, *Demeas' neighbour*

A COOK

PLANGON, *Nikeratos' daughter,* MYRRHINE, *Nikeratos' wife,*
    ATTENDANTS (*silent parts*)

CHORUS (*indicated in the text only by a stage direction*)


## Synopsis

Demeas, a rich merchant, and Nikeratos, who is poor, live next
door to each other but at the beginning of the play they are on a
trading mission to the Black Sea that has kept them away for many
months. Moschion, Demeas' adopted son, has impregnated
Nikeratos' daughter Plangon in their fathers' absence. Chrysis, the
Samian woman of the title, who is Demeas' unmarried partner,
was also pregnant but her baby died. Moschion plans to ask his
father's permission to marry but in the meantime Chrysis is
passing off the surviving baby as her own. Nikeratos and Demeas,
returning unaware of what has happened in their absence, have
already decided that Moschion should marry Plangon. Demeas is
angry that Chrysis has (apparently) had a baby against his express
wishes but is reconciled until he overhears one of the servants
saying the baby is Moschion's. He therefore assumes that his son
has seduced Chrysis and turfs her out. She takes refuge with
Nikeratos but when Demeas tells Nikeratos that Moschion is the
child's father Nikeratos returns home to throw her out. Moschion
just has time to confess the truth to his father before Nikeratos
returns in fury because he has seen his daughter breast-feeding the

265

baby. Demeas manages to placate him, promising that the marriage will take place as planned. In Act Five Moschion, indignant that his father suspected him of an affair with Chrysis, decides to pretend to leave home to be a soldier but is eventually reconciled with him and marries Plangon.

## About the play

Whereas *The Malcontent* begins with a divine prologue, it seems that *The Woman from Samos* began with a human one. This sets up some interesting differences between the plays since it means that here there is no suggestion that the action is part of a divine plan. In *The Woman from Samos* everyone is clearly responsible for their own actions and the audience knows the crucial facts from the beginning. There is no parental opposition to Moschion's marriage to Plangon but everyone's initial desire to be considerate of other people's sensitivities leads to catastrophic misunderstandings and the erection of barriers at every turn. Each time there is a partial resolution of the plot, a further complication springs from the circumstances of that resolution. The key relationship is the paternal not the marital one. However, Moschion's distress and unwillingness to annoy his father, Demeas' fear that he has been betrayed by his adopted son and even Chrysis' torments are undercut by our knowledge that the situation has been misunderstood and by the ways that Nikeratos, the other father, serves as a foil to Demeas. It is also true that Moschion's willingness to assume his responsibilities looks more rhetorical than real as the play goes on and he can never find the opportunity to reveal the truth. The ability of characters to jump to wrong conclusions on the basis of partial evidence extends the action plausibly across four acts with a final twist in the fifth act as a result of Moschion's desire to punish his father. No one is shirking any obligations but everyone's ability to complicate matters leads to real difficulties.

Of course there are modern objections to much of the plot from feminist viewpoints. With the exception of Chrysis, the women are mute and the men treat them all in ways that would raise eyebrows in modern Western culture. However, it must be recognised that Athenian culture was essentially patriarchal and that arranged marriages were the order of the day. The fathers' decision that their children should marry is a perfectly proper one by the standards of the time; even a generous one since the financial disparity between the families means the poor woman is to marry a rich man. Moschion confesses that he impregnated Plangon at a festival, so he may have seduced her or he may have committed what we would now regard as a rape. However, the audience is clearly not expected to empathise with Plangon and we are encouraged to believe that Moschion does want to marry her. Moreover, marrying the victim of rape was regarded by Athenian and by other more modern societies as a fair recompense for the initial crime.

Our responses to the presentation of Chrysis may be more complex. According to archaeological evidence (a mosaic of a scene from the play), Chrysis may have worn a bejewelled headdress to indicate her wealth. She would have worn a mask identifying her as a courtesan, thus helping the audience to see both the possibility of her being thrown out of her current situation and why Moschion might have found her attractive. She cannot marry Demeas because she is not a citizen and so her status is entirely dependent on his goodwill. Although she is the title character, her feelings are not a central concern of the play. In more recent forms of comedy the fact that Demeas himself is so violent and abusive to Chrysis would demand some form of comic revenge and a final reconciliation scene between them. Although Menander does use the cook as a safety valve to reduce some of the harshness of Demeas ejecting Chrysis from their home, he appears to believe that dramatically he only needs to establish that Demeas is basically a good person and that he is only trying to protect Moschion from legal complications.

Very little energy is spent in the play as we have it on Chrysis' dead child. This is another stark reminder that contemporary and ancient attitudes are very different: perinatal death was much more common and we may presume that this affected the way in which both society and individuals regarded infant death. Certainly nothing in the extant play suggests that we are meant to be concerned about the dead child, which in fact operates simply as a plot device to make it possible for Chrysis to be breast-feeding the other child and thus be assumed to be its mother.

Theatrically the play is very effective, using different verse forms to underpin the comedy. Trochaics are used for the bustling wedding preparations of the final act, as well as for the energetic confrontations of Act Four – particularly the sequences in which poor Chrysis is chased from her home with the baby and then from the neighbour's, all to musical accompaniment. The play is skilfully plotted, deploying its characters across a range of archetypal situations. With *The Malcontent*, it established the literary and theatrical conventions that would dominate much of the Western comedic tradition.

# Aristotle's *Poetics* and Greek Tragedy

**Aristotle (384–22 BC)**

Aristotle developed a research method which could be applied to subjects of all kinds: animal movement, the nature of the gods, ethics, politics, the phenomena of the physical universe. The method consisted of amassing as much evidence as possible, arranging and collating it according to the principles of logic and then drawing theories and explanations from it. He is credited with some 400 writings, of which a quarter survive. Some read like notes or summaries, others (including *Poetics*) like verbatim accounts of lectures, others again like works revised and polished for publication.

## *Poetics*

*Poetics* (*Peri poietikes*, 'about [literary] composition') appeared *c.*336 BC. It dealt with all the arts, but concentrated on the principal forms of literary fiction in Aristotle's time: tragedy, comedy and epic. Twenty-six short sections survive, about half the original. They cover tragedy and to a lesser extent epic, mentioning music, dance and the fine arts in passing; the section on comedy does not survive.

*Poetics* was known for two or three centuries after Aristotle's death, but then, although studied in Arabic-speaking countries, it disappeared in Europe for some 1,500 years, when it was rediscovered by a group of Italian Renaissance scholars. Their accounts of Aristotle's ideas were enormously influential, affecting the study of Greek tragedy and the aesthetics of European drama for 300 years. It was not till the late nineteenth century, when systematic investigation began of the literary aspects of Greek tragedy, that it became clear just how different some of their views were from Aristotle's, not to mention those of the extant playwrights.

## The nature and function of tragedy

> Tragedy is the imitation of an action that is serious, complete and substantial. It is written in artistically heightened language, some sections in spoken verse, others using music. It arouses pity and fear in the spectators, and by so doing purges those emotions. (*Poetics* 6)

This pithy definition puts Aristotle's argument in a nutshell. Tragedy is fiction: not reality but an imitation of reality. It shows a group of people involved in a sequence of actions. That sequence is an organic whole, without irrelevance or omission. It is serious, making points of general concern as well as telling a specific story. It is substantial, more than just the account of a single moving or terrifying incident.

The idea of 'imitation' is crucial to our engagement with tragedy and to its effect on us. Because we know that what we are seeing is pretence, we are able to balance our emotional involvement with objective appreciation of the issues. We react to Medea's plight or Ajax' suicide, for example, completely differently from if a real mother announced that she was about to kill her children or we saw a real person committing suicide. The human race, Aristotle says in *Poetics*, learns by watching and imitating, and we also enjoy comparing an imitation (say a portrait or a dance of rage) with the real thing. This enjoyment gives pleasure: the main function of the arts. But the 'high' arts, and tragedy in particular, can also affect their spectators, as we become involved with the characters' plight, feel for their suffering and think about our own attitudes to the issues – perhaps even changing as a result. This process is a form of emotional purgation or cleansing.

## Hamartia

The heroes' sufferings are caused by *hamartia*. (*Poetics* 13)

The Greeks believed that when the universe was functioning properly there was a kind of order, a harmony, and that this depended on everyone and everything in it keeping an allotted place. An enormous mesh of laws, customs, hierarchies and relationships had to be sustained, and the slightest tear in that mesh could lead to the collapse of the whole. For Aristotle, *hamartia* was just such a tear, and had to be corrected if order was to be maintained. By his day the word *hamartia* was used of any kind of 'error': mispronouncing a word, tripping over a stone, losing a battle, committing a crime.

Greek myth is about the establishment and maintenance of the universal mesh, both generally and in detail. In particular, myth-stories show examples of relationships – between supernatural powers and each other, between mortals and the supernatural, between mortals and each other – and of what happens when those relationships are disturbed. By its nature, myth talks less about 'ordinary' people than what Aristotle called those 'of high degree': gods, heroes, rulers, warriors. Since the Greek tragic dramatists based most of their work on myth-stories, presenting and shaping them to bring out resonances and point up general themes, this meant that the principal characters of tragedy were people 'of high degree' rather than commoners. By implication, the *hamartia* of a 'high' character has a more disastrous effect on the mesh of universal order, and can be repaired only by equally exemplary suffering.

Renaissance scholars, writing from a Christian perspective in which the whole human race was tainted with the guilt of original sin and in need of God's redemption, restricted Aristotle's idea of *hamartia* to mean moral failure only. All tragedy, they said, concerns some 'high' person's sin and the working-out of his or her redemption. The sin they most frequently claimed for tragic heroes was *hubris*, the arrogance which makes mortals think themselves equal to gods – and they praised those surviving plays (such as Sophocles' *Oedipus Tyrannos*) where it seemed to exist and condemned those (such as many of Euripides' plays) where it did not. The idea is one of the most seminal in all Western dramatic criticism, but it is fundamentally un-Greek.


## *Anagnorisis* and *peripeteia*

*Anagnorisis* ('recognition') is a change from ignorance to knowledge. Characters recognise what has been hidden from them till now, that they are related or have long been enemies.

*Peripeteia* ('reversal') is a change in the hero's circumstances, from happiness to unhappiness. It should arise not from wickedness but from *hamartia* in the hero. (*Poetics* 11)

In *Poetics*, *anagnorisis* and *peripeteia* are straightforward technical expressions. *Anagnorisis* is when a character onstage realises something about someone else, something that the audience has known for some time (for example, that the person is a long-lost relative) – and the discovery changes his or her behaviour. 'Recognition scenes' are a standard feature of surviving Greek tragedy: those between Elektra and the long-lost Orestes are typical. *Peripeteia* is a 180-degree turn in the fortunes of the play's hero, from security at the beginning to degradation at the end. Oedipus in Sophocles' *Oedipus Tyrannos* begins the play secure and confident, and ends it blind and miserable. Pentheus in Euripides' *Bacchae* begins as a ruler in all his pride, and ends up torn to pieces.

Renaissance scholars, developing their view that *hamartia* meant a specific moral failing in the hero, redefined both *anagnorisis* and *peripeteia*. They said that the process of tragedy requires a climactic moment when the hero realises his or her moral failing and that destruction is inevitable, and that this realisation triggers a reversal not just in his or her physical circumstances (from good to bad) but in moral status (from bad to good). The moment of realisation, *anagnorisis*, is not a public event but a private one and involves a recognition of guilt and an acceptance of punishment analogous to those of a Christian taking part in the sacrament of confession.⟧ ⟦The moment of reversal, *peripeteia*, leads the hero into an irreversible spiral of physical suffering, but also into the state of moral grace induced by the admission of personal guilt⟧ *-deep* ·

## The unities

*Unity of time*
So far as possible, tragedy endeavours to confine itself to a single revolution of the sun, or very slightly longer. (*Poetics* 5)

*Unity of action*
The sequence of actions imitated in the play should be single and unified, in such a way that if any of the actions were to be displaced or removed, the whole would be disjointed and disturbed. (*Poetics* 8)

Aristotle's concept of unity derives from his passion for logic and elimination of the inessential. Everything that happens in a play must 'fit' without incongruity or forcing the story. The action, if possible, should take place in a single, comprehensible time-span. A third kind of unity is followed in most (but not all) of the surviving tragedies: they take place in a single location.

In the Renaissance, scholars elaborated this into the 'rule of the three unities', which went on to become a staple ingredient of dramatic theory and of the criticism of ancient tragedy. (Scholars still sometimes profess 'surprise', for example, that Aeschylus and Sophocles use two locations in *Eumenides* and *Ajax* respectively, or that Euripides appears to tell two stories in such plays as *Herakles' Children* or *Suppliants*.) The three unities are those of time, place and action. The unity of time requires that the events shown in the play must take place in a single time-span of not more than twenty-four hours. The unity of place requires that there should be a single location throughout the play. The unity of action requires that everything in the play should involve one group of people, one set of circumstances and a single narrative from start to finish.

# KEY MYTHS

This brief guide presents some key elements of the myths most commonly used by the Greek dramatists. Most of the myths have a number of variants, which makes it impossible to give a definitive version. For fuller accounts, see Robert Graves' *The Greek Myths*, the Larousse *Encyclopedia of Mythology*, or Kenneth McLeish's *Myths and Legends of the World*.

AJAX: see Troy

ALKESTIS
(Euripides, *Alkestis*)
Alkestis was one of the daughters of Pelias persuaded by Medea to boil their father alive to restore his youth. She fled to Pherai and married King Admetos. In some accounts, Pelias' soldiers pursued her to kill her, Admetos fought for her but was captured and she saved his life by agreeing to be killed in his place. In others, he fell mortally ill, and she persuaded Death to let her go to the Underworld instead of him. In both accounts she was saved by Herakles, who visited Pherai, admired her love for her husband and successfully wrestled Death for her.

ANDROMACHE
(Euripides, *Andromache, Women of Troy*)
Andromache was Hektor's wife and senior princess of Troy during the Trojan War. After Troy fell, the victorious Greeks hurled Andromache's baby son Astyanax to his death from the city walls, and gave Andromache herself as war-spoils to Achilles' son Neoptolemos. He took her back to his palace in Epiros, then left for the Delphic Oracle (in some accounts, to plunder it, in others

to ask Apollo's forgiveness for blaming him for the death of his father Achilles). While Neoptolemos was away, his wife Hermione and father-in-law Menelaos plotted to kill Andromache, but were prevented by Neoptolemos' aged grandfather Peleus. In the meantime, Orestes quarrelled with Neoptolemos at Delphi, and killed him. Andromache married Helenos, Hektor's brother (who had also been given to Neoptolemos as war-spoils), and the pair of them ruled Epiros.

APOLLO

(Aeschylus, *Eumenides; passim*)

Apollo, son of Zeus and Leda and twin brother of Artemis, was the god of the rays of the sun. His light was like an arrow fired from a bow, bringing enlightenment or death. When he was still a baby he killed the sacred snake which guarded Mother Earth's prophetic sanctuary at Delphi, and became the resident god. He brought order to the world by music and dancing, and taught these skills to favoured mortals, partly through his servants the nine Muses. He and Dionysos symbolised the order of the universe, and the union of intellect (Apollo's prerogative) and emotion (Dionysos' prerogative) by dancing hand-in-hand on the peaks of Mount Parnassos above Delphi, leading their devotees. Apollo was benevolent to his followers and merciless to those who challenged his skills (for example, the flute-playing satyr Marsyas, whom he defeated in a contest and then flayed alive) or who rejected his sexual favours (for example, Kassandra of Troy, whom he offered the gift of infallible prophecy if she had sex with him, and when she refused cursed by giving her the gift anyway, with the additional curse that no one would believe a word she said). Apollo's oracles, throughout the world but especially at Delphi, were supervised by priestesses known as Sybils, who went into trances to speak the god's words, knew the secrets of the Underworld, and always spoke true prophecy, if you could only understand their words.

ARGOS

(Aeschylus, *Oresteia*; Sophocles, *Elektra*; Euripides, *Elektra*, *Iphigeneia at Aulis*, *Iphigeneia in Tauris*, *Orestes*)

Two brothers, Atreus and Thyestes, quarrelled over the throne of Argos. Atreus banished his brother, then invited him to a banquet of reconciliation and served him a stew made from the bodies of his own children. Thyestes cursed Atreus and all his descendants, and the gods fulfilled the curse.

Agamemnon succeeded Atreus his father. He married Klytemnestra, and his brother Menelaos married her sister Helen, princess of Sparta. Agamemnon and Klytemnestra had three children, Iphigeneia, Elektra and Orestes. Prince Paris of Troy stole Helen from her husband, and Menelaos and Agamemnon raised a Greek army to win her back. The fleet assembled at Aulis, but Agamemnon offended the goddess Artemis, who held back the winds and refused to release them until Agamemnon sacrificed Iphigeneia. Agamemnon summoned her to Aulis, pretending that she was to marry Achilles, and killed her (in some versions, but see also the final paragraph of this entry).

The fleet sailed and the Trojan War began. During the ten years it lasted, Klytemnestra ruled Argos in Agamemnon's absence. Brooding on revenge for Iphigeneia's death, she took as a lover Aigisthos, the last surviving child of Thyestes (too young to be butchered and stewed with his brothers and sisters). She sent Orestes to grow up in exile in Phokis, and married Elektra to a farmer, far from Argos.

Agamemnon returned from Troy, loaded with spoils and bringing with him his concubine Kassandra, daughter of King Priam of Troy. Klytemnestra laid a red carpet to welcome him into the citadel of Mycenae, then invited him to the bath-house, trapped him in a net and held him while Aigisthos butchered him. She and Aigisthos continued their tyranny, and the people were powerless to stop them.

In due course, Orestes, now grown-up, arrived from Phokis with his friend Pylades. He had been to Delphi to ask Apollo who his real father was, and Apollo had replied that he was destined to kill his mother for murdering his father. He went in secret to Elektra, and she persuaded him to butcher first Aigisthos and then Klytemnestra. As soon as these murders were committed, the Furies swarmed from the Underworld to avenge Klytemnestra's murder, driving Orestes insane. He and Pylades roamed the world, making offerings at the shrines of the gods, until finally Apollo and Athene pacified the Furies and restored Orestes' wits. Orestes married Hermione, Helen's daughter, and ruled in Argos; Elektra married Pylades and ruled in Sparta.

One side-myth, used by Euripides, said that Iphigeneia was not killed in Aulis, but was rescued by Artemis, who substituted a fawn and carried Iphigeneia off to the remote country of Tauris. Here, as Artemis' priestess, her main duty was to make human sacrifice of any Greek visitors who reached her shores. In due course Orestes and Pylades arrived, on their quest to recover Orestes' sanity, and Iphigeneia was about to sacrifice them when Artemis revealed Orestes' true identity. The three of them escaped from Tauris, taking a statue of Artemis which they set up at Brauron near Athens, where it was worshipped ever afterwards.

### ATHENE

(Aeschylus, *Eumenides*; Sophocles, *Ajax*; Euripides, *Ion, Iphigeneia in Tauris; passim*)

Athene was the embodiment of Zeus' thought, born from her father's forehead. She was the goddess of wisdom, and of skill in war, and ranked with Apollo as leader of the younger generation of Olympian gods, Zeus' children. She contested with her uncle Poseidon the right to become patron of Athens, and won, thanks to her gift of olives. In the Trojan War she supported the Greeks, particularly Odysseus, to whom she suggested the plan of the Wooden Horse.

CASTOR AND POLLUX: see Kastor and Polydeukes

CYCLOPS

(Euripides, *Cyclops*)

On their eventful journey home from the Trojan War, Odysseus and his crew landed in Sicily, and took shelter in a cave full of vats of sheep's milk and sheep's cheeses. They hoped that the owner of the cave would help them on their way home, but when he returned in the evening he proved to be a one-eyed, flesh-eating giant, Polyphemos the Cyclops. He drove his sheep into the cave for milking, barred the entrance with an enormous boulder and tore two of Odysseus' men apart to eat for his supper. The next day he ate two more men for breakfast before driving his sheep out to pasture and blocking the entrance once more.

Odysseus and his men spent the day sharpening an olive-wood stake and hardening it in the fire. That evening, when Polyphemos prepared his dinner of human flesh, Odysseus gave him a gift of wine. The Cyclops asked him his name, and he answered 'Nobody'. Polyphemos offered him a gift in return for the wine: of all his men, he would eat Nobody last of all. That night, while Polyphemos snored in a drunken sleep, the crew drove the pole into his eye, blinding him. His groans brought the other Cyclopes running, but when they asked who'd hurt him and he answered 'Nobody', they went away in disgust. Odysseus and his crew escaped next morning by hanging under the fleecy sheep as they were driven to pasture, and they left the island as fast as they could while the furious Polyphemos hurled boulders after the sound of their splashing oars.

DANAIDS

(Aeschylus, *Suppliants*)

Danaos and his brother Aigyptos, descendants of Io, jointly ruled Egypt. Aigyptos wanted his fifty sons to marry Danaos' fifty daughters, but Danaos, thinking this incest, fled with his daughters to Greece, where the people of Argos gave them sanctuary. Aigyptos' sons pursued their cousins, and fell into a trap. Danaos pretended to accept the marriage, but arranged with his daughters to murder their husbands on the wedding night. All obeyed except

Hypermnestra, who spared her husband Lynkeus. The gods made Danaos, Hypermnestra and Lynkeus joint rulers in Argos, and punished the murderous daughters by compelling them to spend eternity bailing a lake of tears with sieves.

DIONYSOS: see Thebes

### FURIES

(Aeschylus, *Eumenides*; Sophocles, *Oedipus at Kolonos; passim*)
The Furies (Erinyes, 'curses', 'madnesses') were daughters of Night and of Acheron, the river of tears in the Underworld (or, in some accounts, were born after Mother Earth was impregnated by blood-drops when Kronos castrated his father Sky at the beginning of time). The three main Furies, Allekto, Megara and Tisiphone, led a pack of lesser beings; some myths added a fourth leader, Nemesis, feared even by the gods. The Furies punished mortal sinners, particularly those who murdered blood relatives. In the Underworld they wielded goads and iron whips and supervised the torments of the damned. In the Upper World they appeared as hunting dogs or swarms of flies, maddening their victims and blighting the earth they lighted on. They had shrines here and there on earth (for example at Kolonos near Athens and in caves in the rock of the Acropolis), and were worshipped there as Eumenides, 'benevolent ones' whose magic could help, not harm.

### HERAKLES

(Sophocles, *Philoktetes, Women of Trachis*; Euripides, *Herakles, Herakles' Children, Alkestis*)
Herakles was the son of the mortal queen Alkmene and Zeus, who took the form of Alkmene's husband Amphitryon to have sex with her. Zeus' immortal consort Hera was determined to keep him out of Olympos, and he spent his time on earth, the noblest and most powerful hero ever seen. When he was eighteen he killed a huge lion which was savaging the cattle of King Thespios of Thespiai, and was rewarded by being allowed sex with every one of the

king's fifty daughters. (Each later bore twins.) Outside Thebes, he defeated an army invading the city, and was rewarded by marriage with the king's daughter Megara. They had several children.

Herakles always found it hard to confine immortal power and strength in a mortal body, and Hera took delight in testing him, trying to drive him to madness or to overreach himself. In one version of the story, he killed Megara and their children in a fit of madness, and was punished by being forced to undertake twelve Labours. These were chosen by King Eurystheus of Mycenae, whom Herakles was obliged to obey in every particular, and consisted of carrying out superhuman tasks (such as cleaning out the byres of the cattle-lord Augeias) or fighting supernatural monsters such as the hundred-headed Hydra of Lerne or Cerberus, guard-dog of the Underworld. Helped by his mortal brother Iphikles, Herakles succeeded in doing them all.

As well as his Labours, Herakles had other exploits. He sailed with the Argonauts to steal the Golden Fleece, fought the Erymanthian boar, rescued the daughter of King Laomedon of Troy from a sea-monster and, when Laomedon refused to pay him, he killed the king and replaced him with the infant Priam. He entered an archery competition whose prize was Princess Iole, and when he won and was refused the prize he killed Iole's brother Iphitos. For this crime, and for arguing with Apollo who refused to purify him afterwards, he was punished by being enslaved for a year to Princess Omphale of Lydia, who dressed him as a woman and made him sit and spin with the other palace slaves.

After his time with Omphale, Herakles at last made his peace with Hera: he rescued her from some drunken centaurs who were trying to rape her, and she agreed to let him shed his mortality and enter Olympos. This would happen, Hera predicted, after he was killed by his own dead enemy. Herakles married Princess Deianeira of Pleuron, after winning her by wrestling her other suitor, the river-god Acheloös. He set out with Deianeira to travel to Thebes. They came to a river, and a passing centaur, Nessos, offered to carry Deianeira across. On the far bank, however, he tried to rape her. Herakles shot him dead with a poisoned arrow –

and with his dying breath Nessos told Deianeira that if she made his shaggy hide into a shirt for Herakles, Herakles would never look at another woman. Deianeira did so, and the shirt, still poisoned with arrow-venom, caused Herakles such agony that he went alone to the peak of Mount Oita, built a funeral pyre, lay down on it, and begged the first passer-by, the shepherd Philoktetes, to light it. In exchange for Herakles' unerring bow and arrows, Philoktetes did so, Herakles' mortality was burned away and he was free to enter Olympos as an immortal god.

## HIPPOLYTOS
(Euripides, *Hippolytos*)

Hippolytos was the son of King Theseus and his Amazon concubine Antiope. He was devoted to Artemis, goddess of purity, and had sworn eternal virginity. Theseus made a dynastic marriage with Princess Phaedra of Crete (where he had long ago killed the Minotaur), and when Antiope tried to interrupt the wedding celebrations, he murdered her. The gods punished him by making Phaedra fall in love with Hippolytos – and when Hippolytos refused to have anything to do with her, they inspired her first to send Theseus a message that Hippolytos had raped her, and then to hang herself. Theseus prayed to Poseidon to punish Hippolytos, and the god answered his prayer, sending a wave to swamp Hippolytos' chariot as he was riding by the sea, and drowning him. In some versions of the myth, Artemis indignantly went down to the Underworld, rescued Hippolytos and took him to Italy, where he served as her priest for the rest of his time on earth.

## IO
(Aeschylus, *Prometheus Bound, Suppliants*)

Io was an Argive river nymph and a priestess/prophetess of Hera. Zeus raped her, and to hide her from Hera's jealousy turned her into a white cow. Hera knew who Io really was, begged Zeus to give her the cow as a present, and then punished her by making her a cow for ever and putting her in the herd guarded by Argos of the Hundred Eyes. Zeus asked Hermes' help, and Hermes lulled Argos asleep with music and rescued Io, still in the form of a cow. When Hera found out what had happened, she sent a stinging fly to torment Io (as cows have been tormented by flies ever since), and Io, driven mad by pain, ran all over the world to escape it. She came on Prometheus, tormented on Mount Caucasus, and in a prophetic trance told him what he had to do to end his agony. At last she found her way to the banks of the Nile in Egypt, where Zeus freed her from madness and from her cow-disguise. She was pregnant with his child, and when the baby was born it was part bull, part human. Both Io and her child were later worshipped as gods in Egypt: she as Isis and he as the bull-god Hap (Greek Epaphos or Apis).

## ION
(Euripides, *Ion*)

Ion was the son of Apollo and the Athenian princess Kreusa, whom Apollo raped in a cave on the Acropolis. Kreusa gave the child at birth to the shrine at Delphi, and Ion was brought up as a temple servant, not knowing his parentage. In the meantime, Kreusa married Xouthos, a warrior-king from Euboia. They were childless, and after some years went to the Delphic Oracle to ask advice. The prophetess told Xouthos that he would find a son, the first person he met on leaving the temple – and that person turned out to be Ion. Kreusa, furious that Xouthos was taking back, as she thought, a complete stranger to be prince in Athens and usurp her own authority, tried to kill Ion, and he tried to save himself by killing her. Just in time, Apollo intervened, revealed the truth, and the mortals left for happiness in Athens.

## KASTOR AND POLYDEUKES
(Euripides, *Orestes; passim*)

Kastor and Polydeukes are also known by their Latin names Castor and Pollux, or as the Dioskouroi ('sons of Zeus'), Latin Dioscuri. Their birth was complicated. Zeus took the form of a swan and raped Leda, wife of the mortal King Tyndareus of Sparta. Leda produced two eggs, and from each egg hatched a pair of twins: Kastor and Polydeukes, Helen and Klytemnestra. One of each pair was mortal and the other immortal. In the women's case, Helen was immortal and Klytemnestra mortal; in the men's case, the issue was not settled until they quarrelled with another pair of twins, Lynkeus and Idas, and Kastor was killed. Polydeukes begged their father Zeus to let him share his immortality with Kastor, and Zeus agreed, letting them die, alternately, and be reborn, once every day (or, in some accounts, once every six months). Zeus also made the twins a constellation in the sky and gave them the duty of guiding and rescuing sailors lost at sea.

## MEDEA

(Euripides, *Medea*)

Medea was a priestess of Hekate, goddess of black magic. She was the Sun's grand-daughter and the daughter of King Aeetes of Colchis who guarded the Golden Fleece. When Jason brought his Argonauts to Colchis to steal the Fleece, she fell in love with him and told him how to fulfil Aeetes' savage conditions for survival. She then drugged the Fleece's dragon-guardian, helped Jason steal the Fleece, and slowed down Aeetes and his pursuing sailors by chopping her own brother Apsyrtos to pieces and throwing the pieces overboard.

Jason and Medea went first to Jason's native town of Iolkos, and Jason claimed the throne from the usurper Pelias who had sent him to Colchis in the first place. When Pelias refused to abdicate, Medea persuaded his daughters that a magic way to bring back his youth and vigour was to boil him alive in a cauldron of herbs – and she and Jason were forced to flee with their two sons to Corinth. Here Jason, anxious to consolidate his position, arranged to marry Princess Glauke, daughter of King Kreon. Medea punished him by sending Glauke wedding-presents smeared with poison, and then killing her and Jason's sons. In some accounts she soared with the bodies into heaven in the Sun's sky-chariot. In others she escaped to Athens (where King Aegeus had offered her sanctuary if she used magic to end his childlessness).

NIOBE
(*passim*)

Queen Niobe of Orchomenos had six sons and six daughters (or, some say, seven or ten of each). She boasted that she was a luckier mother than Leto, the divine mother of Apollo and Artemis – and the gods punished her by shooting the children dead and turning Niobe herself into a mountainside, endlessly weeping waterfalls of tears. All Greek dramatists use her as a symbol of unbearable, unquenchable sorrow.

OEDIPUS: see Thebes

PHILOKTETES: see Troy

PHILOMELA: see Tereus

PROKNE: see Tereus

PROMETHEUS
(Aeschylus, *Prometheus Bound*; Aristophanes, *Birds*)

One of the Titans who existed before the gods, Prometheus helped Zeus and his brothers defeat them and seize control of the universe. Later, however, he angered Zeus, first by moulding dolls from mud and giving them the breath of life (the first mortals), and then by stealing the fire of intelligence from heaven and giving them divine understanding. Zeus punished him by pegging him on Mount Caucasus, in the wild boundary between Earth (being) and Chaos (not-being), and sending a vulture each day to gorge on his liver (which was miraculously renewed each night).

The punishment was fated to end only when another immortal

agreed to take Prometheus' place and when Prometheus told Zeus a secret which only he knew and which affected the future of the universe. Prometheus hung in torment for 30,000 mortal years, resisting all appeals to tell the secret and win his freedom. Then Cheiron the centaur, wounded by one of Herakles' poisoned arrows, was in such pain that he begged Zeus to let him take Prometheus' place, and Mother Earth persuaded Prometheus to tell his secret. The secret was that the sea-nymph Thetis, about to marry Zeus' brother Poseidon, would bear a son greater than his father – and the gods hastily married her to the mortal Peleus. (Her son was Achilles, and so the prophecy came true without harming the immortal universe.) Cheiron stood ready to take Prometheus' place, but instead Zeus turned him into a star-constellation and sent Hermes to kill the vulture and set Prometheus free.

### SPHINX
(Sophocles, *Oedipus Tyrannos*)
Sphinx ('throttler') was a winged dog with a lion's claws and teeth, a snake's tail and a human head. Hera sent it to plague the Thebans. It posed a riddle: 'In the morning four legs, at noon two, in the evening three: what am I?' – and each day the citizens failed to find the answer, it ate one of their children. Oedipus, visiting the city on his way from the Delphic Oracle, gave the right answer ('a human being'), and Sphinx flew angrily up in the air, fell to earth and dashed its own brains out against a rock. The grateful Thebans made Oedipus ruler of the city.

### TEREUS
(Aristophanes, *Birds; passim*)
King Tereus of Thrace raped his sister-in-law Philomela, and cut out her tongue to stop her telling. She however included a picture of the rape in an embroidery she was making, and showed it to her sister Prokne, Tereus' wife. Prokne punished Tereus by killing their son Itys and serving him to his father in a pie. The gods

turned all four of them into birds: Tereus into a hoopoe, Philomela into a nightingale, Itys into a sandpiper and Prokne into a swallow. The nightingale and swallow have wept ever afterwards for Itys, and the image of weeping birds and the cries of 'Itun, Itun' ('Itys! Itys!) were regularly used by Greek poets describing outpourings of lyrical sorrow.

## THEBES

(Aeschylus, *Seven Against Thebes*; Sophocles, *Antigone, Oedipus at Kolonos, Oedipus Tyrannos*; Euripides, *Bacchae, Phoenician Women, Suppliants*)

Thebes was founded by Kadmos, who killed a dragon, sowed its teeth and fought the warriors who grew from them. The survivors accepted him as king, and their descendants – the Spartoi or Sown People – were the leading aristocratic families of Thebes.

Zeus lusted after Kadmos' daughter Semele and asked her what gift she would take to have sex with him. Hera, disguised as a servant, told Semele to ask that she be allowed to see Zeus in all his majesty. Semele did so, and Zeus entered her in the form of one of his own thunderbolts. Semele and the palace were destroyed, but Zeus rescued her infant, Dionysos, and sewed him in a second womb in his own thigh until the child was grown.

When Dionysos returned to Thebes to claim his inheritance, the women of the city accepted him, dancing as Maenads in his honour on Mount Kithairon. But his mortal cousin King Pentheus refused to welcome him or recognise his divine nature. Dionysos disguised him as a woman and took him to Kithairon to spy on the dancing women. They fell on Pentheus and tore him apart, and the king's mother Agave led the procession back to Thebes, carrying her son's head on her Maenad pole under the impression he was a lion.

Several generations later, King Laios and his queen Jokasta were told by Apollo's priest Teiresias that the child in Jokasta's womb would grow up to murder his father and marry his mother. As soon as the baby was born they exposed him on Mount Kithairon – but a Corinthian shepherd rescued him and he was brought up as prince of Corinth. His name, Oedipus ('swell-foot'), indicated the way his ankles had been pinned together when he was born. As an adult, Oedipus went to ask the Delphic Oracle who he really was, and the oracle repeated Teiresias' prophecy. Thinking that this referred to his adoptive parents in Corinth, Oedipus hurried in the opposite direction, and on the way quarrelled with an old man at a crossroads and killed him. He arrived in Thebes, drove away the monstrous Sphinx which was tyrannising the people, and married Queen Jokasta. They reigned peacefully for several years, and had four children. Then the gods revealed the truth: Oedipus was the son of Laios (the old man at the crossroads) and of Jokasta. Jokasta hanged herself, Oedipus blinded himself and rule in Thebes passed to Jokasta's brother, the Sown Man Kreon, until Oedipus' sons grew up.

Oedipus' sons were Polynikes, the elder, and Eteokles, the younger. When they reached adulthood they agreed to share the throne equally, one year each in alternation. They also quarrelled with their father, who cursed them (saying that they would divide their inheritance with iron, and each kill the other on the same day) and went into exile – in some accounts to Athens, where King Theseus gave him shelter until he died. Eteokles reigned for the first year, then refused to surrender the throne to Polynikes. Polynikes went to Argos and raised an army led by seven champions (the Seven Against Thebes). They besieged the city, each champion at one of the seven gates. Eventually, the two brothers faced each other in single combat, and killed each other at the same moment – exactly as Oedipus had foretold.

Rule in the city passed once more to Kreon. He buried the Theban dead with honour, but refused to allow the Argive dead the ceremonies necessary to bring them entry to the Underworld. Antigone, his niece and sister of Eteokles and Polynikes, defied him by sprinkling Polynikes' corpse with dust and saying funeral prayers, and he punished her by walling her in a cave to die. She hanged herself, and Kreon's son Haimon, her lover, found the corpse, cursed his father and killed himself. The Argive heroes' relatives went to Theseus of Athens and begged him to make

Kreon release their sons and husbands for burial. Theseus led a second expedition (the Sons of the Seven Against Thebes) who sacked Thebes, executed Kreon and razed the city to the ground.

## THESEUS

(Sophocles, *Oedipus at Kolonos*; Euripides, *Suppliants, Hippolytos*)
Although Theseus figures in some of the major Greek myths, he is only a character in three extant plays. In *Oedipus at Kolonos* he allows Oedipus sanctuary at Kolonos, in *Suppliants* he intervenes to force the Thebans to allow the Argives who died attacking Thebes to be buried. His major appearance is in *Hippolytos* (see above). His father Aegeus figures in *Medea*.

Theseus' adventures include killing the Minotaur in the labyrinth of Crete with the help of Ariadne. He subsequently took the Amazon Antiope as his mistress, defeating an Amazon army that attacked Athens, and their son was Hippolytos. When Theseus married Phaedra, Antiope attempted to stop the wedding and Theseus killed her. This led Ares, Antiope's father, and Artemis to seek revenge on Theseus. Their revenge is the subject of *Hippolytos*. After the death of Hippolytos, Theseus went mad, and was trapped in Hades until rescued by Herakles. Unfortunately his legs were severely damaged in the rescue and on his return to Athens he went unrecognised. On his way to Crete he was murdered on Skyros by King Lykomedes at Artemis' instigation.

## TROY

(Sophocles, *Ajax, Philoktetes*; Euripides, *Andromache, Hekabe, Helen, Rhesos, Women of Troy*)
When Apollo and Poseidon rebelled against Zeus, he punished them by enslaving them for one mortal year to a human: King Laomedon. Their task was to build him a walled city, Troy, and ever afterwards Troy was particularly dear to their hearts.

A generation later, Hekabe (wife of Laomedon's son King Priam) dreamed that Paris, the child she was expecting, was a firebrand which would destroy the city. Priam and Hekabe ignored the gods' advice (to kill Paris at birth) and instead exiled him to be brought up by shepherds on Mount Ida. Here he was asked to settle an argument between three goddesses, about which was the most beautiful, and each offered a bribe to place her first. Hera offered him rule over all Asia, Athene rule over all creation, Aphrodite sex with Helen, the most beautiful woman in the world. Paris chose Aphrodite, and soon afterwards went to Greece and stole Helen, wife of King Menelaos of Sparta.

Menelaos and his brother Agamemnon gathered a huge war fleet, with princes and soldiers from every state in Greece, and sailed for Troy to win Helen back. The princes included some of the noblest heroes in Greece: Achilles, Ajax, Diomedes, Odysseus, Nestor. On the Trojan side the warriors were led by Priam's son and heir-apparent Hektor. The gods took sides: Athene and Hera favoured the Greeks, Poseidon and Apollo the Trojans. Zeus remained impartial, and Aphrodite darted at whim from side to side, until Diomedes grazed her with his spear-point and she withdrew to Olympos to complain to her father Zeus, and sulk.

Because the sides were so evenly matched, the war continued for ten years. The gods prophesied that it would not end until Philoktetes joined the fighting, armed with the unerring bow and arrows of Herakles (given to him when he lit the hero's funeral pyre and released his soul to join the gods). But Philoktetes had trodden long ago on a sacred snake, which had bitten him in the foot. The wound tormented him, and the Greeks, unable to stand the sound of his groaning or stench of his gangrene, banished him to the remote island of Lemnos. As the war dragged on, Odysseus and Achilles' young son Neoptolemos went to Lemnos to fetch Philoktetes. The gods had promised that if he went to Troy his wound would be healed, he would kill Paris and Achilles with magic arrows and victory would come to Greece. Philoktetes obeyed, but he was still resentful of the Greek lords for the way they'd banished him in the first place. Equally resentful was Ajax, prince of Salamis and bravest of all Greek warlords. After Philoktetes killed Achilles, Ajax claimed the hero's armour (made by Hephaistos, craftsman of the gods), and Odysseus tricked him out of it. Maddened by fury, Ajax first slaughtered a herd of sheep and cattle, mistaking them for the Greek commanders, and then committed suicide – deeds which outraged the gods and turned them against the Greeks.

By now, however, no god's anger could prevent the city's destruction. Athene, still loyal to Odysseus, whispered the idea of the wooden horse to him: the Greeks should build a vast hollow horse, fill it with soldiers, leave it on the plain and pretend to sail away. The Trojans would drag the horse into the city and offer it in Athene's temple. In the night, the soldiers should climb out and open the gates to their companions. All this was done, and the Greeks sacked Troy, slaughtered its men, distributed its wealth and enslaved its women and children.

The women, led by Queen Hekabe, were kept in tents by the shore, ready for collection by the warlords who now owned them. The allocations were savage: Hekabe was the prize of Odysseus, Andromache went to Neoptolemos (whose father Achilles had killed her husband Hektor), Kassandra the prophetess to Agamemnon (who lusted for sex with Apollo's virgin priestess), and Helen to her former husband Menelaos, who was to take her home to death in Sparta. Before they finally sacked the city, the Greeks offered Hekabe's youngest daughter Polyxena as a blood-sacrifice over Achilles' grave and threw Andromache's baby son Astyanax from the battlements, to ensure that the Trojan dynasty was wiped out for ever.

In the main myth-account, the Greeks then sailed for home – and the gods who had supported Troy saw to it that their journeys were difficult and their arrival unwelcome (Odysseus' adventures are typical). There are also two variant myths, used by Euripides. In one, Hekabe never sailed with Odysseus. Driven mad by grief for Polyxena, and for her son Polydoros (murdered by the scheming Polymestor, a former friend of Priam who had defected to the Greeks), she prayed for deliverance, was turned into a dog yapping at Odysseus' heels, and finally ran up the mast of his ship, jumped into the sea and drowned. In the other, Helen never went to Troy at all. Instead, the gods made a phantom Helen which sailed with Paris, and marooned Helen herself in Egypt, far from the fighting. After the war, Menelaos' ship was carried to Egypt by storms, he was reconciled to the real Helen and took her home to Sparta.

*alazon*   a character type used by Aristophanes in many minor roles. *Alazons* boast loudly of qualities they do not posses. They often try to extract a favour from the hero but are defeated and quickly ejected, with much slapstick. Sometimes the *alazon* is a blustering rival.

**antistrophe**   see **strophe/antistrophe**

**buskins**   soft leather boots worn by actors. In later times they had built-up soles, which led to the subsequent misapprehension that actors wore platform-boots to enhance visibility, teetering about as if on stilts. Vase paintings suggest that the soles were actually no more than a few centimetres thick.

**comedy**   play designed to be amusing, normally with an original story and satirising current attitudes or character-types. Old Comedy (the kind written by Aristophanes) is surreal, slapstick, viciously satirical (often of real-life people), and blends natural and supernatural events in a way uniquely its own. New Comedy (the kind written by Menander) is domestic, everyday and concerned with character types rather than specific satirical targets. Its plots are full of repartee (particularly between slaves and their masters), coincidences, impersonations and mistaken identity. Middle Comedy (that of Aristophanes' *Women in Power* and *Wealth*) comes historically between the two, and uses elements of both. The word 'comedy' literally means 'village-song', some say because the form's origins were in rural celebrations.

*deus ex machina*   appearance, at the end of a tragedy, by a god who sorts out the tangle of the plot and tells the characters what will happen next. Often, these appearances were made 'above', either on the roof of the *skene* or on a special raised platform called the *theologeion* ('god-speaking-place'). Latin scholars in later times therefore gave them the name *deus ex machina* ('god from the stage-effect').

**dithyramb**   choral song performed by a choir of men or boys, accompanied by a flute player, in the sanctuary of Dionysos. The performers were amateurs, groups competing in an annual festival. Dithyrambs were, apparently, formal and austere, religious celebrations in general and not specific to Dionysos. Sometimes the words and movements were divided between two groups (see **strophe/antistrophe**), and some poets also introduced solo singers to contrast with the choir. Although dithyrambs continued to be written during the heyday of Athenian tragedy, authorities suggest that the rise of drama – in part a development of the dithyramb form – stole their thunder and reduced their popularity. No one knows what the word 'dithyramb' literally means.

*ekkuklema*   ('roll-out') a device used in tragedy perhaps to reveal the results of murder 'inside' (for example, the corpse of Klytemnestra in the *Oresteia*), and in comedy for jokes (as when Euripides in *Acharnians* is too lazy or too busy to come to his own front door, and has himself 'rolled out' instead). It used to be thought that the 'roll-out' was some kind of wheeled platform or sofa, but it is more likely to have been a screen or screens, wheeled aside at the appropriate moment.

**machine** (*mechane*)   a crane used to fly actors, perhaps in tragedy (for example, *Ajax*, *Philoktetes*, *Orestes*, *Elektra* and certainly in comedy (for example, *Peace*, *Festival Time* and *Birds*).

**monody**   lyric song for single actor, sometimes brief, sometimes in **strophe/antistrophe** form. Monodies often occur at moments of high emotion, particularly joy or mourning.

**ode**   lyric song, usually for the chorus and in **strophe/antistrophe** form.

*orchestra*   circular performing area at the heart of a Greek theatre, used principally by the chorus. The word 'orchestra' literally means 'dancing-place'.

*parabasis* in some Aristophanes comedies, a choral section in which the chorus-members speak directly to the audience, discussing the state of the country, the poor quality of Aristophanes' rivals, the blessings that will accrue to the judges if he wins the competition and the misfortunes they will suffer if he doesn't. The *parabasis* is in **strophe/antistrophe**, involves dance as well as song and speech, and often ends with a *pnigos* ('choker'), a one-to-two-minute-long speech by the chorus-leader intended to be spoken in a single breath. The word '*parabasis*' literally means 'stepping-aside', and refers to the chorus stepping out of the illusion of the play-plot (though they remain in character as wasps, frogs, or whatever their identity in the action).

*parodos* side-passage leading into the *orchestra* of a Greek theatre. Originally merely paths, allowing entrance to the chorus and actors, *parodoi* were decorated in later theatres with elaborate stone paving and entrance-arches. The word '*parodos*' literally means 'side-path'.

**pastoral** see **satyr play**

**satyr play** pastoral comedy burlesquing characters from myth (for example, in Euripides' *Cyclops*, the only surviving example, showing Polyphemos as a gluttonous, brainless giant). The form was said to have been invented by Aeschylus' predecessor Pratinas, and its name comes from the chorus, who are always satyrs, the half-human, half-animal wood-spirits who, in some Dionysian myths, were the god's dancing followers. They were innocents, spirits of nature, and in the plays their tastes ran to the joys of the flesh, particularly drink and sex. (Their costume included the notorious 'phallus', a large, padded, erect penis, represented in some vase paintings as being as long as the dancer's arm and curving up almost to touch his chin.) Although only fragments of their satyr plays survive, both Aeschylus and Sophocles are said to have been masters of the form – and, if the tradition is true which says that playwrights took the lead in their own plays, not only in writing them but in performing them, not perhaps the first activities we might associate with either of these playwrights.

*skene* building at the rear of the acting-area of a theatre. Originally a tent or hut, in front of which the actors performed or on which the play's setting was painted, the *skene* in later theatres became ever more elaborate, until in Roman times it was built of stone, with a façade of pillars and high, arched doorways.

**stichomythia** dialogue between two characters in which the speeches are exactly paired, the actors answering one another in swift repartee. Passages of stichomythia often end long, rhetorical scenes, and each actor has single lines or half-lines. The effect is to speed things up enormously, the scene galloping towards its conclusion. 'Stichomythia' literally means 'words in ranks'.

**strophe/antistrophe** passages of lyric verse, solo or chorus, which echo each other exactly in metre, style and often content. The words literally mean 'turn' and 'counter-turn', and referred originally to movements of the chorus as they danced, making reflecting patterns across the *orchestra*. All tragedies and all Aristophanes' plays use the idea, a major component of the formality of the original performing-style.

**tragedy** a serious, or mainly serious, play usually based on a story from myth, telling its events in a mixture of fast dialogue, more formal spoken rhetoric and lyrical song and dance, and drawing out from the material moral, political and social meanings – sometimes philosophical (as in Aeschylus' *Prometheus Bound*), sometimes religious (as in Sophocles' *Oedipus Tyrannos*), sometimes topical (as in Euripides' *Women of Troy*), often all at once. The word 'tragedy' was once taken to mean 'goat-song' (*tragos*, 'goat', *oidos*, 'song'), and fanciful explanations were provided, for example that the prize at the earliest festivals was a goat for sacrifice. But it may equally come from the dialect word *tragein*, still used in modern Greek, to strike or strum a stringed instrument, and may mean no more than 'accompanied singing'.

| | |
|---|---|
| *c.* 534 | Thespis first presents tragedies |
| ?525/4 | Aeschylus born |
| *c.* 500 | Pericles born |
| ?496 | Sophocles born |
| 490 | First Persian invasion: Battle of Marathon |
| 486 | First comic dramas at the City Dionysia |
| 484 | Aeschylus wins his first first prize |
| 480 | Second Persian invasion. Battles of Artemision, Thermopylai, Salamis |
| *c.* 480 | Euripides born |
| 479 | Battle of Plataia |
| 472 | Aeschylus, *Persians* |
| 469 | Socrates born |
| 468 | Sophocles wins his first first prize |
| 467 | Aeschylus, *Seven Against Thebes* |
| 463 | Aeschylus, *Suppliants* |
| 458 | Aeschylus, *Oresteia* |
| 456 | Aeschylus dies |
| 440s | Sophocles, *Ajax* |
| 449 | Prize for best actor in tragedy introduced |
| 449–*c.* 420 | Building of the Parthenon and of Precinct of Dionysos as a playing space |
| *c.* 448 | Aristophanes born |
| 442 | Prize for best actor in comedy introduced |
| *c.* 440 | Euripides wins his first first prize<br>Sophocles, *Antigone* |
| 438 | Euripides, *Alkestis* |
| 431 | Euripides, *Medea* |
| 431–404 | Peloponnesian War between Athens and Sparta |
| 430 | Plague in Athens |
| ?430–28 | Sophocles, *Oedipus Tyrannos* |

| | |
|---|---|
| ?430–27 | Euripides, *Herakles' Children* |
| ?430–13 | Sophocles, *Elektra* |
| 429 | Pericles dies |
| 428 | Euripides, *Hippolytos* |
| c. 427 | Plato born |
| 425 | Aristophanes, *Acharnians* |
| ?425 | Euripides, *Andromache* |
| 425–13 | Euripides, *Elektra* |
| 424 | Aristophanes, *Knights* |
| c. 424 | Euripides, *Hekabe* |
| 423 | Aristophanes, *Clouds* (first version) |
| 422 | Aristophanes, *Wasps* |
| c. 422 | Euripides, *Suppliants* |
| 421 | Aristophanes, *Peace* |
| | Peace of Nikias |
| ?c. 417 | Euripides, *Herakles* |
| 415 | Euripides, *Women of Troy* |
| 415–13 | Sicilian Expedition |
| 414 | Aristophanes, *Birds* |
| c. 413 | Euripides, *Iphigeneia in Tauris* |
| 412 | Euripides, *Helen* |
| c. 412 | Euripides, *Ion* |
| 411 | Revolution of the Four Hundred at Athens |
| | Aristophanes, *Lysistrata* and *Festival Time* |
| 409 | Sophocles, *Philoktetes* |
| c. 409 | Euripides, *Phoenician Women* |
| 408 | Euripides, *Orestes* |
| 406/5 | Euripides and Sophocles die |
| 405 | Battle of Aigospotomi |
| | Aristophanes, *Frogs* |
| c. 405 | Euripides, *Bacchae* (posthumously produced) |
| | Euripides, *Iphigeneia at Aulis* (posthumously produced) |
| 404 | Sparta defeats Athens; rule of the Thirty Tyrants |
| 403 | Civil war in Athens and restoration of democracy |

| | |
|---|---|
| 401 | Sophocles, *Oedipus at Kolonos* (posthumously produced) |
| 399 | Socrates executed |
| 390s | Aristophanes, *Women in Power* |
| 388 | Aristophanes, *Wealth* |
| c. 387 | Plato starts Academy |
| 386 | Regular revivals of tragedy introduced at the City Dionysia |
| ?386/80 | Aristophanes dies |
| 384 | Aristotle and Demosthenes born |
| 367 | Aristotle joins the Academy |
| 359 | Philip II king of Macedon |
| 356 | Alexander (the Great) of Macedon born |
| c. 350 | Theatre of Epidaurus built |
| 347 | Plato dies |
| 342/1 | Menander born |
| 336 | Philip of Macedon dies |
| c. 336 | Aristotle, *Poetics* |
| c. 330 | Lycurgus builds the first stone theatre in Athens |
| 323 | Alexander the Great dies |
| 322 | Aristotle and Demosthenes die |
| c. 316 | Menander, *The Malcontent* |
| c. 305 | Menander, *The Woman from Samos* |
| c. 290 | Menander dies |

# BIBLIOGRAPHY

## The plays

The Methuen *Classical Greek Dramatists* series includes translations of the works of Aeschylus in two volumes, Euripides in six and Sophocles in two; there are two volumes of plays by Aristophanes and one containing two plays by Aristophanes and two by Menander. Penguin have published translations of the fragments of Menander's other plays in Theophrastus *The Characters*, Menander *Plays and Fragments*, trans. P. Vellacott, 1967.

## Selected further reading

Arnott, P. D. *Greek Scenic Conventions in the Fifth Century* BC, Oxford, Clarendon Press, 1962
   *Public and Performance in the Greek Theatre*, London, Routledge, 1989

Aylen, L. *The Greek Theater*, Cranbury, New Jersey, Associated University Presses, 1985

Bain, D. *Actors and Audience*, Oxford University Press, 1977

Baldry, H. C. *The Greek Tragic Theatre*, London, Chatto & Windus, 1971

Bremmer, J. *Greek Religion*, Oxford University Press, 1994

Brooke, I. *Costume in Greek Classical Drama*, London, Methuen, 1962

Cartledge, P. A. *Aristophanes and his Theatre of the Absurd*, Bristol, Classical Press, 1990

Csapo E. and W. J. Slater *The Context of Ancient Drama*, Ann Arbor, University of Michigan Press, 1994

Dover, K. *Aristophanic Comedy*, London, Batsford, 1972

Easterling, P. E. ed. *The Cambridge Companion to Greek Tragedy*, Cambridge University Press, 1997

Else, G. F. *The Origin and Early Form of Greek Tragedy*, Cambridge, Mass., Harvard University Press, 1967

Evans, A. *The God of Ecstasy: Sex Roles and the Madness of Dionysus*, New York, St Martin's Press, 1988

Goldhill, S. *Reading Greek Tragedy*, Cambridge University Press, 1986

Graves, R. *The Greek Myths*, Harmondsworth, Penguin, 1955

Green, J. R. *Theatre in Ancient Greek Society*, London, Routledge, 1994

Hall, E., F. Macintosh and O. Taplin *Medea in Performance 1500–2000*, Oxford, Legenda, 2000

Halleran, M. *Stagecraft in Euripides*, London, Routledge, 1984

Hornblower, S. *The Greek World 479–323 BC*, 2nd ed., London, Routledge, 1991

Hubbard, T. K. *The Mask of Comedy*, Ithaca, Cornell University Press, 1991

Jones, P. V. *et al. The World of Athens*, Cambridge University Press, 1984

Mackinnon, K. *Greek Tragedy into Film*, London, Croom Helm, 1986

Kitto, H. D. F. *Greek Tragedy*, 3rd ed., London, Methuen, 1961

Lattimore, R. L. *Story Patterns in Greek Tragedy*, London, Athlone Press, 1964

Lefkowitz, M. R. *The Lives of the Greek Poets*, London, Duckworth, 1981

Lesky, A. *Greek Tragedy*, trans. H. A. Frankfort, 3rd ed., London, Benn, 1978

Lever, K. *The Art of Greek Comedy*, London, Methuen, 1956

McDonald, M. *Euripides in Cinema: The Heart Made Visible*, Philadelphia, Centrum, 1983

*Ancient Sun, Modern Light: Greek Drama on the Modern Stage*, New York, Columbia University Press, 1992

*Sing Sorrow: Classics, History and Heroines in Opera*, Westport, Conn., Greenwood Press, 2001

McDowell, D. M. *Aristophanes and Athens*, Oxford University Press, 1995

McLeish, K. *The Theatre of Aristophanes*, London, Thames & Hudson, 1980

*Myths and Legends of the World*, London, Bloomsbury, 1996

Meier, C. *The Political Art of Greek Tragedy*, trans. A. Webber, Cambridge, Polity Press, 1993

Pickard-Cambridge, A. W. *The Theatre of Dionysus in Athens*, Oxford, Clarendon Press, 1962

*The Dramatic Festivals of Athens*, 2nd ed., revised J. Gould and D. M. Lewis, Oxford, Clarendon Press, 1988

Pomeroy, S. B. *Families in Classical and Hellenistic Greece*, Oxford, Clarendon Press, 1997

Sandbach, F. H. *The Comic Theatre of Greece and Rome*, London, Chatto & Windus, 1977

Scodel, R., ed. *Theatre and Society in the Classical World*, Ann Arbor, University of Michigan Press, 1993

Seale, D. *Vision and Stagecraft in Euripides*, London, Croom Helm, 1982

Segal, C. *Tragedy and Civilization*, Cambridge, Mass., Harvard University Press, 1981

*Interpreting Greek Tragedy*, Ithaca, Cornell University Press, 1986

Segal, E., ed. *Oxford Readings in Aristophanes*, Oxford University Press, 1996

Stanford, W. B. *Greek Tragedy and the Emotions*, London, Routledge, 1984

Taplin O. *Greek Tragedy in Action*, London, Methuen, 1978

*The Stagecraft of Aeschylus*, Oxford, Clarendon Press, 1997

Trendall, A. D., and T. B. L. Webster *Illustrations of Greek Drama*, London, Phaidon, 1971

Walcot, P. *Greek Drama in its Theatrical and Social Context*, Cardiff, University of Wales Press, 1976

Walton, J. M. *Living Greek Theatre: A Handbook of Classical Performance and Modern Production*, Westport, Conn., Greenwood Press, 1987

*The Greek Sense of Theatre: Tragedy Reviewed*, London, Methuen, 1984; 2nd ed., Amsterdam, Harwood, 1996

*Greek Theatre Practice*, London, Methuen, 1991

Walton, J. M. and P. D. Arnott *Menander and the Making of Comedy*, Westport, Conn., Greenwood Press, 1996

Webster, T. B. L. *Greek Theatre Production*, 2nd ed., London, Methuen, 1970

Whitman, C. H. *Aristophanes and the Comic Hero*, Cambridge, Mass., Harvard University Press, 1964

Wiles, D. *The Masks of Menander*, Cambridge University Press, 1991

*Greek Theatre Performance*, Cambridge University Press, 2000

*Tragedy in Athens*, Cambridge University Press, 1997

Winnington-Ingram, R. P. *Euripides and Dionysus*, Cambridge University Press, 1948

*Sophocles: An Interpretation*, Cambridge University Press, 1980

Zimmermann, B. *Greek Tragedy*, Baltimore, Johns Hopkins University Press, 1985

# INDEX

*Figures in bold are main references.*

*Acharnians* (Aristophanes) 1, 15, 195, 196, 197, **203–7**; Dikaiopolis 15, 198, 200, 203–4, 206; Euripides 8, 204, 205, 206; Lamachos 25, 203, 204, 205, 206, 207

Achilles 3, 286, 290, 291; in *Iliad* 3, 34, 35; in *Iphigeneia at Aulis* 161–2, 163

actors 2, 10, 35, 71, 72, 218–20, 258

Admetos 275; in *Alkestis* 114–15, 116–17

Aegeus 285, 287; in *Medea* 169, 171–2

Aelian 164

Aeschylus viii, 1, 3, 5, 10, 31–2, 67, 70, 72, 107; characters 25, 26, 34, 35, 109; chorus 10, 34, 35, 111; irony 74; language and metaphor 28, 36, 37–8, 40–1, 110–11; lost plays 32, 52, 56, 60, 64; messengers' speeches 33–4; and politics 23, 41; portrayed in *Frogs* 222–3, 224, 225, 226; see *Oresteia* trilogy; *Persians*; *Prometheus Bound*; *Seven Against Thebes*; *Suppliants*

Agamemnon 3, 35, 165, 277, 290, 291; in *Ajax* 76, 77, 78; in *Hekabe* 136–7, 139; in *Iphigeneia at Aulis* 161, 162, 163; see *Agamemnon*

*Agamemnon* (Aeschylus) 21, 33, 35–6, 39, **42–4**, 46; Agamemnon 35, 36, 39, 42, 43, 44, 46; chorus 10, 11, 36, 40, 42, 43, 44, 58, 116, 117; the gods 46; Kassandra 36, 40, 42–3, 46, 65; Klytemnestra 10, 24, 33, 35, 36, 42, 43, 44; messenger 33

Agathon 197; in *Festival Time* 217, 219, 220

Agave 287; see *Bacchae*

Agorakritos: in *Knights* 227, 229

Aigisthos 277, 278; in *Elektra* (Euripides) 132, 133, 134, 135; see *Agamemnon*; *Elektra* (Sophocles); *Libation-Bearers*

Aigyptos 64, 279

*Ajax* 290–1; see *Ajax*

Ajax (Sophocles) 17, 21, 22, 68, 69, **76–9**, 97, 101, 112, 273; Ajax 19, 25, 73, 146; Menelaos 73, 77, 78; Odysseus 76, 77, 99; Teukros 73, 77, 79

*alazon* scenes 234, 293

*Alexandros* (Euripides) 192

Alkestis 275; see *Alkestis*

*Alkestis* (Euripides) 105, 106, 113, **114–18**; Herakles 108, 114–15, 117

Alkmene 102, 280; in *Herakles' Children* 148, 149

Allekto 280

Amphitryon 141; in *Herakles* 144, 145, 146, 147

*Amymone* (Aeschylus) 64

*anagnorisis* 272–3

*anapaests* 13

Andromache 3, 26, 275–6, 291; see also *Andromache*; *Women of Troy*

*Andromache* (Euripides) 106, **119–23**, 162

Antigone 288; in *Oedipus at Kolonos* 88, 89, 91; in *Phoenician Women* 178, 179, 181; in *Seven Against Thebes* 59, 60, 61; see *Antigone*

*Antigone* (Sophocles) 21, 68, 69, 71, **80–3**, 112, 180; Antigone 65, 68–9, 71, 72, 73, 80–1, 82, 83; chorus 11, 71, 80, 81, 82, 83; Haimon 71, 80, 81, 82, 83; Kreon 24, 71, 72, 73, 80–1, 82–3; Polynikes 80, 82, 180

Antiope 282, 289

*Antiope* (Euripides) 106

antistrophe 296

Aphrodite 111, 141, 290; in *Hippolytos* 153, 154, 156

Apollo 105, 112, 276, 281, 283, 289; in *Alkestis* 114, 115; and Delphic Oracle 275, 276, 277; in *Oresteia* 10, 40, 42, 48–9; in *Orestes* 174, 176–7; see *Eumenides*; *Ion*

Araros 196

Ares 289

Argos: myth–cycle 85, 166, 277–8

Argos, King of: in *Suppliants* (Aeschylus)

63, 64, 65
Aristophanes viii, 3, 5, 10, 17–18, 21, 22,
   32, 105, 107, 109, 121, 195–8, 259;
   characters 25, 196–7, 198–201; chorus
   10–11, 17, 18–19, 199–200, 259;
   language 15, 28; and politics 23, 197,
   255; reputation 201–2; see Acharnians;
   Birds; Clouds; Festival Time; Frogs;
   Knights; Lysistrata; Peace; Wasps;
   Wealth; Women in Power
Aristophanes of Byzantium 254
Aristotle 37, 253, 269; Ethics 24; Poetics
   viii–ix, 2, 21, 66, 68, 71, 78, 93, 94,
   95, 107, 108, 129, 163, 194, 269–73
Artemis 141, 276, 282, 289; in Hippolytos
   153, 154, 155, 156
Astyanax: in Women of Troy 191, 193
ate 54
Athene 3, 9, 278, 290, 291; in Ajax 76,
   78, 79; in Ion 157, 158; in Iphigeneia
   in Tauris 166, 167; in Suppliants
   (Euripides) 187–8, 189, 190; in
   Women of Troy 191; see also
   Eumenides
Athens 22, 41, 70, 196; education 215;
   euthune 242; festivals 2, 3–6, 11, 21,
   107; 'The Fifty Years' 22–3, 32; 'The
   Four Hundred' 232; 'Melian affair'
   192, 209–10; theatre 1–2, 6–11, 12, 56,
   107, 256; see also Peloponnesian War;
   Persian Wars
Atreus 277
Ayckbourn, Alan: Intimate Exchanges 258

Babylonians (Aristophanes) 195, 205
Bacchae (Euripides) 66, 106, 113, 124–7;
   Agave 9, 124, 125, 127; chorus 11,
   124, 181; Dionysos 65, 112, 124–5,
   126–7; Kadmos 108, 124, 126, 127;
   Pentheus 124–5, 126, 272;
   soldier–messenger 109; Teiresias 108,
   124, 126
Banqueters (Aristophanes) 195
Bdelykleon: in Wasps 240, 241
Beethoven, Ludwig van: The Creatures of
   Prometheus 57
Birds (Aristophanes) 8, 197, 208–12;
   Chairis 200, 208; chorus 11, 209, 210;
   Prometheus 211, 285–6; Tereus 208,
   286–7; wedding procession 15, 209,
   210–11
Blepyros: in Women in Power 248, 249
Brasidas, General 188, 238
buskins 9, 293

Caesar, Julius 254
Calderón de la Barca, Don Pedro: Life is
   a Dream 160
Cassandra see Kassandra
Castor and Pollux see Kastor and
   Polydeukes
Chaereas: in The Malcontent 260, 262,
   263
Chairis see Birds
characterisation 24–7; see also specific
   playwrights
Cheiron 286
Choephoroi see Libation-Bearers
choreography 10, 13
choriamboi 13
chorus, the 2, 4, 10–11, 71, 72, 257; in
   comedies 17, 18–19, 247, 257, 259;
   and language 13, 14; in tragedies
   15–16, 17
Chremes: in Women in Power 248–9
Chremylos: in Wealth 244, 245–6
Chrysippos 60
Chrysippos (Euripides) 106
Chrysis: in The Woman from Samos 265,
   266–8
Circe 3
City Dionysia 3, 4, 5, 31, 39, 51, 60, 67,
   129, 154, 204, 209, 214, 232, 253
Clouds (Aristophanes) 5, 6, 197, 199,
   213–16, 241; Strepsiades 213–14, 216,
   245
Clytemnestra see Klytemnestra
comedy 2, 11, 17–19, 293;
   characterisation 24, 25; 'New' 18, 24,
   142, 197, 201; 'Old' 18, 197, 201
costumes 8–9, 258–9, 295
cranes see mechane
Cyclops (Euripides) 10, 106, 128–31, 295;
   Polyphemos 128–9, 130, 279, 295

Danaids 279–80; see Suppliants
   (Aeschylus)
Danaos 279, 280; in Suppliants
   (Aeschylus) 63, 64, 65
Daos: in The Malcontent 261, 262
Deianeira 281–2; see Women of Trachis
Demeas: in The Woman from Samos 265,
   266, 267
Demetrios of Phaleron 253
Demos see Knights
Demosthenes: in Knights 227, 228
deus/dea ex machina 17, 107, 134, 135,
   164, 175, 176, 185, 187–8, 293
Dikaiopolis see Acharnians

Diomedes 290; in *Rhesos* 183–4, 186
Dionysos 1–2, 3, 9, 20, 25, 130, 131, 207, 276, 287; in *Frogs* 222–4, 226; *see Bacchae*
Dionysos, Theatre of 6–11, 56, 107
Dioskouroi *see* Kastor and Polydeukes
diptych structure 78
dithyrambs 2, 294
*dochmiacs* 14
Dolon: in *Rhesos* 183, 184, 185, 186
*Dyskolos see Malcontent, The*

*Ekklesiazousai see Women in Power*
*ekkuklema* ('roll–out') 8, 172, 204, 264, 294
Elektra 272, 277, 278; *see Libation-Bearers; Orestes* and below
*Elektra* (Euripides) 85, 106, 109, 113, **132–5**, 162, 175; chorus 108, 132–3; Elektra 9, 132–5; Orestes 111, 132, 133, 134, 135
*Elektra* (Sophocles) 9, 39, 68, 69, 74, **84–7**, 91, 133, 175; chorus 72; Elektra 72, 73, 74, 84–7; Klytemnestra 72, 73, 84–5, 86, 87, 175
Eleusis/Eleusinian Mysteries 31
Ephesus: theatre 12
*epitrites* 14
Eteokles 80, 122, 189, 288; in *Oedipus at Kolonos* 88–9; in *Phoenician Women* 178, 179, 180; *see Seven Against Thebes*
*Etneans* (Aeschylus) 32
Euelpides: in *Birds* 208, 210
*Eumenides* (Aeschylus) 10, 33, 34, 39, 41, **48–50**, 101, 273; Apollo 48–9, 276; Athena 10, 34, 48–9, 50; chorus 15, 44, 49; Furies 15, 36, 40, 46, 48, 49–50, 280; trial 40, 41, 48, 50
Euripides viii, 1, 3, 17, 22, 23, 70, 105–6; characters 25, 26, 110, 111, 112–13; chorus 10, 111; irony 108, 151, 155, 159, 160, 177; language 14, 111, 112; lost plays 106, 192, 205; messengers 20; portrayed by Aristophanes 8, 204, 205, 206, 217, 218, 219, 220–1, 222–3, 224, 225, 226; *see Alkestis; Andromache; Bacchae; Cyclops; Elektra; Hekabe; Helen; Herakles; Herakles' Children; Hippolytos; Ion; Iphigeneia at Aulis; Iphigeneia in Tauris; Medea; Orestes; Phoenician Women; Rhesos; Suppliants; Women of Troy*
*euthune* 242

Evadne *see Suppliants* (Euripides)

*Festival Time (Thesmophoriazousai)* (Aristophanes) 8, 9, 18, 197, 198–9, **217–21**, 141, 232; Scythian policeman 130
festivals viii, 2, 3–6, 11, 21, 107
*Frogs* (Aristophanes) 5, 18, 154, 197, **222–6**, 235; Xanthias 222, 224, 256
Furies 278; *see Eumenides*

Getas *see Malcontent, The*
Glauke 169, 170, 172, 284
gods, the 21, 111–12; *see* Apollo; Athena; Hera; Poseidon; Zeus
Goethe, Johann von 57
Gorgias: in *The Malcontent* 260, 261, 262, 263

Haimon 288; *see Antigone*
*hamartia* 271, 272
Hekabe 289–90, 291; *see Hekabe; Women of Troy*
*Hekabe (Hecuba)* (Euripides) 21, 78, 101, 106, 113, 120, 121, 122, 129, **136–9**, 162; Hekabe 136–8, 139, 289, 291; Polymestor 129, 136–7, 138, 139
Hektor 3, 35, 290, 291; in *Rhesos* 183, 184–5, 186
Helen 277, 290, 291–2; in *Orestes* 173, 174, 175, 176; *see Helen; Women of Troy*
*Helen* (Euripides) 9, 39, 106, 109, 113, **140–3**, 162, 166, 219; Helen 140–1, 142–3, 290, 291–2; Menelaos 22, 39, 140, 141, 142, 143
Hera 141, 286, 287, 290; and Herakles 102, 144, 146, 147, 149, 280, 281; and Io 55, 282–3
Herakles 102, 148, 149, 280–2; *see Alkestis; Herakles; Philoktetes; Women of Trachis*
*Herakles (Hercules)* (Euripides) 21, 78, 106, 113, **144–7**
*Herakles' Children* (Euripides) 66, 106, 113, 145, **148–52**, 273
Hermes 283, 286; in *Ion* 157, 158, 160; in *Prometheus Bound* 56
Hermione 276, 278; in *Andromache* 119, 120, 122; in *Orestes* 173, 174, 175, 176
Herodes Attikos, Theatre of 6
Herodotus 141
Hesiod 26, 37
Hieron 32

INDEX

*Hippolytos* (Euripides) 5, 106, 113,
153–6; Hippolytos 22, 153–6, 282;
Phaedra 25, 153–6, 282; servant 108–9;
Theseus 153–4, 155, 156, 289
Homer *see Iliad; Odyssey*
hubris 54, 78, 79, 193, 194, 271–2
Hugo, Victor 57
Hyllos 148; in *Women of Trachis* 100,
101, 102
Hypermnestra 64, 280

*iamboi* 13, 14, 15, 257
*Ichneutai* (Sophocles) 129
*Iliad* (Homer) 2–3, 12, 25–7, 34–5, 37,
62, 70, 98, 109, 184
Io 63, 282–3; *see Prometheus Bound*
Iole 281; *see Women of Trachis*
*Ion* (Euripides) 22, 106, 109, 113,
157–60, 166; Apollo 112, 157, 159; Ion
22, 157, 158, 159, 160, 283; Kreusa 22,
157–8, 159, 283; Xouthos 157, 158,
159, 283
Iphigeneia 42, 277, 278; *see below*
*Iphigeneia at Aulis* (Euripides) 106,
161–4, 278
*Iphigeneia in Tauris* (Euripides) 93, 106,
109, 141, 162, 165–8; chorus 108, 165,
166, 168; letter scene 19
Iris 25; in *Birds* 208, 211; in *Herakles*
144, 146
irony 20; in Aeschylus 52; in
Aristophanes 25, 198; in Euripides
108, 151, 155, 159, 160, 177; in
Sophocles 74–5, 86, 97, 99, 102
Ixion 141

Jason 284; *see Medea*
Jokasta 287, 288; in *Phoenician Women*
178, 179, 180, 181; *see Oedipus
Tyrannos*

Kadmos 178, 287; *see Bacchae*
Kalistratos 204
Kallippides (actor) 220
Kallippides: in *The Malcontent* 261, 262
Kalonike: in *Lysistrata* 231, 234
Karion *see Wealth*
Kassandra 276, 291; in *Women of Troy*
191; *see Agamemnon*
Kastor and Polydeukes 283–4; in *Helen*
140, 141; in *Orestes* 175
Kilissa *see Libation-Bearers*
Kinesias: in *Lysistrata* 231, 232, 233, 234
Kleisthenes 31; in *Festival Time* 217, 219

Kleon 188, 195, 205, 215, 228, 229–30,
238, 242, 243
Klytemnestra 277–8; in *Iphigeneia at
Aulis* 161–2, 163; in *Oresteia* 8, 39,
174–5; *see Agamemnon; Elektra*
(Sophocles); *Libation-Bearers*
Knemon *see Malcontent, The*
*Knights* (Aristophanes) 197, 199, 204,
227–30, 241; Demos 25, 227, 228–9,
230
Krateinos 197
Kreon 288, 289; in *Medea* 169, 170; in
*Oedipus at Kolonos* 88, 89, 90, 91; in
*Oedipus Tyrannos* 92, 94, 95; in
*Phoenician Women* 178–9; *see Antigone*
*Kresphontes* (Euripides) 106
Kreusa 283; *see Ion*
Kritylla: in *Festival Time* 217, 218, 219

Laios 60, 92, 93, 94, 95, 287, 288
*Laios* (Aeschylus) 60
Lamachos, General *see Acharnians*
Lampito: in *Lysistrata* 231
language and metre 12–15; Aeschylus
37–8; comedies 13, 15, 17, 257;
Sophocles 69, 71, 72; tragedies 13,
14–15, 16–17; and translation 27–9
*lazzi* 200–1
Lenaia, the 3, 4, 5, 204, 227, 232, 241
*Libation-Bearers* (Aeschylus) 33, 39, 40,
45–7; chorus 37, 44; Elektra 10, 43–4,
45, 46, 47; Kilissa 40, 45, 47;
Klytemnestra 33, 45, 46, 47; messenger
33; Orestes 10, 45–6, 47, 85
Lykos: in *Herakles* 144, 145
*Lysistrata* (Aristophanes) 18, 196, 197,
199, 218, 219, 231–5, 250; chorus 220,
231, 234

Makaria: in *Herakles' Children* 148, 151
*Malcontent, The* (Menander) 1, 254, 256,
258, 260–4, 266; Getas 258, 260–4;
Knemon 258, 260, 261, 262–4;
Sostratos 258, 260, 261, 262, 263
*Man from Sikyon, The see Sikyonios*
Marathon, battle of 22, 31, 150, 151
masks 9, 257, 258; 'silent' 10
*mechane* (machine; crane) 8, 56, 294
Medea 275, 284–5; in *Pelias' Daughters*
106; *see below*
*Medea* (Euripides) 6, 21, 91, 106, 110,
113, 169–72; Jason 22, 169–72, 284;
Medea 25, 111, 169–72, 284–5
Megara (Fury) 280

307

# INDEX

Megara (Herakles' wife) 281; in *Herakles* 144–5
'Melian affair' 192, 209–10
Menander vii, viii, 1, 10, 11, 24, 197, 253, 255; and Athenian theatre 256–9; characters 255–6; chorus 10, 11, 247, 257; language 15, 257; lost plays 253; reputation 254, 259; *see Malcontent, The; Woman from Samos, The*
Menelaos 26, 116, 117, 276, 277, 290, 291, 292; in *Andromache* 119–20, 122; in *Iphigeneia at Aulis* 161, 163; in *Women of Troy* 192, 193; *see Ajax; Helen; Orestes*
messengers 19, 20; in Aeschylus 33–4
metaphor, use of 37, 40–1, 93, 112
metre *see* language and metre
Mnesilochos: in *Festival Time* 217, 218, 220–1
Molossos: in *Andromache* 119–20
Moschion: in *The Woman from Samos* 265–6, 267
Myrrhine: in *Lysistrata* 231, 232, 233, 234
myths, use of 15, 70, 112–13, 133, 180, 271, 275–92

narrators 19, 20
Nausikaa 67
Nemesis 280
Neoptolemos 275–6, 290, 291; absence in *Andromache* 119, 121, 122; *see Philoktetes*
Nessos 281–2
Nestor 290
Nikeratos: in *The Woman from Samos* 265, 266
Nikias: in *Knights* 227, 228
Niobe 285

Ocean *see Prometheus Bound*
Odysseus 3, 26, 67, 98–9, 279, 290–1; in *Cyclops* 128–9, 130; in *Hekabe* 136, 139; in *Rhesos* 183–4, 186; *see Ajax; Philoktetes*
*Odyssey* (Homer) 2–3, 12, 25–7, 37, 70, 98–9, 109, 130
Oedipus 12–13, 16, 20, 25, 286, 287–8; in *Phoenician Women* 178, 179, 180; *see below*
*Oedipus* (Aeschylus) 60
*Oedipus at Kolonos* (Sophocles) 1, 21, 68, 75, 85, **88–91**, 112; Oedipus 71, 73, 88–90, 91; Theseus 88, 89, 91, 289

*Oedipus Tyrannos* (Sophocles) 21, 68, 69, 89, **92–5**, 180, 272; irony 74; Jokasta 20, 92, 93, 94–5; Oedipus 71, 73, 74, 92, 93, 94–5, 272
*orchestra* 6, 7, 16, 294
*Oresteia* (Aeschylus) 8, 9, 10, 21, 32, 33, **39–41**, 60–1, 174–5; *see Agamemnon, Libation-Bearers, Eumenides*
Orestes 16, 39, 272, 276, 277–8; in *Andromache* 120, 122, 123; in *Elektra* (Sophocles) 84–5, 86, 87; in *Eumenides* 48–9; in *Iphigeneia in Tauris* 165–6, 167; in *Orestes* 173–4, 175–6; *see Elektra* (Euripides); *Libation-Bearers*
*Orestes* (Euripides) 106, 121, 122, 160, 162, 173–7; chorus 16; Elektra 16, 173–6; Kastor and Polydeukes 175, 283–4; Menelaos 22, 173, 174, 175, 176

*Palamedes* (Euripides) 192
Panathenaic Festival 2, 39, 41
Paphlagon: in *Knights* 227, 228–9
*parabasis* 17, 19, 199, 201, 205, 214, 225, 238, 247, 249, 251, 295
Paris 277, 289–90
*parodoi* 7, 7, 295
*Peace* (Aristophanes) 8, 15, 195, 196, 197, 199, **236–9**; chorus 11, 236, 238; Trygaios 200, 236, 237, 238, 241, 250
Peithatairos: in *Birds* 208–9, 210–11
Peleus 276, 286; in *Andromache* 119, 120, 122
Pelias 275, 284
*Pelias' Daughters* (Euripides) 106
Peloponnesian War 22, 23, 67, 106, 121–2, 125, 137, 151, 170, 175, 188, 192, 195–6, 204–5, 232, 245; Peace of Nikias 237; Sicilian Expedition 205, 209, 211–12, 232
Pelops, King 60
Pentheus 287; *see Bacchae*
Pericles 22, 52, 67, 81, 121, 201
*peripeteia* 272, 273
Persian Wars 22, 23, 31, 53, 141–2
*Persians* (Aeschylus) 1, 9, 15, 22, 29, 31, 32, 33, **51–4**, 103; chorus 11, 51, 53; ghost scene 36, 51; messenger 33; Xerxes 36, 51, 52, 53, 54, 58
Phaedra 282, 289; *see Hippolytos*
Pheidippides: in *Clouds* 213–14
Philokleon *see Wasps*
Philoktetes 282, 290; *see below*
*Philoktetes* (Euripides) 106

*Philoktetes* (Sophocles) 8, 9, 17, 21, 68, 69, 85, **96–9**, 112; Herakles 8, 96, 97, 98; Neoptolemos 73, 74, 96–8, 99; Odysseus 74, 96–7, 99; Philoktetes 73, 74, 96–7, 98, 99

Philomela 286, 287

*Phoenician Women* (Euripides) 106, 113, **178–82**

Phrynichos: *The Phoenician Women* 52; *The Siege of Miletos* 52

Plangon: in *Woman from Samos* 265, 266, 267

Plato 37; *Apology* 215; *Republic* 209; *Symposium* 195, 197

Plautus vii, 196, 253, 254

Plutarch 11, 254

politics and drama 22–4

Pollux 257

Polydoros 136, 291

Polymestor 291; *see* Hekabe

Polynikes 122, 189, 288; in *Oedipus at Kolonos* 80, 82, 88–9, 91; in *Phoenician Women* 178, 179, 180; in *Seven Against Thebes* 59, 60; *see* Antigone

Polyphemos 3, 279; *see* Cyclops

Polyxena 193, 291; in *Hekabe* 136, 137, 138

Poseidon 286, 289; in *Women of Troy* 8, 191

Pratinas 295

Praxagora: in *Women in Power* 248, 249, 250

Priam 3, 35, 277, 289

Prokne 286–7

*Prometheus Bound* (Aeschylus) 8, 16, 19, 21, 33, 34, **55–8**, 91; chorus 15, 37; Io 34, 36, 55, 65, 112, 282–3; Ocean 8, 55, 56, 112; Prometheus 19, 25, 34, 37, 285–6

props 8–9; *see also* mechane

*Proteus* (Aeschylus) 39

Pylades 277, 278; in *Iphigeneia in Tauris* 165–6, 167; in *Libation-Bearers* 45, 46, 47; in *Orestes* 173–4

Racine, Jean 27, 139

'recognition scenes' 272

*Rhesos* (Euripides) 105, 106, 162, **183–6**

Salamis, battle of 22, 31, 33, 52, 53

satyr plays 2, 4, 5, 10, 32, 39, 64, 68, 106, 129, 192, 295

scenery, stage 8; painted 71, 72

Semele 127, 287

Seneca: *Medea* 170

*Seven Against Thebes* (Aeschylus) 33, **59–62**, 64, 65, 66, 91, 139, 180, 190; chorus 11, 16, 59; Eteokles 16, 36–7, 58, 59, 60, 61, 62; messenger 33, 59

Shakespeare, William 13, 27, 107, 160, 257; *All's Well That Ends Well* 143; *Hamlet* 14, 19; *Henry V* 56; *Henry VI Part One* 164; *King Lear* 65, 89–90; *Macbeth* 19, 24; *A Midsummer Night's Dream* 264; *Othello* 19; *Pericles* 179; *The Tempest* 89, 130; *Twelfth Night* 143

Shelley, Percy Bysshe 57

Sikon: in *The Malcontent* 260, 261, 264

*Sikyonios* (*The Man from Sikyon*) (Menander) 254

Silenos: in *Cyclops* 128–9

Simiche: in *The Malcontent* 260, 261, 263

*skene* 6–7, 7, 293, 296

Socrates 6, 65, 142, 201; in *Clouds* 25, 213, 214, 215, 216

Sophocles viii, 3, 5, 20, 23, 34, 67–8, 69–71, 107; characters 25, 26, 71, 73, 109, 111; chorus 10; irony 74–5, 86, 97, 99, 102; language 69, 71, 72; technical innovation 71–2; *see* Ajax; Antigone; Elektra; Ichneutae; Oedipus at Kolonos; Oedipus Tyrannos; Philoktetes; Women of Trachis

Sostratos *see* Malcontent, The

Sparta/Spartans 22, 23, 120, 121, 150, 151, 188, 196, 249; *see also* Peloponnesian War

Sphinx 286, 288

*Sphinx* (Aeschylus) 60

*stichomythia* 17, 138–9, 296

Strepsiades *see* Clouds

strophe 296

*Suppliants* (Aeschylus) 8, 33, 34, **63–6**, 91, 139; chorus 37, 63, 64; Danaids 63, 64, 279–80

*Suppliants* (Euripides) 21, 22, 66, 106, 110, 113, **187–90**, 273; chorus 11, 187, 188–9; Evadne 8, 19, 109, 187; Theseus 22, 24, 110, 187, 189, 289

Talthybios: in *Hekabe* 136, 139; in *Women of Troy* 191, 192, 193

Taormina: theatre 12

Teiresias 287, 288; in *Antigone* 80; in *Oedipus Tyrannos* 92, 94; in *Phoenician Women* 178, 179; *see* Bacchae

Tekmessa: in *Ajax* 76, 77, 78

*Telephos* (Euripides) 106, 205
Terence vii, 253, 254
Tereus: in *Birds* 286–7
Teukros: *in Helen* 140, 142; *see Ajax*
Thamyras 67
theatres 11–12; *see* Athens
Thebes 287–9
Theoklymenos: in *Helen* 140, 141, 143
*theologeion* 8, 172, 293
theomachy 40
Theonoe: in *Helen* 140, 141, 143
Theophrastos 253; *Characters* 24
'theory of forms' 142
Theseus 122, 282, 288–9; in *Hippolytos*
  153–4, 155, 156; in *Oedipus at Kolonos*
  88, 89, 91; *see Suppliants* (Euripides)
*Theseus* (Euripides) 106
*Thesmophoriazousai see Festival Time*
Thespis 2, 35
Thetis 286
Thoas: in *Iphigeneia in Tauris* 165, 166,
  167
Thucydides 205, 228
Thyestes 277
Tisiphone 280
Titans, the 40
tragedy 2, 9, 129, 179, 194, 296: actors
  10; and Aristotle's *Poetics* 269–73;
  characterisation 24–7; chorus 15–16,
  17; language 13, 14–15, 16–17;
  rationale 21–2; representation and
  narration 19–20
translations 27–9
*tribrachs* 13, 14
*trochees* 13, 14
Trojan War 26, 33, 39, 193, 277, 278,
  290

Troy 289–92
Trygaios *see Peace*
Tyndareos: in *Orestes* 173, 174, 175, 176

unities, the 273

*Wasps* (Aristophanes) 197, **240–3**; chorus
  200, 240, 242; Philokleon 15, 240–1,
  242
*Wealth* (Aristophanes) 1, 18, 23, 24, 196,
  197, **244–7**, 293; chorus 11, 244, 246,
  247; Karion 244–5, 246, 256
*Woman from Samos, The* (Menander) 1,
  253–4, 258, **265–8**
*Women in Power* (*Ekklesiazousai*)
  (Aristophanes) 18, 23–4, 78, 101, 196,
  197, 235, 246, **248–51**, 293
*Women of Trachis* (Sophocles) 68, 69,
  **100–3**; Deianeira 73, 100–1, 102;
  Herakles 73, 100, 101, 102–3; Iole 72,
  100
*Women of Troy* (Euripides) 6, 22, 66,
  106, 110, 113, 162, **191–4**, 210, 233;
  Andromache 9, 191, 193; Athene 8,
  191, 193; Hekabe 14–15, 25, 108,
  191–2, 193, 194; Helen 108, 192, 193,
  194; Poseidon 8, 191

Xanthias *see Frogs*
Xerxes *see Persians*
Xouthos 283; *see Ion*

Zeno 142
Zeus 35, 40, 102, 141, 276, 283–4, 290;
  and Apollo 289; and Athene 278; and
  Io 282–3; and Prometheus 55–6, 57,
  285–6; and Semele 127, 287